Advance Praise for
Merry-Go-Round Broke Down

"You might think that it would be impossible to write a novel that helps the reader put her arms around the complex issues raised by globalization. Yet, David Woo and Margalit Shinar have done precisely this. The result is most engaging and insightful. It is also one that even globalization experts such as myself can profit from."

—**Jagdish Bhagwati,** University Professor of economics and law at Columbia University, author of *In Defense of Globalization*

"What a fantastic tapestry of wordsmithing and storytelling! It left me with a much better understanding of how the world was woven so tightly by globalization, all through the dramatic stories of fascinating cultures and characters that are relevant to this day."

—**Paul Tudor Jones,** Chief Investment Officer of Tudor Investment Corporation

"*Merry-Go-Round Broke Down* depicts the key socio-economic developments of the last quarter-century. It brings to life the people who put them into effect, as well as those who were affected by them. Few were untouched."

—**Howard Marks,** the co-founder and co-CEO of Oaktree Capital and international bestselling author of *The Most Important Thing*

MERRY-GO-ROUND BROKE DOWN

DAVID WOO ★ MARGALIT SHINAR

A REGALO PRESS BOOK
ISBN: 979-8-89565-580-1
ISBN (eBook): 979-8-89565-581-8

Merry-Go-Round Broke Down:
A Novel of Guilt, Greed & Globalization

Cover Design by Noma Bar

Publishing Team:
Founder and Publisher – Gretchen Young
Managing Editor – Caitlin Burdette
Production Manager – Kate Harris
Production Editor – Rachel Paul

As part of the mission of Regalo Press, a donation is being made to Sheldrick Wildlife Trust USA, as chosen by the author. Find out more about this organization at: www.sheldrickwildlifetrust.org.

Regalo Press
New York • Nashville
regalopress.com

Published in the United States of America
2 3 4 5 6 7 8 9 10

Dedicated to

Ada and Adya Gour, Zhong Biao Hu and Hao Yuan Woo

TABLE OF CONTENTS

PROLOGUE

New York City, USA, September 2008

"The problem is no longer that with every pair of hands
that comes into the world there comes a hungry stomach.
Rather it is that, attached to those hands are sharp elbows."

—Paul Samuelson

JUST ANOTHER DAY IN THE bar deep in the bowels of a famous Manhattan hotel.

The signature bronze centerpiece of a bull and bear, polished to a soft velvety luster, glinting serenely under the light of the heavy chandelier. Small knots of regulars, hotel guests, and tourists milling around and murmuring softly. Refugees from a conference being held upstairs, a mix from the world of policy and finance, nametags dangling from their necks, placing their orders for drinks at the mahogany counter.

Shattering the discreet hush of this September afternoon, two armed men come crashing into the bar.

Where on earth are the security guards?

Securing the conference upstairs.

Not here.

The cloudburst of screams and cries of hysteria as this chilling realization sinks in.

One of the gunmen, the more heavyset of the two, races across the burgundy expanse of carpet through the thump and crunch of overturned barstools and splintering barware.

He leaps up into the air. Wild-eyed, he shouts.

Even as some people run toward the street entrance and escape, the second gunman rushes to the door and locks it.

Seven people are trapped inside: a Chinese tycoon, an American CEO, a London hedge-fund manager, a Wall Street bond salesman, and a Norwegian environmentalist. A Japanese TV celebrity, too, in New York to promote her book. The seventh, a waiter, an illegal immigrant from Mexico, walks out of the bathroom straight into the unfolding drama.

The first gunman declares that they are all hostages now.

"*Madre de Dios!*" the illegal immigrant cries, trembling.

The Chinese tycoon mutters under his breath, outraged. Who's ever heard of a hostage crisis in a five-star Park Avenue hotel in the middle of New York City?

And they all think:

Who are these men? What do they want?

Chapter 1

LIANG DACHENG

Shangcheng, China, May 1999

"Let China sleep, for when the dragon awakes, she will shake the world."

—attributed to Napoleon Bonaparte

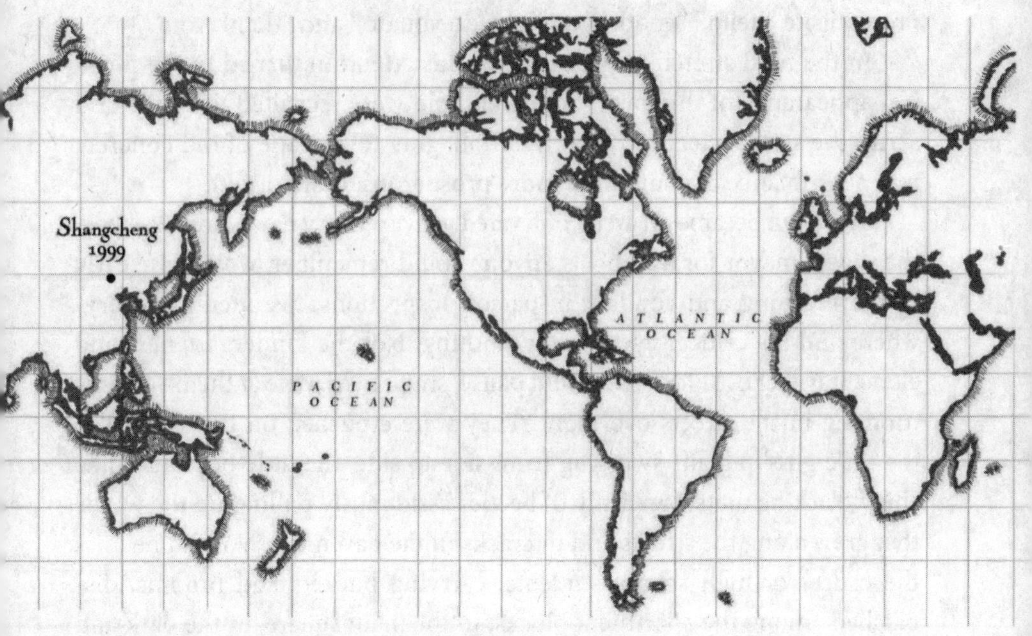

THE AMERICANS ARE COMING! FOR an entire month, a frenzy of directives streamed over the dormitory and factory loudspeakers. *Personal hygiene top priority! No public spitting! No toothpicks in mouths! Neatness and tidiness at all times!*

The Americans are coming! Anything and everything had to be done to present the best face the town could offer. Nothing could be allowed, vowed its determined mayor, to stand in the way of the projection of a healthy and well-run community. To this end, he mandated that all must show up at the crack of dawn to attend daily exercise classes in the town's central park. Shirkers would be punished. But there was a carrot, too: free haircuts for the menfolk, plastic hair clasps and kerchiefs for the women, and new T-shirts for all.

And in an additional push to whip the populace up to standard, the mayor, who was known for never leaving anything to chance, issued a short instruction manual on foreign manners and English greetings, distributing thousands of free copies in the streets. This last effort was quite successful: By the end of a few short weeks everyone knew how to say the prerequisite "hello," "good-bye," "how do you do," and "thank you."

In the final stretch of preparations, his attention turned to the physical appearance of the town. Young and old were recruited to sweep and scrub the streets clean, to turn the drab, gray townscape of old concrete into a semblance of something more prosperous, more bright.

The town became an arena of fevered activity. Every day, Liang Dacheng, the town's mayor for as long as anyone could remember, would rise early in the morning and conduct in-person inspections, his attention everywhere and his critical eye missing nothing. Not the kindergarteners and elementary school kids—he would pause, smiling, to wave at them—mushrooming in the streets overnight. They were crouched on the sidewalks, the little girls' pigtails swinging from side to side, the little boys' hair like shiny black helmets—an army of beetles assiduously pulling up the weeds that grew along the streets and in cracks in the pavement. Nor did he miss the cadres of high school students, carrying buckets and brooms, dispatched among the apartment blocks, in the main square, in the park and at the train station, to hose down roads, collect the trash, and dispose of it. Nor the unmarried factory employees pouring out of the dormitories to whitewash the dirty, liver-red bricks of the factory walls. Nor the pluckier amongst them climbing tall wooden ladders and hanging red plastic banners emblazoned with golden Chinese letters across the avenues. Some even had the English word *WELCOM* painted on them, missing the final *E*, despite the best efforts of Li Li the town translator, the mayor's wife.

Groups of volunteers joined in as well, to adjust crooked signs and wash shop windows and paint the wooden doorframes of the buildings that abutted the central square. And, most importantly, to burnish the towering concrete image of Chairman Mao (his hand raised in a gesture of triumph—or perhaps a blessing) standing in the middle of the square until it gleamed an imperial yellow in the early morning sun as eager hands arranged wreaths of flowers at its feet.

The entire town was in an uproar: all fifteen thousand of its residents. The communal spirit had never been stronger. They would have dusted the very leaves on the trees if they could have.

But then, in the small, uneventful factory township of Shangcheng, the fortunes of the government-owned factory touched them all.

• • •

A fly landed on the back of Liang Dacheng's hand and he woke up with a jolt. He had fallen asleep in the conference room. As he lifted his head from the hard glass tabletop, his first thought was that Li Li would give him hell for not returning home last night.

He rubbed his face, bloated by sleep and sticky with sweat. The slow, lazy rotations of the ceiling fan were useless against the stifling heat.

He felt stiff all over, his neck hurt, and his back ached. His plump cheek was sore where it had lain on the glass. He got up to stretch his cramped legs. He was getting too old—he would be turning fifty-one this year—to be giving up the comfort of his bed, he thought. When he was younger, though, it was many a night that, working all hours, he had slept on the factory floor.

The gray light of dawn seeped through the empty room like a gentle mist. But for him, Liang Dacheng, the coming of daybreak was more like a warning clap of thunder.

Looking out from the soot-streaked window strategically placed above the factory yard, Liang surveyed his domain. At this early hour, the grounds were empty except for some chickens running about. Beyond, at the far side of the yard, were the entrance gates, still locked.

The first day of his arrival to the factory. He could see a young man, weighed down by a suitcase on his back, approaching these very same gates in the pouring rain. Hungry, exhausted, his heart pounding with excitement and nervous anticipation.

Fresh out of university with an engineering degree, he had been dispatched by the party secretariat to this remote place, far from his home and family in the south. Back then, the nearest train station had been twenty-five kilometers away, and he had walked the entire night to reach the town.

The factory workers had welcomed him warmly and chatted with him cheerfully in their regional accent that he could barely understand. They had brought him steamed buns and soymilk, a thick quilt for his dormitory bed, and had seen to it that he wanted for nothing. He was so touched by their hospitality that he promised himself that he would work hard to repay their kindness.

Liang Dacheng turned away from the window. He patted down the far fewer hairs he had left on his head.

They had given him a home. And he—thirty years of his life. Thirty years of loyalty and excellence in service to reach his position of top dog in Shangcheng town. Factory director. Communist Party secretary. Mayor.

• • •

No possibility of a cup of tea—the kitchen was still closed at this early hour. The communal bathhouse across the yard, however, was unlocked and, after a quick shower, Liang found himself back in the second-floor conference room that doubled as his office. With a touch of trepidation, he glanced out the window again at the heavy iron gates to the factory complex. Nothing stirred, not even a leaf on the elm trees that lined the avenue beyond the gates.

On the desk was a neatly folded sheet of paper. It was the speech over which he had labored for hours last night. There was a lot riding on his choice of words, and he had spent much time on the right turn of phrase, even practicing the precise tone of voice for his delivery. He reread the speech with a frown. Its reception would determine the outcome of this fateful day that would change his future—and the town's future—forever.

A soft knock interrupted his musings. A tired-looking, timid face appeared at the door.

"Vice Secretary Shi, what are you doing here? Why aren't you at the exercise session?" Liang Dacheng asked.

"I thought you might need me on this big day," said Shi Chi, a thin man in his early forties.

Liang Dacheng wondered if Shi Chi, whose face was flushed, had already been drinking. "Everything must be ready before the Americans arrive. How are the preparations coming along?"

"Very well, Secretary Liang. Not to worry. The welcome committee is on top of everything, and the heat hasn't dampened the citizens' spirits."

Not to worry? Not to worry? What was his vice secretary going on about? A thousand worries buzzed like gnats in his head. The fish they had procured for the banquet dinner could turn bad in the heat! With no air-conditioning, a guest might faint! The little show they had been rehearsing at the school—would it be well received? And Shi Chi, could he be trusted not to show up drunk, shaming them all? As for the deal, it was still not 100 percent secure, and the Americans—perish the thought!—may yet walk away at the very last moment. The neighboring town, he had heard, was actively courting the very same company. And perhaps—despite his well-placed bribes—the deputy provincial governor would not sign off on the agreement in the end.

But the worst of it was, appearances notwithstanding, not all was harmony and solidarity in the town. If he failed to win over the opponents to his carefully laid plans in the coming showdown, it would all be over.

Liang Dacheng felt like a man besieged. His mouth was dry, and he kept kneading his right earlobe, a nervous habit when under stress. Shooing Shi Chi out of the room, he turned his attention to his speech again.

• • •

A couple of hours later, there was a second timid knock at the door.

"Come in!" Liang Dacheng called out irritably. Shi Chi slithered in.

"They're coming, Secretary Liang. They're here at the gates!"

There was no escaping the moment. Wearily, Liang Dacheng rose from his chair. "I will deal with this. You," he said, motioning to the dirty office window, "get that cleaned up right away."

He could hear the faint din of slogans infiltrating his office. *Down with America! Down with imperialism!*

Blast that Kosovo War. Damn those Americans. Why did they have to bomb the Chinese embassy in Belgrade at precisely the time he was trying to sell the factory? He felt like a magnet for all the bad luck in the world.

Liang adjusted his suit, tried to smooth down the rebellious tuft of white-flecked hair that grew stubbornly on the top of his head, threw back his shoulders with determination, and hurried downstairs. He just had to defuse the situation before the Americans arrived.

It won't be easy, he thought. The bombing had provoked a nationalist backlash, fueling anti-American sentiment across the country, with American consulates and businesses like McDonald's becoming targets of public rage.

He strode across the canteen towards the entrance of the factory building, his thoughts smoldering, the cooling effect of his recent shower having worn off already. Rivulets of sweat trickled down his back and legs.

The din from outside grew louder.

Down with America! Down with the foreign devils!

He pulled open the heavy doors and stood motionless on the landing of the steps overlooking the yard. From his vantage point he could see the heaving crowd of workers pushing and rattling the gates thirty meters in the distance. There had to be a couple of hundred people out there on the sidewalk with fists raised and waving placards, their faces ugly with fury.

They were roaring now.

Open up the gates! Open up, Secretary Liang! Down with imperialism! We want no truck with foreign devils!

Quietly he surveyed the scene. He knew each and every one of the protestors. In a small town such as Shangcheng, the boss and his subordinates were constantly in and out of each other's lives, and thirty-odd years of a shared fate created strong bonds.

He wanted to think that he had earned their trust, and that they would give him a chance to make his case. But he also knew that a crowd could turn into a violent mob in the blink of an eye.

Shi Chi suddenly materialized at his side.

"Do you want me to call in the police, Secretary Liang?" he asked in a trembling voice.

Liang Dacheng didn't answer, holding the sheet of paper with his speech limply in his right hand. A minute or two ticked by. "Unlock the gates."

"But, Secretary!"

"Do as I say. And go get me a megaphone, a stool, and a glass of water."

• • •

Liang Dacheng took off his jacket, folded it up neatly, and put it down on the ground. He got up on the small stool. He crumpled his speech into a ball and shoved it into his trouser pocket, having now decided that the appearance of spontaneity would be the best course. This was his plan: appeasement and charm, followed by straight talk and firmness.

First the charm.

Angry faces stared up at him, the collective as one restive, multi-headed beast.

Liang Dacheng, standing firm on the stool in his rolled-up shirt-sleeves, his hands on his hips, broke out in a wide, avuncular smile that radiated commiseration and understanding. He nodded, turning his head from side to side and making small bows like an actor on a stage.

He stood there, silent in the oppressive heat, his face shiny with perspiration, smiling and nodding, a beacon of stability above the tumultuous sea. He knew that despite his small stature and rumpled shirt and trousers he had an imposing presence.

He must have stood for a full five minutes, until—

"Quiet, comrades! Let Secretary Liang speak!" boomed a commanding voice. It was the voice of Wang Min, a senior machinist and the leader of the protest.

The roar subsided somewhat.

"Thank you, Wang Min," Liang Dacheng said into the megaphone in a jovial tone. Then singling out a dour man with his back slouched against the trunk of the single tree that grew in the yard, he continued, "I see that Little Lu, who was on sick leave—at death's door I was told—is back in full health and full voice this morning. Let us thank the sky and earth—a miracle!"

The crowd tittered, wavered a moment, then opted to laugh.

"My dear comrades and compatriots," Liang Dacheng continued. "I, of all people, understand your anger. I, of all people, have your best interests at heart."

"Traitor Liang Dacheng!"

Liang Dacheng ignored the interruption.

"My dear comrades and compatriots. Please bear with me and listen patiently to what I have to say. I ask—no, beg—for your trust. We've been through many good and bad times—together. Up the hills and down the valleys—together. Have you ever known me to let you down?"

No! everyone answered in unison.

"Have I not always looked out for everyone's interests? Who worked tirelessly to get Grandma Peng a bed at the People's Hospital in Shenyang? Who petitioned the provincial government to send our brilliant Tang Maylin to Beijing University? I am a good man. All present here can attest to my character. So how can I be a traitor? Didn't I give the best years of my life for our ideals? We seek an egalitarian utopia—and you all know as I do that while I'm above you in rank, I live as frugally as any man in this town. I cycle to work. I live in an apartment block no different from your own. My belly is no fuller than yours. Do I lie?"

No! responded the crowd with warmth.

"I despise capitalism like each and every one of you."

The demonstrators, still restless, repeated as one: *Down with capitalism!*

"But here's the thing. We have no choice."

"There is always a choice!"

This came from Wang Min, who, breaking from the ranks of protestors, jumped up, agitated, right in front of him.

Liang Dacheng set down his megaphone. Beckoning to Wang Min, he climbed down from the stool and descended from the landing, till he stood only one step higher than his challenger. He addressed him in a hushed tone, as to a person of equal importance.

"No, Comrade Wang," he said, looking directly into his eyes. "There *is* no choice. We're out of options. We must catch the mice, to paraphrase Comrade Deng Xiaoping. And time is running out. If we don't accept the American buyout, I tell you now, the factory will shut down in two weeks."

Climbing back onto his perch, he repeated the same words through the megaphone so that all could hear.

The protestors fell into an uneasy silence.

Liang Dacheng continued hammering on the unpleasant reality.

"We are, I'm telling this to you straight, flat out of cash. There is barely enough in the bank to cover your salaries this month. We can't meet our production target, and the subsidies from the provincial government have dried up. The order has come directly from Beijing. Sell—or shut down."

Liang Dacheng finally had the protesters' full attention. Everyone knew that the factory paid for the town's healthcare, education, and pensions. If the factory were to close, it would mean the end of the town, their livelihoods, and everything they had worked for. As the realization of their predicament began to sink in, worried faces, open-eyed, were now staring up at him with attention.

And he went on, mercilessly, "Comrades, I am sorry to be the bearer of bad news, but we simply can't afford to keep all of you employed, take care of the retirees, and provide jobs for your children. We kept going as long as we could, but now we've truly reached the end of the line."

"Gross mismanagement!" someone shouted.

"It's your fault, Liang Dacheng," cried another.

Liang held up his hand as if by this gesture he could arrest the tide of blame.

"No! It's not my fault. Nor anyone else's. It's just that times have changed. Change is like the wind, comrades. Some build walls against it, but others build windmills to harness its power. I say—no, I insist—we build the windmills that will allow us to compete. *Compete or die* will be our new goal. For the good of our factory. For the good of the town, for the good of China—"

"But it'll be the end! We'll lose all our achievements. Everything!" Wang Min, sticking to his Marxist guns, broke in. "No way can we cave to rotten American capitalism!"

"He's right! I stand with Wang Min!" yelled another protestor. "Selling out China to foreign devils is treason!

Liang could not give up now. To additional cries of *Treason! Treason!* he held on fast, trying to control his temper—

"Attention, all of you! Listen carefully! Especially you, Comrade Wang. My heart still sings: From each according to his ability, to each according to his needs. But today," Liang Dacheng called out, his voice rising, "but today, the time has come for a new phase of our socialist revolution. If we once had to erase the bourgeois dogs in our midst, today it is our duty to raise the triple banner of flexibility, pragmatism, and reform."

"It's a sellout, that's what it is," Wang Ming thundered with undisguised rage. "You're selling out to our enemies! Giving in to those turtle eggs!" And the entire crowd, revived, shouted out in one beat: *Turtle eggs! Turtle eggs! Say no to the turtle eggs!*

The pivotal moment had arrived. It was now or never. Liang Dacheng, his shirt soaked through with sweat from the heat and the strain, his cowlick more rebellious than ever, tried once more.

"Yes. I agree the Americans are sons of bitches. Imperialist dogs. But hear this: We are *not* selling out. We are *not* giving in. Never. Collect your thoughts calmly, all of you. Consider the advantages. In this deal with the Americans you get to keep your jobs. I get to keep my job. With a new injection of capital, we'll be able to get the up-to-date technology and know-how we need to compete in the world. Our town will thrive. *You* will thrive. Remember the words of Comrade Deng Xiaoping: Poverty is not socialism! Like it or not, for the good of our factory, for the good of China, we need those foreign devils! But here's the thing…." He paused dramatically. "We are all patriots, right?"

Right! the crowd roared in agreement.

"So, join me in beating the turtle eggs at their own game. Help me, my comrades! Help make China strong and respected. Help make socialism strong and respected. We'll learn, adapt, and rise to the top of the world. Be part of our second revolution! Be part of history in the making!"

A timely tear appeared in his eye—and it was not a fake tear. It was quite genuine. Liang Dacheng was moved by his own words. He accepted that times were changing. But he had been a true believer once, and the tear was shed not least in mourning for the passing of the ideals of his youth.

"We are all loyal citizens here! We are all loyal to government directives! The government knows best how to lead us to success and victory!"

With tears now flowing freely down his plump, shiny cheek, Liang Dacheng began singing in a cracked voice, "*The East is Red*…. Come. Join me in saluting our country."

The demonstrators, who had in turn been angry and defiant, confused and frightened, were now ready to bathe in the warmth of national solidarity, the ultimate balm. Moved by Liang Dacheng's singing, the collective was tamed and the multi-headed beast deconstructed back into a throng of worried individuals. They all joined in, singing along with their leader.

Afterwards, the demonstrators dispersed quietly.

For the first time that day, Liang Dacheng breathed easy. He had successfully defused the bomb. Through his arguments, communism and capitalism were, for the moment at least, reconciled.

• • •

The cooking smells wafting down the stairwell reminded Liang that he was ravenous. He threw down his bike in the hallway and tore up the two flights of stairs to his apartment.

Li Li was standing in the kitchen doorway, a dishcloth in her hand. Only a couple of years younger than Liang Dacheng, she had been very pretty once, with small, delicately drawn features. She bore her years well, her tall figure still slim and her short, bobbed hair still raven black.

She did not look pleased at the sight of her husband.

"Where on earth have you been?" she demanded in a shrill, plaintive voice.

"Before I tell you anything I need something to drink, food, and a nap. And in that order."

Li Li obediently set the table in their little kitchen and put down a bowl of beef noodle soup that Liang Dacheng gobbled up in a flash and washed down with three cups of hot water. Despite her prodding, he refused to say anything.

It was only when Liang Dacheng had emerged from the bedroom after his nap that he finally declared, "Well, Li Li. Tell me you're proud of me. I've just saved us from disaster. I think we'll make it."

Li Li's tired features lit up. She smiled coyly. "Good for you, Dacheng. Good for you! So I gather it's safe for me to show it to you now."

"Show me what?"

Li Li disappeared into their bedroom. Liang Dacheng heard the creaking of the old closet door and the rustling of paper. A few minutes later, Li Li, her eyes sparkling, entered the small living room wearing a bright purple dress.

"The color looks really good on me, don't you think?" She twirled coquettishly a couple of times.

The purple hue struck Liang Dacheng as somewhat loud and forward—a tad too triumphant, not to say expensive.

"You're incorrigible, Li Li. The money isn't in our pockets yet."

Li Li frowned with displeasure. "But you know damned well I've nothing to wear to the banquet."

"I know, I know," Liang said. "But it's too early to go shopping. People will talk."

"Bah. You're just an old worrier. Our lives are finally going to improve. What's to stop us now?" she bubbled enthusiastically. "Can you imagine? Our daughter will be guaranteed the education she deserves. We'll have a new house, a car for you, an eyelift for me—I'll be beautiful again, Dacheng. And we'll go on a real vacation. Oh, Dacheng—there are so many places we haven't seen!"

"Stop! Li Li! Stop right there. Please. Don't get so carried away."

"Carried away? How dare you! I followed you to this godforsaken place more than thirty years ago and have been holed up in it ever since! It's you who carried *me* away."

True. Liang Dacheng had aggressively courted his princess, the well-educated daughter of a doctor. For him, their courtship had always smacked of a fairy tale—because he had nothing to offer her except his degree and a future riddled with uncertainty. As a result, he always carried within himself a pang of remorse for having snatched her away from a life of relative comfort in Shanghai. Not only had he put some two thousand kilometers between her and her family, he had subjected her to decades of hardship and want. He had even deprived her of Wu Shunjun, the young man she had loved like the son they never had.

"Just stop fantasizing, that's all," he said softly. "We're not out of the woods yet. We mustn't spend one yuan before I close the deal."

Li Li was in no mood for conciliation.

"You're so small, *Chi*," she sneered. "Forever tiptoeing around the drops so as not to get your feet wet. My brother says that the Americans get rich because they take risks. But you, oh no." Her thin lips curled with disdain.

As always, the mention of his brother-in-law felt to Liang Dacheng like a poison dart. Beyond reach in a fabulous America, he was also beyond reproach: the measure of all success, of all that was good in his wife's eyes, while he, her husband, never failed to fall short.

But if he could tame a mob of angry protestors, couldn't he tame his own wife? So Liang Dacheng tried again: "If word came out that I paid bribes we could be in very hot water."

"Bribes? So what? Everybody does that. My brother once said—"

"Hang your brother!" Liang snapped. "I don't give a fig what he does or doesn't say! He should've been sent away for re-education years ago! How dare you mention risk to me? To *me*!" He was almost shouting, hurt by the unfairness of it all. Hadn't he sunk their meager life savings into bribing the provincial deputy to get approval for the deal? Hadn't his first thought been for Li Li, who he knew hated their life in this town?

"I broke the law for you! I am party secretary. Factory director. I've betrayed the state!"

"So what? What has the state ever done for you? Haven't you given it your entire life? And mine?" she whipped back. "Come on, we're just taking back a bit of what is owed to you, of what is rightly yours."

They were standing opposite each other in the living room, glowering at each other like two wrestlers in a ring.

Liang rarely quarreled with his wife. Their lives had been entwined for so long that he often felt that the innermost recesses of his mind were connected by some secret passage to hers. But on this occasion, he had to keep the door to the passage firmly shut. He would endanger her if he revealed what had really happened: What he had done went far beyond a mere greasing of the system. If his true transgression were found out, the penalty would be unbearably severe. He was not only risking his own life but possibly Li Li's as well.

A shudder of apprehension coursed through Liang's body. It was too late now. What he had set in motion couldn't be stopped. The truth was, he wouldn't have minded for them to continue as they were: He was used to the tattered beige sofa in their spartan living room, to the bleakness of the neon lighting that matched the bleakness of their lives—he had no dreams of expensive clothes or fancy vacations. And yet, all those years of loyalty to the factory and to the party with so little to show for it, yielding no more than a take-home pay of a measly $200 a month. If they could manage for the present, there was the future to contend with. How could they retire—expensive vacations or no—on that? Besides, the guilt he felt towards his wife kept churning in his gut. He still loved her companionship, still remembered his youthful passion for her beauty that drudgery—not just time—had stolen from her.

Turning away abruptly, he strode over to their dingy sofa and sat down. He sat very still, his head bowed, his chin sunken onto his chest, his pulse racing. Up to this very moment, swept up by the momentum of events, he had stifled any thought of wrongdoing. And his wife had egged him on the whole way. *Go ahead, do it, just do it, do whatever it takes to sell the factory, to get our hands on some*—and she had used that tainted capitalist word: *money*. "From each according to his ability, to each according to his needs." But who was to say, let alone dictate, what those needs were?

Life was just too hard, he complained to himself, sighing, overcome by a surge of self-pity. Li Li was right—the system had exploited him. He had climbed to the top of this particular ant heap by dint of tenacity and hard work. He was a prize-winning manager—an engineer to boot—and his superiors had bought his services at a bargain-basement price. His own brother-in-law, that worthless prick, had somehow wrangled his way to America on a student exchange program and had stayed there, making, at some shit job, twenty times as much as he did as the star manager of Liaoning Province.

From the depth of his self-absorption, he hardly noticed Li Li going out of the room and returning, having changed back into a pair of well-worn blue trousers and a T-shirt. He hardly noticed when she knelt meekly before him on the bare concrete tiled floor. But then the touch of her hands on his trousered knees reminded him of some long-forgotten desires.

Liang Dacheng lifted his head and looked at his wife. Ever so gently, he gathered her hands between his own, and began tenderly kissing, one by one, the tip of each chapped and callused finger, each broken fingernail.

"Do you remember, Dacheng?" Li Li whispered. "Do you remember how smooth and ivory white the skin of my hands was?"

He remembered. The hands of a princess, soft, without blemish, with cuticles in the shape of perfect half-moons.

All at once, he calmed down. He beckoned to her to sit down beside him, patting the hard cushion at his side. And when she sidled up to him, he pulled her to him, hugging her tightly.

Beautiful hands were more important than fancy clothes.

"You must hurry and get yourself a manicure before the Americans arrive," he said. "That much we can afford," he added, not without a tinge of bitterness.

• • •

Back in his office, there was a letter waiting for him on his desk, his name neatly spelled out on the front of the envelope. Puzzled, Liang Dacheng flipped it over. No return name or address.

Impatiently, Liang ripped open the letter. He quickly scanned the few lines scribbled down the sheet of paper.

"Shi Chi," he bellowed. "Who delivered this?"

Shi Chi shrugged his shoulders. "No idea. Found it on the floor near the door."

"I have to go out. I'll be back soon. Don't tell anyone I'm gone," he barked.

• • •

It was the perfect hiding place. The bed of the river ran lower here, in a gully-like depression between two steep slopes, so that it could not be seen from the main road. A field of tall sorghum that grew to within a few feet of the bank provided additional protection from prying eyes.

The bike Liang Dacheng had pedaled furiously for more than half an hour to this secluded spot was leaning against a nearby rock, and he was pacing back and forth impatiently, lighting one cigarette after another, waiting.

It was unbearably hot. The noontime sun in the inverted bowl of pale blue above beat down on his bare head like a hammer, the odor of rotting vegetation and sour mud strong in his nostrils. And it was silent: a pastoral silence, disturbed only by the steady chirping of crickets and the swift coursing of the river's waters.

Liang Dacheng swatted away an iridescent dragonfly that alighted on his bare arm and glanced impatiently at his watch.

He took the letter out of his pocket and with sweaty fingers smoothed out the creases, trying once more to figure out who had sent it.

It had been written by a local. Only a local would have asked to meet him at this old, abandoned fishing dock, a favorite rendezvous for young couples in search of privacy, that scarcest of commodities.

He wiped away the beads of sweat from his forehead with the back of his hand and tugged pensively at his right earlobe.

Far away, on a distant hillock to his right, he thought he could see a colorful blob moving against the horizon. But it was getting smaller and smaller, moving away, not toward him.

A sudden rustling in the growth behind him made him jump. But no, it was only a bird. Having freed itself from the tangle of stalks in the field, it soared upward into the sky.

The waiting was agony.

He glanced at the letter yet again, as if by examining the words one more time he could penetrate their underlying message.

The words were transparent enough: *I know all about your treason.*

Liang checked the hands of his watch, which showed that half an hour had elapsed. Whoever it was, his nemesis was late.

He scanned the horizon. Still nothing.

It was hard to think clearly in the debilitating heat. But suddenly a name broke through to the surface of his consciousness. Wang Min! His overladen mind had forgotten Wang Min. Of course! It could only be him! The pieces of the puzzle tumbled rapidly into place one after the other. Wang Min regarded the sale of the factory as an act of treason against socialism. The demonstration had failed to stop the sale. Wang Min was out to sabotage the meeting with the Americans. By luring him out here, Wang was free to stir up trouble in his absence. Ergo, no one was meant to show up. No one was going to show up. Mystery solved. Liang exhaled at length with pleasurable relief. He would wait just a little while longer and—

"Congratulations!"

Startled, Liang Dacheng swung round to face the figure that emerged theatrically from the dense cover of the sorghum field. The figure paused for a moment, chewing on a stalk with studied nonchalance, hovering a couple of meters above Liang Dacheng before scrambling down the steep slope to the river's bank.

"You!" exclaimed Liang Dacheng.

It was the boyish Wu Shunjun, his former protégé, the one he and his wife had welcomed into their family like a son. But also the disgraced offender. He was the very last person he had expected to see.

"What on earth are you doing here?"

"As I said. Congratulations," Shunjun repeated, slowly clapping his hands. "So, you pulled it off. Well done! You'll be a rich man." Turning his head to one side, he spat out the stalk of sorghum.

Liang Dacheng still had a soft spot for Shunjun. When Shunjun arrived at the factory from the orphanage, Liang took him under his wing, mentored and promoted him. And Li Li would have him over for Chinese New Year and other holiday meals as though he were a member of the family. Then, not a year ago, disaster struck. Shunjun was caught red-handed, embezzling the factory's funds.

It was a terrible stain on the factory's sterling reputation and reflected badly on Liang's stewardship. Though Liang Dacheng—despite Li Li's entreaties—expelled him from the factory forthwith, he hadn't had the heart to prosecute him. Even now, his fatherly feelings got the better of him.

"Where have you been all this time? Have you any idea how upset Aunt Li Li was when you left without bothering to say good-bye? She was worried sick something bad might have happened to you."

The young man paid no heed. He rocked slowly back and forth on his heels, with a smile that revealed his crooked teeth, gazing insolently at Liang Dacheng.

Liang could hardly recognize his golden boy. "Answer me! Where have you been?"

"What is it to you?" said Wu Shunjun flatly, shrugging his shoulders. "But if you must know, I've been around and about, and doing a lot of thinking."

Liang Dacheng responded, upset at Shunjun's unflappability, "Oh, really? I'll tell you what's it to me. I am a very busy man and I don't have time for your little games."

"You can't fool me, Liang Dacheng. As I said, congratulations. You've made it. But you can't play the high and mighty with me anymore."

His presumption was boundless. Taking a quick look at his watch again, Liang Dacheng interrupted angrily, "I see I've been too good to you, you ingrate," his narrow eyes hardening into little black bullets. "So out with it! What the hell do you want from me?"

"Fifty thousand dollars or I'll spill the beans," was Shunjun's cool reply.

Stunned, Liang Dacheng took a step back, almost losing his footing on the muddy ground. He stared at Shunjun in disbelief.

"I know what you did," said Shunjun quietly.

"I don't know what you're talking about," Liang Dacheng countered, more distraught than he let on. He knew very well what he had done.

Shunjun took a step closer.

"What did the Americans pay to buy you, huh? To sell out your country, Liang Dacheng? Undervaluing the factory for your own gain—clever, I'll give you that," Shunjun went on, goading him, stepping ever closer to his erstwhile benefactor, his mocking grin unchanged.

"How dare you!" Liang Dacheng retorted, incensed. "Wipe that sneer off your face! I'm still Secretary Liang to you."

Liang Dacheng had not reached the top for lack of iron nerve. But he was now genuinely scared for the first time in his life. Fear rose from the depths of his belly like nausea. The American CEO—the one with the unpronounceable name of Ryan Forrester—had indeed offered, in exchange for lowering the price of the factory even further, to pour $250,000 into an offshore account on top of the agreed-upon 5 percent commission in stocks. Liang had conducted the last round of negotiation personally, and in utmost secrecy. Had taken all the necessary precautions to keep the details under wraps. Or so he thought.

Somehow Shunjun had sniffed out the truth.

"I read about the sale in the *Shenyang Daily*. They said the factory was going for five million dollars. Well, I know that the land alone is worth much more. By my own calculations it is worth double that...."

"Mere conjecture! You've no proof!" Liang Dacheng shot back.

"Maybe. But then, maybe not. I've compiled an inventory of all the assets of the factory, you see. My estimate of their value comes to around ten million dollars. One word from me, as the former chief accountant of the factory—"

"A position you held upon my own recommendation, don't forget—"

"One word from me," Shunjun repeated, unruffled, "to the Liaoning committee secretary should be quite enough, don't you think? The mere whiff of wrongdoing would bring the whole deal crashing down. And you along with it."

Despite the heat feeling like burning fire, Liang shivered. He knew he was trapped. Shunjun was right. Would his future inquisitors believe his claims that Ryan Forrester had threatened to take his business elsewhere if he did not comply? That to save the factory and the workers he had had no choice but to accept the American's bribe?

Damn, damn, damn*!* He was in touching distance of his prize. He couldn't possibly allow this turtle egg to spoil everything. Turning his back on Shunjun, Liang stomped up the steps to the jetty. He needed a moment to gather his thoughts. With every passing second, with every whirr of an insect in the air, with every burble of the river's waters, his heart drummed more wildly in his chest. He just had to figure a way out of this mess.

But Shunjun wouldn't let go. Liang could hear his footfalls on the wooden planks following him, his voice calling after him,

"Come on now, Secretary Liang. Give me the money, and I promise I'll never bother you again."

Liang Dacheng swung around.

"And what are the promises of a double traitor worth? How can I count on you not to hound me for more?"

"You needn't worry about it. You'll never see me again. I know I'm branded in this town. I'm getting out of here. For good."

Liang Dacheng ran his fingers through his hair, the stubborn tuft refusing to be tamed.

"Come on," said Shunjun. "There's no other way out, Secretary Liang. Neither for me nor for you."

Looking down at the dark water through the gaps in the half-rotten boards of the jetty's platform beneath his feet. Liang thought hard. If he gave in to Shunjun, there was no telling if he would actually keep his word. But his plan did make sense. And if he did keep his promise to disappear…

"Please, Secretary," said Shunjun, pleading now. "I don't want to report you. Honestly, I don't. If I destroy you, I destroy myself. Come on, you must see the reasonableness of my demand."

"To be rewarded for your treachery?"

"Hypocrite. Are you the only one entitled to money and a new life? The only difference between us is that I got caught and you're getting away with it."

Liang Dacheng's face darkened, flushing deep red under his tan from the heat and his mounting rage.

"How dare you, you ungrateful turtle egg! Shame on you! After all I've done for you. And Li Li..." He almost choked on the enormity of Shunjun's betrayal. "She loved you."

He couldn't control his temper anymore. Exploding at last, Liang Dacheng lashed out with his fist. With all the weight of his heavy body, he landed a resounding punch on Shunjun's jaw.

Shunjun reeled. Slipping on a slimy spot on the worn floorboards of the dock, he almost lost his balance.

But Liang Dacheng was on the rampage. "Do you want another go? I don't have patience for the likes of you!"

And he landed another blow, which sent Shunjun's thin frame tumbling backward, his arms flailing. He fell right over the edge of the pier into the river with a splash.

Liang Dacheng, left standing on the jetty, looked down at him. He burst out laughing, his temper subsiding. "Serves you right! That should cool you down a bit," he shouted at him.

The water was deep. Shunjun was thrashing about wildly, trying, unsuccessfully, to grasp one of the wooden posts supporting the jetty, his eyes full of terror—

"Secretary, help!" he called out.

Liang Dacheng had already unbuckled his belt to pull him out.

"Comrade, I can't swim!" Shunjun called out desperately again between gasps for air.

For a moment Liang Dacheng examined his conscience, squinting at the empty river, the empty horizon.

They used to go fishing together, over there, upstream.

The big smile on Shunjun's face when he caught his first fish ever. A warm, merry, and sunny smile.

Li Li would be heartbroken. But the town had too much to lose. They all had too much to lose. He couldn't risk the only chance to save the town. Not for Shunjun. Not for anyone. He looked at his watch. The Americans would be arriving very soon now. He should not make Ryan Forrester wait.

Turning his back to the river, blinking away the sting of tears in his eyes, Liang Dacheng strode resolutely toward his bicycle.

• • •

When Liang Dacheng marched into his office, Shi Chi was waiting for him.

"Good news, Secretary Liang. We just had a phone call from Beijing. The Americans have boarded the train to Shenyang. They'll be here in a couple of hours. It seems that everything is on schedule."

After emerging from the shower, Liang Dacheng spent the next hour practicing the CEO's name. "Ryan," he repeated to himself over and over, trying his best not to pronounce it as "Lion."

• • •

Liang Dacheng had been unable to fall asleep. After tossing and turning for a couple of hours, he had slipped out of the house in the wee hours of the night to walk about the deserted streets of the town, hoping some mild exercise would quell the nagging of his troubled conscience.

He should have been pleased and relieved by the day's turn of events. After all, his careful preparations had borne fruit. The banquet had gone without a hitch and the small spectacle the high school students staged was well received. At the signing ceremony, Ryan Forrester's handshake had been firm, and the deputy governor of the province of Liaoning had signed the contract for the sale of the factory at the agreed-upon price without a flicker of hesitation.

Even that nasty business with Wu Shunjun seemed resolved. The chief of police had informed him later on that evening that a couple of fishermen had pulled his body out of the river, and the verdict was that the poor man had taken his own life. Li Li cried bitterly when she heard the news, which was unfortunate, but time and their newfound money would soon help her overcome her loss.

Yet sleep escaped him, the memory of his grandmother Nai-Nai's admonitions, about hell's eternal hounding by those seeking justice, giving him no peace.

• • •

Was it a ghost?

Liang Dacheng's body quaked. Drops of cold sweat dripped into his eyes. In the shadows of the darkened factory buildings, he could make out the blurred silhouette of a slender male figure with dark hair leaning against one of the brick walls.

Shunjun?

Though his heart pounded, Liang took a brave but tentative step forward. He would confront the apparition. As he had always done toward the living, he would do now in face of the dead.

Incredibly, the thing was moving toward him! Liang froze in his tracks as he saw it detaching itself from the wall.

"Hello there! Imagine finding you here so late at night!" the figure emerging from the shadows pronounced cheerily.

It was Ryan Forrester, very much alive.

The relief Liang felt left him momentarily speechless. And then finding his tongue, he uttered, stupidly, "*Ni hao ma*," as if an exchange of greetings at this abnormal hour were the most normal thing in the world.

Ryan looked back at the placid mask of Liang's face, and replied, in halting Mandarin, "I couldn't sleep, either."

If Liang was startled by Ryan's knowledge of the language, which he had kept well-hidden until now, he showed no sign of it.

"The excitement, you know," Ryan continued, glancing up, ecstatic, at the factory walls. "It isn't every day that I buy a factory. It's my first, in fact."

"What are you going to do with it?"

"Everything. Big things," Ryan replied, throwing his arms up in the air. "Things that are going to change the world."

He reached for the pack of cigarettes in his pocket. "Smoke?"

Liang shook his head. Ryan Forrester was crazy, he thought. How could an old, decrepit factory full of rusting machinery change the world, even if he did pour millions into it?

Besides, he didn't believe the world could change. Not anymore. Not after having spent the better part of his life fighting for communism, for a dream that had led to nothing but misery and deprivation. He was done with grand schemes and ambitions. The only concerns that preoccupied him in defeat were the more mundane and modest aims of bettering his lot and that of his town.

"I see a great future here in China, my friend," Ryan went on, this time in English. "With our know-how and your labor, the future glows bright."

Ryan flicked the ash off his cigarette. "I like this town. You will be seeing a lot of me from now on."

"What about your wife and children?" said Liang.

"I'm divorced," Ryan answered rather curtly. "No wife, no kids."

So, a lonely man, thought Liang.

"You're still young. You can find another wife," Liang countered.

"Not that young," Ryan laughed. "Just turned thirty-eight. And no. Being married once was plenty enough for me. Now I have all the time in the world to focus on my work. Sorry, our work. We are going to do great things together. It's a promise."

And with that, Ryan strode away, waving his hand in a lighthearted gesture of farewell, leaving Liang alone in the darkness, staring down at the glowing end of the unfinished cigarette that Ryan had thrown casually onto the ground.

Chapter 2

RYAN FORRESTER

Cleveland, USA, September 2002

"If you deprive yourself of outsourcing and your competitors do not, you're putting yourself out of business."

—Lee Kuan Yew, *prime minister of Singapore*

"We used to make shit in this country."

—Frank Sobotka *in the second season of* The Wire

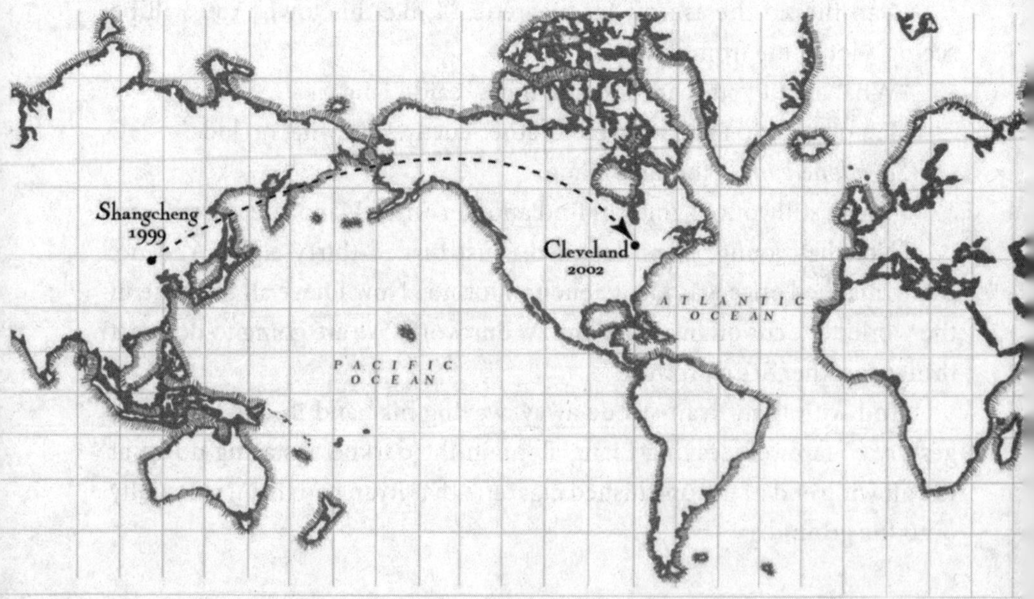

THE AIRPLANE FROM LOS ANGELES began its descent into Hopkins International Airport, its nose breaking through the blanket of cloud to reveal the great flat expanse of Lake Erie.

Ryan Forrester, compelled, finally, to shut down his laptop, gave way to a host of emotions and memories messing with his normally disciplined mind.

He was thinking of Cleveland, the city they were rapidly approaching. The city in which he had been born and raised. From which he had escaped.

As the plane descended, its wheels dropping, Ryan looked out wistfully through the porthole. The runway was speeding closer and closer into view. Then the plane, regaining the reality of its mass, landed with a bump on the tarmac.

• • •

At the baggage claim a driver held up a large placard with Ryan's name on it. It was a superfluous precaution given that the airport was half empty on this day of ill omen, the first anniversary of 9/11. Superfluous, too, because Ryan instantly recognized the portly, greying figure.

"Well, whaddya know! Adam Kuczinski!"

The recognition was mutual. "Mr. Forrester! Welcome home! Great to see you." Adam broke out in a smile and vigorously shook Ryan's hand. He took charge of Ryan's carry-on as they exited the terminal.

"How've you been doing, Adam? How are the wife and kids? It's been so long," said Ryan as they walked to the car.

"Yes, too long. And everyone's doing well, thanks for asking."

Ryan slid onto the soft cushy leather of the back seat of the company limousine. Good thing they sent it. He was tired and overworked and had to cram this last-minute trip into his busy schedule.

"We'll be in Gates Mills in no time," said Adam as they set out in the direction of the I-71, northward to the city.

Ryan shifted in the back seat and leaned forward to speak to Adam. "How about taking the long way and driving through town? I feel like seeing the old neighborhood."

The afternoon was slowly turning into dusky evening as they drove across the bridge that spanned the bend of the Cuyahoga River, Industrial Valley stretching out below them to their right. Machinery, warehouses, and factories were scattered throughout the valley. Ryan watched the familiar landscape glide by. In the failing light, the low bank of rolling grey and blue clouds, streaked with the orange hues of the soon-to-be-setting sun, created an impressionistic haze upon which the dark steel trusses of iron bridges, of great cranes, and of soaring electric pylons were etched as if in black ink.

But it was the idiosyncratic silhouette of the onion domes of the cathedral of St. Theodosius rising beyond the white conical-roofed water tanks that caught Ryan's eye and gave him pause. It reminded him of what his uncle used to say: that piety and industry were the twin pillars of American success. Not that his uncle, as far as he knew, had ever set foot in a church.

"Say, Adam, how many years you been working for my uncle?"

"Thirty years come November. Mr. Payne says that at this rate I'll be driving him to his funeral," he said with a chuckle.

Ryan laughed politely. "Speaking of, how's the old man doing?"

"Mr. Payne's not so good, I'm afraid. He's all broken up over John's injury. Haven't seen him in such a state since your mother passed."

Ryan felt sorry for what had happened to John, Clifton's youngest son, who had lost both legs in Afghanistan. But it was the recollection of Clifton's breaking down, being helped into a chair, at his mother's wake that really affected him. Clifton's ashen face, his eyes brimming with tears.

"The only thing keeping him alive now is the factory, I reckon," Adam went on.

The factory. Of course. Somehow, he wasn't surprised.

"Even though Graham runs it now, Mr. Payne can't let go. Shows up every other day, rain or shine. My two sons have jobs there, you know, and they say Mr. Payne is still the living soul of the place."

He didn't know Clifton was still so deeply involved with the factory. He felt sorry for the old guy—not easy letting go of a life's work.

The car sped on and more church spires came into view. Hadn't Ryan read somewhere that Cleveland boasted more than a thousand churches? Too much piety and too little industry. He wasn't fooled by the chimney stacks puffing plumes of white steam into the air, by the bright yellow glow of occasional flares from the distant steel mills dotting the horizon. It was a romantic vision of industry that he knew was quite false. The golden flares from the blast furnaces out there no longer a show of power but merely the shrunken remnants of Ohio's once-thriving steelworks, which had, for the most part, relocated to China.

Ryan lowered the window to let in some fresh air. It smelled good, almost sweet. All those clean-air acts and regulations were having an effect all right, their punishing costs most likely the death blow to the country's ailing manufacturing industry. Suddenly, unbidden, the noxious pollution of China's industrial cities was vividly present in his nostrils. *Breathe good air and you got no job,* he thought. *Choke and you got one.*

Ryan was not insensitive to his own role in this decline. In the three years that had passed since buying the factory in Shangcheng, he had perfected the art of the vulture, picking and tearing away at the flesh of the sick and dying American rustbelt, taking apart entire production lines and reconstituting them in China. He had done well, thanks to his East Asian studies major at Stanford and the experience gained over a decade at General Electric. With the capable Liang Dacheng at his side, he had succeeded beyond even the high expectations he had set for himself. CEO of a company valued at more than $250 million, with branches in five countries and a fancy office in LA, he was now a wealthy man. But it wasn't the money he cared about. That stuff was only a by-product of his ambition.

No, he envisioned himself as something of a pioneer, out there on the frontier, harnessing the wild, untamed horses of globalized capitalism for the benefit of the common man, helping the third world catch up with the first. He had meant every word when he told Liang Dacheng that they were going to do "great things together." The town of Shangcheng had flourished as a result of their partnership. The townsfolk realized this, and whenever he went for a visit, which was a couple of times a year, they showed their appreciation by coming up to shake his hand in the street.

• • •

As they exited the freeway, the skyscrapers of downtown Cleveland loomed ahead. Terminal Tower, Cleveland's own Empire State Building, stood as tall as ever. Built in the thirties when Cleveland was still one of America's biggest cities, the Terminal Tower was at the time the fourth-tallest building in the world.

For a moment, Ryan imagined Superman, Cleveland's native son, flying over the Terminal Tower. Superman, the hero of his childhood: *Kerpow! Bang! Garrgh!*

"Still a Tribe fan?" Adam's voice interrupted his reverie.

"Of course."

They were almost upon Jacobs Field, the huge baseball stadium erected a few years previously on the southeast corner of downtown. It was a festive structure, topped with a tiara of bristling lights that looked like the teeth of a ring ready to be set with a huge diamond—but missing the diamond.

An altogether pathetic, almost desperate, attempt by the city to sparkle, to project success, to call attention to herself like some aging beauty queen. *Look at me, I'm still alive, still vital!*

The city some called the "Mistake by the Lake."

"Lost to the Blue Jays last night," said Adam with sorrow in his voice. "Blown any chance of making the playoffs this year." He shook his head. "Should never have traded Colón to Montreal."

"Well, they had a pretty amazing run in the last eight years," Ryan replied, flushed by the recollection of happy times, going to games at the old Municipal Stadium with his father. The flavor and crunch of crackerjacks revisited, for a fleeting instant, his tongue and palate.

"Good things don't last," said Adam. "It sure feels like the end of an era."

• • •

Euclid Avenue, one of the city's main arteries downtown, was quiet; *too quiet,* thought Ryan, even for a business district emptying out at the end of the day. He could see entire buildings in disuse, with boarded-up storefronts and entrance doors. As they turned onto Cedar Avenue the rot became worse, the city dissolving into a dreary wilderness of decaying warehouses with broken windows and abandoned lots. Thorns, tumbleweed, and clumps of dried-up grass grew in the cratered sidewalks and in what had once been parks. Blooms of rusting soda cans, of broken beer bottles and junk; piles of old tires, twisted iron, and hillocks of trash and assorted debris. The only signs of activity they drove by—a rundown establishment that called itself a discount store, a decrepit, shuttered bar with its roof half caved in—seemed on the verge of collapse, like the old, toothless Black man squatting folded up on a stoop.

It was as if the city had willed itself into poverty, thought Ryan; as if it had simply given up the ghost. And the windows of the abandoned factories that had no panes at all seemed to gape at him accusingly like gouged-out eyes in faces of dirty brick.

Dispirited, Ryan looked away.

• • •

Away from downtown, the monotonous flatness gave way to rolling hills. Neat houses with well-tended front yards lined the street, as did the commercial signifiers of prosperous suburban America: supermarkets, fast-food restaurants, and chain stores of all kinds.

They passed by some familiar storefronts. It was here that he had grown up, in Cleveland Heights, in a modest house on a modest street at the edge of this solidly middle-class neighborhood.

"Be sure to keep your window up," said Adam. "There's been some shooting around here lately, and it's my responsibility to deliver you in one piece."

"Here? Really?" Ryan's eyes scanned the quiet streets with disbelief.

"Yep. Haven't heard of the Bicycle Shooter, eh?"

"Can't say I have."

"Some thug on a bicycle took potshots at people three times in the last two weeks. The latest victim was hit right around here, sitting in his car in his driveway."

"Nasty." So this was his welcome home.

But was it home? Adam pulled the limousine up to the curb opposite Ryan's parents' old house. Ryan sat there, very still, staring at it from the car window. It had been repainted a vulgar shade of strident blue his mother would have hated, though the bushes at the edge of the small front garden were trimmed into neat spheres just as he remembered them. Though he'd been living in California for more than twenty years, he never felt truly at home there. But was this place home?

Growing up, he had been pulled between two worlds: the working-class one of his father, owner of a small car repair shop, and that of the rich, patrician one of his mother. Though his mother loved his father, she never did adjust to his world. Everything about her set her apart, including the well-ironed shirts and ties she made Ryan wear to school that turned him into a laughingstock in their blue-collar neighborhood. When his father died in a car crash, she hadn't thought twice of whisking him off to her brother Clifton when he offered them to live under his roof.

For Ryan, the trauma of losing his father, his house, and his school in the space of a few short months only reinforced his natural introversion. Soon after, when his mother fell ill with multiple sclerosis and began secluding herself in a room somewhere in the large rambling house like some eccentric character from Dickens, his loneliness was sealed. Though

Clifton was unfailingly kind and came to tuck him in at night as he would his own children, Ryan could never rid himself of the feeling that he was an unwanted burden, and that, as his father's son, he would never quite belong.

And now? Now that he had made it, out there in the real world, could he finally cast the doubts aside? He was not looking forward to finding out. The car moved on. Catching his reflection in the driver's rearview mirror, he smoothed down his dark hair uneasily and readjusted his tie.

• • •

In the twilight, the simple clapboard church and spire stood out in numinous pallor against the background of shadowed green, against the darkening sky where early stars peeked out from among the clouds.

They had arrived in the tiny, pristine center of Gates Mills village, and at Ryan's request had parked on the shoulder of Chagrin River Road, just across from the churchyard's white picket fence.

He needed to stretch his legs and give his overactive mind a rest before girding up to confront his mother's family.

He stepped out of the car, inhaled the damp evening air and, leaning back on the stout trunk of a chestnut tree, took out his lighter and lit up a cigarette.

Here in Gates Mills, nothing, as far as he could see, had been touched by change or decay. Not so much, it seemed, as a single blade of grass or a single board in the white picket fence. It was uncanny. Perhaps Gates Mills was ordained from its founding to remain unchanging and genteel forever—a secluded, hilly, wooded enclave, a shelter for the old rich and superrich: Ohio's version of Martha's Vineyard.

Ryan stood for a while, quietly smoking and contemplating the Episcopal church of St. Christopher's, standing aloof on its generous and spotless lawn, wrapped in its stillness. The services he would sometimes attend with his cousins as a child, the time he spent at his uncle's house, seemed to belong to another life.

But enough dawdling, he chided himself; enough with maudlin sentiment. It was time.

He stubbed out his cigarette on the asphalt and, as if to avoid any possibility of desecration, slowly and deliberately stooped down to retrieve the butt, cramming it among the remaining cigarettes in the pack.

He climbed back into the limousine and, with a resounding slam of the car door, they drove off into the green, now turned indigo in the shadows.

• • •

A couple of miles and a number of twists and turns later, they drove through a tall wrought-iron gate onto a gravel driveway. At the end of it lay the imposing mass of the Payne family estate. The Cape Cod revival–style house, with its white cladding, black shutters, and shingled roof, was deceptively simple and modest. And it was even bigger than he remembered.

Adam jumped out of the car, removed Ryan's bag from the trunk, and opened the car door for him. "Thanks for a lovely ride, Adam," said Ryan.

He skipped up the wide porch steps and lifted the familiar, eagle-shaped brass knocker, letting it fall against the front door. A maid appeared. After a few words of introduction, he was ushered discreetly inside.

• • •

The notes of a piano playing filtered through the tall, heavy double doors of the music room off the entrance hallway.

Ryan pushed them open a crack—

"Julie?"

The Steinway grand piano, perfectly poised at an angle in a corner, seemed to be hovering above the polished hardwood floor.

"Jule?" he repeated.

The music stopped abruptly mid-phrase, and his cousin swiveled around on the piano stool and stood up somewhat unsteadily.

"Here already? You're early!"

It was not quite the welcome Ryan expected. But he was happy to see her, and he hugged her tightly and pressed his lips to her cheeks.

Long ago, in another lifetime, her willowy blondness had never failed to make his heart race a little faster.

"You haven't changed one whit, Jule," he lied politely. Dropping his arms, he tried to hide his shock at her appearance. He hadn't seen her since her wedding five years before. She was only forty-three, but she looked older. Her mid-length hair hung down in lank strands and her once-creamy skin was marred by faint spidery lines that crept across her forehead and fanned from the corners of her nervous, light blue eyes.

"Flatterer," she protested, her lips twisting in a wry smile. "Drink?" she asked as she started to drift away towards the fireplace.

"You know I don't drink," Ryan reminded her.

"Mind if I have one?"

"Go ahead."

He watched her pour out the whiskey—his beautiful Julie—with uneasy eyes.

Frozen in time like the church in Gates Mill village, nothing in the room had changed. Not the oak-paneled walls, not the white limestone of the elaborate fireplace—the eighteenth-century original that Clifton had installed at great expense—not even the angle at which the blue silk-upholstered armchairs were positioned in front of it.

Julie abruptly slumped down into one of them.

"Sit," she commanded.

Ryan raised his eyebrows but obediently sat down.

She leaned over. "Hungry?"

Was that ever so slight a slur he detected in her voice?

"No thanks. I'm good," Ryan answered, loosening his tie. "I ate something on the plane." And he went on brightly, "What do you say we go out for a ride after the party? You know, a good jaunt for old time's sake?"

"I don't think so, Ryan," she drawled slowly, still slouched in her chair, fidgeting with a strand of hair, curling it around her forefinger again and again. "I'm done with that. Haven't been out riding or hunting in years."

What the hell was going on with her? What ever happened to the brilliant horsewoman, the accomplished pianist, the sunshine of the family? Sure, her marriage had been a disaster. But it had been three years since her divorce. Surely plenty of time in which to recover. Instead, here she was, still stuck in her parents' house.

"What gives, Jule?" he inquired gently, as if of a fragile thing. He had a sudden urge to take her by the hand but thought better of it.

"Don't you dare." She looked up at him from under thick dark eyebrows that, once upon a time, had enhanced her pallid beauty.

"Fuck you, Ryan."

And she emptied her glass in one go, like a habituated drinker.

Ryan saw not just the hurt in her eyes but also a new hardness in them.

"Where does this sudden concern come from?" she went on. "You disappear from our lives as if we weren't good enough for you anymore. Do you really think you can suddenly show up and expect everything to be the same?"

Ryan was totally taken aback.

"I realize my brothers were tough on you," she said more softly, "but after all, Dad did put you through high school and college."

Tough?

Tough was all she could call it? Tied down to the bed, helpless, his cousins leering over his face in the middle of the night? The contempt, the mocking, the endless taunts. *Charity boy. Parasite. Leech.* The hissing malevolence of his cousins' name-calling still stung.

Ryan's teeth and lips clenched involuntarily. "I know the debt I owe this family," he said, and calmer now, he placed his hand on hers. "I'm grateful from the bottom of my heart. Truly, I am."

She quickly slipped her hand out of his grasp. "So why have you stayed away? We were such friends! Did you think some Christmas cards and the occasional email would make up for your disappearance somehow?"

Ryan watched his cousin—once his sanctuary and goddess—pour herself a second drink. She had been the only one to stand up for him, the only one who shielded him from her brothers' cruelty. Of all the people in the world, she was the one he could least bear to hurt.

He mumbled some platitudes about his work, and other constraints. But why did he have to explain?

Making love in the dark shadows under the trees in Gates Mills. The white church glistening in the moonlight.

Wasn't it obvious to her that he had to run for his life, even at the cost of abandoning her? And he had vowed he'd never come back until he could stand on his own two feet, owing nothing to no one.

It was the summer before his senior year at Stanford. He was twenty and had just earned a black belt in judo. Life was good. He came back to work at the factory as he did every summer, but that July, the closeness with Julie flowered into something more. He was working in the factory on a Sunday when all hell broke loose. He could still summon up the scene as clear as day.

The particles of dust in the light streaming down from the tall clerestory windows of the main factory hall, the smell of machine oil mixed with the lingering perfume from Julie's kiss. And Frank. Frank, Julie's brother, shouting down at him over the deafening noise of the machines. Lying prone on the ground, his judo skills powerless against both Frank and his brother Graham, Clifton's eldest son, whose booted foot was on his chest. "Hands off Julie, you fucking scum. Is this how you repay us? By getting into Julie's pants? Do you think she'll save you? And just wait till we tell Dad. You'll never be one of us! Dad's leaving it all to his real children. You won't see a dime when he's gone."

That very night he had made his escape. He hurriedly packed his bags, saying good-bye to no one.

"Anyway," said Julie, "what does it matter now? You're here, right? And for what it's worth, I'm glad you are." But she couldn't resist adding, in a hushed voice, "Though I have a feeling Graham invited you only because he wants something from you. Is it the family business, Ryan?"

"I wouldn't know about that," said Ryan. Graham had specifically asked him not to mention anything to the family. Not to Uncle Clifton—and certainly not to Julie.

"I'm in the dark, Ryan. Always in the dark. But I sure hope you can fix whatever needs fixing. Nobody tells me anything," she complained with a sniff. "For one thing, Dad is getting really old. His age shows. He's seventy-five, for heaven's sake! And he hasn't been himself, you know, ever since John-John—sorry—John returned from Afghanistan."

"Yes. Adam told me he has difficulty coping. How bad is it?"

"You tell me. He's taken to having his dinner in his bedroom, alone. He shuns everybody. He's almost never at home, and when he is, he flies off the handle over the littlest things. He and Graham are forever getting into fights—they're barely on speaking terms."

"I see," said Ryan.

"See what?"

Ryan shook his head.

Julie's litany continued, "Then there's Graham's divorce. Messy and expensive. Alexandra's moved to England, and Frank is still out of a job."

Yeah, thought Ryan, *Frank wasn't the only fool to lose his shirt when the dot-com bubble burst.* But he only allowed himself to say, "I understand. But you can't let this drag you down. You've got to get out of this house."

Julie gave him a look not so much of reproach as of weariness.

"And go where, exactly?" she asked almost wistfully. She went on, "I haven't even told you about John. Just a shadow of who he was. He's hooked on opioids, you know, though nobody talks about it. And when he isn't locked in his room, he wheels himself around the house like a zombie. Nobody can get through to him."

"And your mom," ventured Ryan. "How's she taking all this? Holding up?"

"Oh yes. You know Mom, always putting on a brave face." Julie smiled at him wanly. "You know, Dad isn't even looking forward to this birthday party."

"Are you sure he isn't secretly pleased, Julie? Is it going to be a big bash?"

"And how. A huge bash. All the who's who and even those who aren't are coming. How in the hell we can afford it, I don't know."

Julie finally got up, somewhat unsteadily, brushing away an imaginary speck from the front of her thin silk dress. "It's getting late," she said.

Ryan rose from his chair, too, and stood facing her.

"Is that why you're here, Ryan?" Julie asked, looking directly into his eyes. "To help Dad and Graham straighten things out? Is that why you were summoned?"

Hell. Of course, he knew why. He couldn't very well resist what was essentially the family's cry for help, could he? But could he straighten things out? For a fraction of a second, the thought of Superman, his talisman, crossed his mind.

But he sidestepped the question. "Don't let your imagination run away with you, Julie. I was invited, not summoned."

She didn't look convinced.

"But enough about me," Ryan added, flustered. "You still haven't told me what you're up to these days...."

"Oh, there's nothing to tell, Ryan." She shrugged. "Everything's just fine and dandy." There was no light in her light blue eyes.

Fine? Her stars had been aligned from birth. Yet here she was: a has-been already, with no kids and no career. She looked wrung out and drained. Somehow, the life of a modern woman had passed her by.

What a cop-out.

• • •

The family sure knew how to put on a show! Warily, Ryan came down from the steps of the front veranda of the house in the early hours of the afternoon and plunged himself into the pool of the happy sounds of clinking glass and screams of laughter splashing over the great lawn. There were balloons everywhere, hanging in garlands and bunched in bouquets overhead. There were flowers, too: waterfalls of red and white roses cascading around the tables and spilling from pedestal vases. And the snapping of an American flag in the breeze provided crisp counterpoints to the notes of a band playing.

As Ryan wound his way through the crowd of guests and white-jacketed waiters, he could almost feel, like a tangible presence, that peculiar confidence born of old money radiating from the tuxedoed men's faces, from women teetering on the lawn in spiky heels and wide-brimmed straw hats, from little girls chasing each other in almost identical Lilly Pulitzer dresses.

He looked down at his business suit with misgivings: Naturally, Graham hadn't bothered to inform him that the party would be a black-tie affair. The old feelings of belonging-not-belonging rushed back. This was a mistake, thought Ryan: He should have skipped the party and come directly for the meeting the next day.

He hadn't met his other cousins yet and dreaded the coming encounters. Thinking of the devil, he spotted Graham circulating among the guests, tall and imposing, his still-abundant, greying blond hair combed back from his forehead. He cut quite a figure in the crowd, his custom-made tuxedo succeeding, to great effect, in camouflaging his large paunch with the best sartorial expertise that money could buy.

He had to give it to him. Graham had this enviable knack for looking good and making everyone feel at ease. A born politician. On the board of the local high school, of the Hospice of the Western Reserve and several other charities, as well as serving as vice president of the Hunt Club. His social adroitness was an important asset to the Payne family's standing.

Ryan really needed to grab him for a talk to finalize the details of their agreement. Slim chance of that, though. Graham was all over the place and kept motioning to him—*later, later*—with his hand whenever Ryan did manage to catch his eye.

He approached a small group where Alexandra, Julie's younger sister, and her English husband, Simon, were among those chattering about their summer vacations: "The Hamptons," "The Bahamas," and "The Seychelles" flying through the air.

Alexandra was not to be outdone. "We spent a couple of weeks in August at our country house in the Cotswolds. Then we stopped in New York for a few days on the way here. The spa at the Four Seasons was amazing. And the shopping!" she gushed breathlessly. "I went on a rampage. Would you believe it? European designers cheaper in New York than in London? And then, to top it all, Simon here"—she looked up lovingly at her husband—"got us courtside seats for the men's finals at the US Open."

"It was fabulous. An epic match," added Simon, glowing in the light of his wife's attention. He was only twenty-nine and already a senior proprietary trader at Morgan Trust Bank with plenty of money to throw around. "American tennis at its finest. Sampras only barely held off Agassi in the fourth set."

Ryan edged away. Addicted to work, he hadn't taken a vacation in years. And he didn't play tennis. The good life was not for him, he thought. Yet he couldn't help but feel a tinge of envy of these people who were so secure in their own world.

Ryan felt a sudden slap on his shoulder. He swung around.

It was Frank, the last person he wanted to see.

"How much you reckon the party is costing us? The Krug Grande Cuvée alone is about a hundred dollars a pop. Funny, isn't it? That we are putting on this circus to convince the banks that the family is still solvent? Gotta show you got money to get money."

Frank shoved his face too close to his own for comfort, his breath hot on Ryan's cheek.

"So, Superman," he said, looking right through him, "you're the big dick now. Graham says you're here to save us. Not because of your pretty face, I hope."

Kerpow. Every fiber of his being strained to keep himself from punching him in the face.

It was at that moment that Clifton, birthday boy and family patriarch, chose to make his entrance. With a transformed Julie—a vision in peachy pink—on one arm, and his wife, Bitsy, on the other, he stood on the steps to the veranda of the house, commanding everyone's attention. He was tall, like Graham, with an upright posture undiminished by age. Greeted with applause by his guests, he gazed down at them, with an expression of magnificent scorn. He didn't like parties, the fuss and the bother, and he drove home his disdain by choosing to wear, over the protests of his wife, his decades-old navy-blue blazer with the brass buttons. With his mane of white hair, his white handlebar moustache, and his crinkled, weather-beaten face, he could have passed for an old sea dog, which in some sense he was, having served on a battleship during the Korean War.

For a brief moment, Ryan felt as if his heart was doing a somersault in his chest. He hadn't set eyes on Clifton for five years. Yet here he was, bigger than life, just as he remembered him: a lion. He was overwhelmed by ancient feelings of tenderness and love. Of respect. Of gratitude for his uncle's support and encouragement throughout his youth.

Ryan went up to congratulate him. Clifton reciprocated with a firm hug and gripped him with both arms. "Great to see you, son. So glad you could make it," he said with a beaming smile. "I want you to know that you make me proud. Your poor mother would have been so happy to see what you've made of yourself."

His uncle wasn't one given to easy compliments. A rush of warmth melted Ryan's entire being. What had Julie been on about? Like the clapboard church in Gates Mills village, the old man hadn't changed at all. For the first time that day, Ryan felt he had made the right decision in coming.

Julie detached herself from her father's arm. "You seem to have really cheered him up," she murmured in Ryan's ear.

He responded by holding out his hand. "Wanna dance?"

They soon found themselves on the temporary wooden dance floor, swaying to an old-fashioned melody. "You look ravishing," Ryan said. The magic of a gorgeous low-cut gown that revealed the swell of her breasts, a flattering upsweep of blonde hair, and a judicious application of eye shadow and mascara that brought out the cerulean blue of her eyes had transformed Julie, like Cinderella, back into the princess she really was. He held her more tightly than he should have.

• • •

"Speech! Speech!" the guests cried out, tapping their glasses with their spoons.

Afternoon had grown into evening, and tea lights were lit up, winking like stars on the tabletops on the lawn. Clifton Payne was sitting at the long table reserved for the closest members of his family, Bitsy on his right and Graham and Julie, his two eldest, on his left. John was also there, in his wheelchair, along with Frank, Alexandra, and Simon, Alexandra's British husband.

Not having been invited to join them, Ryan retreated to the side, leaning back against a trellised pole entwined with flowers.

Clifton rose and clutched a wine glass in one blue-veined hand and reached for a microphone with the other. His children looked on, trying to mask, with varying degrees of success, their apprehension at what might come next.

"Welcome, my oldest and dearest friends and guests!" he called out while flashing the wide, self-confident grin he was renowned for. "So, you have all gathered here in my home to celebrate. What exactly are we celebrating, I wonder? My seventy-fifth birthday or the countdown to my final decrepitude? On that score this should be my twenty-fifth!"

Everyone burst out laughing.

When they had quieted down, he continued. "Rudy. Hey Rudy! I know you're hiding somewhere. Show yourself!"

All heads turned. A small man sitting in the back row timidly raised his hand.

"Rudy, what are you doing there by yourself? Get yourself over here! Make room for him at my table! Folks, Rudy is my foreman, the pillar of my factory.

"Came to me as a mere slip of a boy, he did. You were fourteen, right, Rudy? And he rose to become my right hand by the sweat of his brow. Folks, a round of applause for Rudy! A round of applause for those who are the bedrock of our success!"

After the applause died down, Clifton continued. "Getting old sucks," he said, in a low voice, drawing closer to the microphone.

More laughter.

"There is one great advantage to it, though. I am not afraid to speak my mind."

Laughter yet again, but more circumspect this time.

"And I have to say that I do not like what I see around me. All I see," he went on, with a mocking, derisive look at Graham, "are fancy-schmancy foreign suits. What's wrong with good ol' made in the USA? Whining and complaining. Chasing easy money. We've turned into a bunch of good-for-nothing sissies." Now Clifton focused his withering gaze on Frank, who seemed to shrivel under its impact.

"Whatever happened to hard work, thrift, and, yes, patriotism? Folks, a round of applause for my son John. A veteran of the war in Afghanistan. He went on the line for us! I salute you, John! All stand for a toast to John!"

Refilling his glass from the decanter in front of him, Clifton raised it high, turning and bowing slightly in the direction of his youngest son. The guests stood up and raised their glasses. But John sat frozen in his wheelchair, his eyes fixed on some distant object.

If Clifton was disappointed, he didn't let on. He wobbled for a moment while he filled his glass again. Unhurriedly, he took a few a sips and then resumed, in a booming voice, "How many of you are actually out there on the factory floor? How many of you make the concerns of ordinary folks your own concern?"

The implied accusation wafted in the air above his guests. Many of them knew Clifton from way back, knew that he was an industrialist of the old school, more at home in his factory than at Cleveland Symphony Hall. The silence hung heavily. Graham and Frank exchanged worried glances.

Ryan hung on to his every word from the sidelines. Yes, he thought to himself, Clifton was still a lion. But it wasn't merely age that made him speak his mind. This jeremiad was quite in character; he had always been outspoken, blunt.

"Folks," Clifton thundered, "times are tough. Since 9/11 last year, our enemies have been watching our every move, looking for any weakness. This is not the moment to waver.

"Now, some of you might have heard rumors that Payne Tool and Die is facing difficulties. I can confirm this is true. I can also tell you that we don't plan to give up. Let me be clear. I want Rudy here to keep his job. And by God, he won't lose it. Not over my dead body. So, this is my solemn promise: I have no intention of ever abandoning my workers and will fight to keep their jobs in my factory."

At this pronouncement, Ryan nearly jumped out of his skin. The task he had come to do, he now realized, would prove much more of a struggle than he had anticipated.

Graham's agitation, too, was palpable. Ever mindful of the family's creditors present at the party, he discreetly pressed down hard on his father's toe under the table. But Clifton ignored him, clearly enjoying himself. All Graham could do was bite his tongue.

An elderly man at one of the tables, a life-long friend of Clifton's, suddenly shouted out. "No, Clifton! Get out while you still can! It's bigger than you. The drought and the economy are bad enough, and now we're going to war in Iraq. Don't play the hero. Not worth it."

Clifton smiled at his friend, pressing a hand to his heart, and went on, "I hear you, my friend. But I'm not 'getting out.' On the contrary. I've decided to sell our estate. Because Payne Tool and Die will remain open for business. We're not quitters. To anyone who is struggling, I say, don't lose heart. If there is ever a time for going all in, it is now. If we stick together, we stand a good chance of beating this downturn. We've done it before. We'll do it again."

Graham, Frank, and Alexandra, Ryan saw, were dumbstruck. They hadn't seen this coming either. Poor Julie looked as if a brick had been thrown in her face.

"Furthermore," Clifton continued, taking his wife's hand, "Bitsy and I have decided to put our tract of land in Toledo on the market. We invite anyone who's interested to make us an offer."

The house *and* the entire estate!? This was a move Ryan had never expected.

With a quick look at Bitsy, Ryan saw she was the picture of serenity. It was clear to him now how the battle lines had been drawn. Where did this streak of idealism come from? He had always known his uncle to be a shrewd businessman. Had he become sentimental in his old age? Yes, he thought, his uncle was a lion, all right, but an old lion, engaged in an old-world battle that he couldn't possibly win. As for himself, he sure didn't relish the now-inevitable confrontation that lay ahead.

In fact, the battle was already on. Graham, his lips grim, crushed his wine glass with such ferocity that the delicate crystal shattered in his hand. Despite his having thought that he had planned for every eventuality, he never expected his father to go so far as to jeopardize the family's last bastion of financial security. His hand bleeding, his carefully cultivated decorum in tatters, he stomped off in a rage, but not before his eyes caught the piercing look of self-satisfied righteousness that his father hurled in his direction like a lance.

His mother, concerned, rushed after him, with Frank and then the rest of the family following suit. Soon the dais was empty, except for Simon, who looked abandoned, out of place, his pale face drawn as he emptied his wine glass. He made an unsteady exit.

Ryan, for his part, couldn't help but be overcome by a profound sadness. His family just didn't get it: didn't get that they were fighting a battle with bows and arrows against cannons. It was only a question of time before the forces of globalization unleashed by the new information age crushed them and their world underfoot. Ironically, it was now the poor cousin they had driven away who was their only chance.

• • •

"We have to bring this business to a close." Graham was conferring in urgent tones with Ryan in the small wood-paneled anteroom, tucked away near the north-wing staircase of the house, where they had gone for some privacy. “I’ve had it with Dad. He’s an old fuddy-duddy who’s out of touch with the world. I want to hold a vote *tonight*.”

It was nine o’clock, and the last of the guests had gone.

There was a soft knock on the door. Julie appeared, her blue eyes reddened by tears. She seemed to be on the verge of hysteria. “Graham, Ryan, can one of you please tell me what’s going on?” she cried. “Dad’s in the study having a fit. Even Alexandra can’t calm him down. If Dad sells the house, what will happen to me?”

Ryan could see that she was battling her conscience.

“I mean, to us?” she quickly corrected herself. “How can he turn against his own family like that? And how on earth can we stop him?”

The door creaked open again and Frank crowded into the tight space, his shoulder almost knocking over one of the family photographs on the wall. It used to be their favorite hideaway as children. The penciled markings of their yearly childhood heights were still visible on a white board. But what had once been home to giggly, juvenile adventure was now a war room.

“We have to vote Dad down, that’s the only way,” Graham urged in a hoarse whisper. “Are we OK on this? Julie? Frank?”

Frank nodded his assent, but Julie, her eyes on a heavily framed photograph of her sitting on her father’s lap as a little girl, was apparently of two minds.

“I don’t know. This will be a big blow to him. Poor Dad.”

“Poor *Dad*, Julie? The business has lost half a million dollars the past six months alone! This isn’t the time to grow all soppy.”

Julie glanced miserably at Ryan. With a slight upward tilt of his chin, he indicated Graham was right. Sighing, she said limply, “I’m in.”

“Good. And get Alexandra on board. You can do that, right? She always listens to you. Let’s meet in the dining room in half an hour. Drag Dad to the meeting if you have to.”

Then swiveling, business-like, to Ryan, Graham continued: “Can you please get your thoughts together for some kind of presentation? Maybe Dad, I dunno, will see the light.”

And in a last aside to Frank and Ryan, Graham added, "So far, so good. We can count on fifty percent of the vote. But we still need John to outvote Dad. I'll go look for him. We can't count him in yet, but I'm going to try and talk some sense into him."

• • •

It had taken some doing and persuasion on Julie and Ryan's part, but Clifton had finally agreed to shift from the study to the dining room where, some twenty minutes later, harried and worried, the entire family, including Ryan and Pete Hancock, the family lawyer, were gathered around the table, arguing in loud voices. Simon, too, had been marshaled in with the rest. Keeping himself discreetly aside, he stared down glumly at the bottle of bourbon in his hand.

Graham rapped his knuckles on the table in a call to order. But before he could utter a word, Clifton leaned forward in his chair, shook a long finger at him, and thundered, "What's the rush, son? Can't wait to get your paws on my business?"

Graham wouldn't be provoked. "Sit down, everybody, sit down and for God's sake, shut up. I know you're all upset, but I have things to say that can't be put off anymore.

"As Dad has said in plain words, Payne Tool and Die is in trouble. Things have gone from bad to worse, and our revenue has halved. We're dropping customers—and with them new orders—by the bucketload. They're either struggling themselves or turning to cheap Asian suppliers."

"You've run our business into the ground, boy! When I was in charge—" Clifton interrupted angrily.

"Let it go, Dad. That was way back when. This is now, and it goes way beyond you and me. Look, we've tried everything short of reducing staff—searching for new markets, cutting costs, and all the rest. But it's like trying to catch up with a runaway train on a bicycle. The hole is simply too big. The business is bleeding cash every day. We have a negative cash flow of a hundred thousand dollars a month. In three months our reserves will be totally depleted, and we're behind on our payments with many of our suppliers. We've been kept afloat thanks only to our credit lines. The only reason why the banks haven't pulled the plug on us yet is because of our name, our standing in the community."

And he added, in an ominous voice, "That can, of course, change on a dime. In case you're wondering, Dad"—his eyes narrowed in on his father—"your brilliant performance tonight did us no favors."

Glued to their chairs, no one dared make a sound in the awkward hush that followed.

"So. We've arrived at a critical juncture. As chairman of the board, it's my duty to inform you that if we were to stay on our current course, we'd be throwing good money after bad and be at risk of losing everything—our house, our land, the family's savings—in short, *everything*. And I don't think any of us want that."

"Why, you little twerp!" Clifton thundered. "Spoiled silly is what you are! Do you have any notion what an extra year, or for that matter a month, of wages means to a working man? Of course you don't! You've never actually done an honest day's work in your life!"

Graham tightened his lips and clenched his fists, his blue eyes scowling at the insult. "Enough, Dad! You old fool! Just stop meddling. You understand nothing! Trust me. Just this once. You might find it hard to believe, but I have only your best interests at heart."

The sudden grating of Clifton's chair on the parquet floor sounded in everybody's ears like a piercing rebuke.

"I understand more than you'll ever know," he shot back as the chair toppled over and he stalked out of the room.

Julie jumped up and ran straight after him. Some long minutes later, she returned with her father in tow. Unapologetic, he sat down again and, with elbows planted firmly on the tabletop, clarified loudly, "I've only returned to hear what Ryan has to say."

Ryan stood up. He had to convince his uncle that the plan he had drawn up for the family was for the best.

With all eyes upon him, as if in expectation of an oracular pronouncement, he took the plunge.

"Uncle Clifton," he began, "You're right. We live in challenging times. The world is changing and with it the way we should be doing business."

He cleared his throat.

"Graham has shown me your books. In my professional opinion, there is only one way out and that is a dramatic reduction of your costs."

Ryan then dropped the bomb in the gentlest way he knew how.

"Fortunately," Ryan smiled limply, "cost reduction is my specialty. I help companies like yours relocate their production lines to China. My expertise can be harnessed to your benefit."

He stole a look at his uncle. Clifton was looking at his hands, studiously turning the wedding band on his left finger.

"The challenge faced by Payne Tool and Die is one that thousands of American companies are confronting. The economy is tough, and pressure on margins is unrelenting. Many of them are opting to offshore to China to stay competitive. Chinese workers are not as good as American ones, but they earn only fifty cents an hour.

"This means that for the price of one American worker, you can hire thirty Chinese. Moreover, they work hard and learn fast. Based on the numbers Graham gave me, my calculations suggest that Payne Tool and Die will be able to save as much as two million dollars a year by moving its main production lines to China."

He tried to measure his uncle's response. Clifton's face didn't seem to register any emotion at all.

Ryan raised his voice. "Uncle Clifton, I know for certain that a number of your major competitors have decided to go to China. This means that if you keep production at home, you'll be placed at a huge disadvantage."

Still, Clifton did not look up.

Ryan was almost pleading now. "Please understand, Uncle Clifton. There really is no alternative. China is the future of manufacturing. There's nothing we can do about it."

Clifton sat still while everyone else raised their voices at once—except for Simon. Ryan couldn't help noticing that he was barely holding himself up, taking big swigs directly from the bottle. Why was Simon, even more of an outsider than himself, taking it so hard?

"This sounds like a no-brainer to me," said Frank. "What are we waiting for? You have my support."

"But what about our workers?" Julie protested.

Alexandra chimed in too, "I agree with Julie. Aren't we responsible for them?"

"Sure, we are," countered Ryan, with one eye on Clifton. "But—that responsibility lies in facing the new reality head-on. If you don't relocate to China, the factory will shut down in a few months. And then what? The jobs will vanish anyway. And you won't have money for severance pay. I know it sounds callous, but you should make a clean break while you still can.

"Remember," he went on, turning to his uncle in one last-ditch effort to move him, "in the long run, what's good for your business is good for the country."

"Ryan is absolutely right," Graham broke in, his store of patience exhausted. "Enough with this twiddle-twaddle! Let's accept Ryan's offer." He grabbed a stack of papers that he had brought into the room and began hastily distributing them.

"These are copies of the draft memorandum of understanding Ryan and I have drawn up. The terms of the agreement are all here. Let's vote on it. Come on, everybody, it's not the end of the world."

Not the end of the world? Graham was being so insensitive. Ryan didn't have the heart to look Clifton in the eye. This surely was the end of his. But much to Ryan's surprise, Clifton just sat there quietly.

At last, Clifton raised his eyes.

"Can't figure you young folks out. Why should we be giving away our jobs to the damned Chinese? To a bunch of foreigners? Ryan, your arguments don't make sense to me. At least my daughters show some compassion. So what if we sell the house? Shouldn't we be prepared to sacrifice for our people and our country?"

An explosion of a loud, sarcastic laughter tore through the room as if a hand grenade had gone off.

It was John, who had kept to himself up till now.

"John-John, I didn't mean—" Clifton spluttered.

"Don't you dare John-John me! It's John, if you please. Sacrifice? Don't talk to me about sacrifice, Dad. Weren't my legs sacrifice enough for you? Now you want the roof over my head, too?"

A barely perceptible smile of triumph appeared on Graham's face.

With a slight tremor in his voice, Clifton said, "From you, Ryan, I expected better. I had high hopes for you."

Ryan hung his head.

"You disappoint me, Ryan. I thought you came to save my company, not to destroy it."

Kerpow. Bang. There could be no happy ending to this story. A tear formed in the corner of Ryan's eye, lingered, but refused to fall. He loved the old man. He would do anything for him, and this was the only reason he came back. But there were no good choices. If he didn't intervene, his cousins would drive the entire family business into the ground, and his uncle would end his days penniless. *Sometimes,* he told himself, *a limb must be amputated to save a life.* But he was less than confident now that he was doing the right thing. Was the operation worth his uncle's suffering?

"Sorry. I'm so sorry," he mumbled, his jaw slackening with emotion.

Clifton's final cut was brutal:

"Is *sorry* the best you can come up with? You may have achieved success in the world outside, but not in mine. You've lost all my respect, my boy. Make no mistake, you're the angel of death, that's who you are. My executioner. Now I know."

Without waiting for a reply, his uncle rose clumsily to his feet and shuffled off, his shoulders slumped, his robust frame, as it passed through the doorway, suddenly showing the true signs of old age.

• • •

Simon had not proffered any opinion of his own throughout the course of the unfolding drama. But now, in one huge, heaving convulsion, Simon threw up all over the dining table, the carpet, and Ryan.

Alexandra's nerves cracked. "For Chrissakes, Simon! Look what you've done! I told you not to drink so much!" she shrieked.

But Simon was in no state to tell his wife why he, too, was in mourning—why his urge to get piss-drunk had grown stronger as the evening progressed. Or why he had become the man who knew too much. A thousand-ton weight was poised to come crashing down on his head.

Chapter 3

SIMON BLACKWELL

London, UK, September–November 2002

"Globalization was exerting a dis-inflationary impact."

—ALAN GREENSPAN

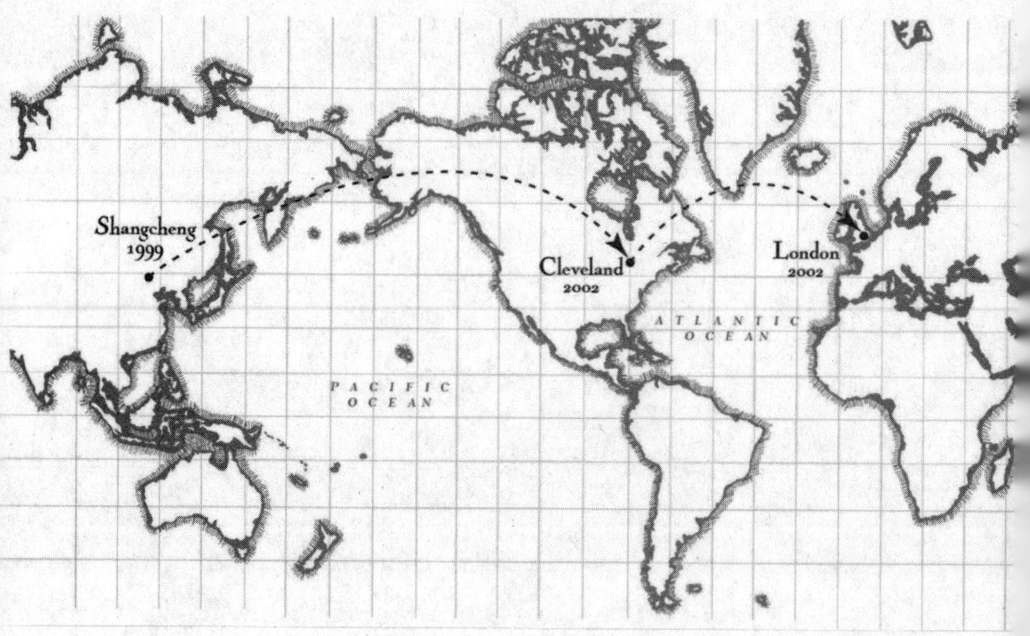

GOD ALMIGHTY. WHAT NOW? AS if he hadn't enough on his mind.

Simon, still in his travel tracksuit, was sitting across the table from Andrew, his boss, in a Pizza Express on King's Road.

"How was it over the pond?"

"Fab, thanks."

Simon had only just landed from Cleveland when he got a call from Andrew. He had rushed directly from Heathrow. In all the three years he had worked under Andrew he had not once been called on like this, out of the blue, to a one-on-one on a Sunday night. What was so urgent that it couldn't wait until tomorrow? It was ten thirty, and the waiters were taking the last orders.

A gust of wind blew into the garden terrace in the back of the restaurant where they were sitting. Simon shivered and sneezed. It was a little cool for September. He ordered a pot of tea.

"There's been a lot of talk in the market lately," Andrew began. There was an intimation of a frown on his face, and his pale-blue eyes looked troubled.

"What about?"

"Your trading."

"Really?" Simon answered, concentrating on pouring himself some tea. "What about my trading?"

"That you have been at it a lot lately."

"Maybe a little more than usual." Simon shrugged. "So what?" But he recrossed his feet uneasily under the table.

Andrew looked at the menu. "Are you sure you don't want something to eat?"

Simon shook his head. Who was talking behind his back? Why couldn't people mind their own business?

"And some malicious tongues, Simon, are saying that you've lost a shitload of money."

Damn. He didn't dare look at his boss directly, alarm bells ringing in his head. *Got to stay calm. Don't let on that you're bothered.*

"Well, you know that's bollocks. You of all people know that I'm having a decent year. I hope you set the record straight." Simon knew that Andrew, as the head of the proprietary trading desk, received a P&L report every day for every trader. Moreover, he knew that the report said that he was up $5 million so far in the year.

"Yes, yes…that's true. But…" Andrew paused, letting the conjunction hang there for an infinitesimally short moment before continuing. "I still wonder where people get the idea that you're actually losing money."

Simon noticed the pause and it emboldened him. "You don't believe it, do you?"

"No, just that there must be a reason for these rumors. Never smoke without fire, eh? Honestly, I don't know what to think. That's why I am sitting here with you," he said with a small smile.

"Are you saying I'm hiding something?" said Simon, pretending to be offended.

"No. Of course not. Look. I can help you if you're in trouble." Then he corrected himself. "In the unlikely event that you're in trouble."

Simon didn't doubt Andrew's sincerity for a moment. Andrew was his mentor as well as his boss, and Simon knew that he had his back.

"Well, I'm not in trouble," he said, digging in.

"Good. But just to make sure, I want you to go through your books with me tomorrow morning. My office. Seven sharp."

Fucking hell. His books! Simon slowly stretched his neck to one side, as if he could feel the noose tightening around it already. He thought he had more time. More time to turn things around, to sort things out. His pulse began to race through his body at a gallop. Was this the beginning of the end?

• • •

Simon stumbled downstairs, his ginger hair tousled, eyelids half closed over bloodshot grey eyes. The stainless-steel kitchen of the South Kensington mews house, washed by downlights, looked particularly uninviting at this early hour of the morning. His eyes adjusted slowly and painfully to the glare. Staggering to the huge Sub-Zero fridge, he swung it open. No succor there but for a couple of 1 percent yogurts and some moldering goat cheese. He slammed the door shut. *Bugger it.* He detested yogurt.

Coffee. He would brew himself some coffee. Their newfangled contraption might, at the very least, provide him with something hot and comforting, as a proper kitchen, the heart and hearth of home and family since time immemorial, should.

Cheerlessly he sipped his macchiato and munched on a Duchy oatmeal biscuit from a pack he had found abandoned in a cupboard. Perched uncomfortably on a stool at the kitchen island, he pondered the streamlined composition of the built-in modular ovens, the black lacquered cabinet doors and the magnificent steel extractor hood. As in a bad dream, the smooth, shiny surfaces of modernity gleamed in the acid light and shifted malevolently, playing tricks on his mind. But this was no bad dream. His problem was as real as it could be. And worse, there was no escape whatsoever.

He squinted up at the clock. The hands indicated four minutes past three. The bloody thing was so silent, of a design so minimalist, it seemed to be keeping the passage of time a secret unto itself, thought Simon, longing for the soothing *tick-tock*, *tick-tock* of the old-fashioned clock in his mum's kitchen.

Three more hours to go. Three long hours before heading for the office. Three long hours before he, Simon Blackwell, on this Monday of September 16, 2002, would set out to the City to exit the game forever.

• • •

It had all begun three months before. Expecting the slide of the US dollar in the wake of September 11 soon to reverse direction, Simon had started shorting the euro against the greenback. But the dollar kept going down. Not discouraged, he bought more and more dollars against the euro to lower his average cost.

As his losses piled up, the trade consumed his every waking hour. Down, down plunged the dollar, and still he held on. His trader's instinct told him to cut his losses, but his bet on the dollar had become personal. It had become a crusade to prove that America was still the greatest economy on the face of the earth.

By the end of August, his position had ballooned to $1 billion, and when the euro rose above parity against the dollar, he was sitting on losses that totaled over $50 million, ten times his stop-loss limit—the amount of its own capital that the bank permitted him to play with and lose before suspending his activities.

• • •

Bleary-eyed, Simon surveyed once again the brand-new Poggenpohl kitchen that had cost him over a hundred thousand quid—a present for Alexandra's twenty-seventh birthday. *Vanity of vanities*, he repeated to himself, over and over. In the high-gloss surface of the countertop, he saw his thin, narrow face with its fine spray of freckles. The stainless steel was like a cruel mirror. He looked like mud. With the heightened pallor of his milk-white skin, he looked dead already.

"Trouble sleeping, honey? You look beat." Alexandra's drowsy voice suddenly roused him.

She was barefoot and he hadn't heard her come downstairs. Through eyes dripping with fatigue, she seemed to Simon like an angelic apparition in her floating white nightgown, her long, chestnut curls mussed by sleep. He had told her nothing.

"I forgot to tell you that I got an email from the Hyde Park Tennis Centre. They've agreed to hold our charity tournament. It will be on October twentieth. Awesome, isn't it?"

"Good for you." Alex was aiming to raise £100,000 for finding homes for retired racehorses.

"Don't forget to put it in your diary."

Alex was bonkers for animals. She did volunteer work three days a week at an animal shelter for abused and abandoned pets. They had no kids yet, but he knew she'd make a great mum someday.

"And now come to bed, honey," she insisted gently. "You must get some sleep."

Lovely, lovely Alex. He adored her so much, his one and only consolation.

"Yeah. I'm knackered," he finally muttered. "Go ahead. I'll follow you up in a moment."

• • •

His love affair with America had started even before he met Alex. Growing up in dull Newcastle upon Tyne in the northeast of England, the son of a civil servant and a teacher, America was his Narnia. America—land of the open road. Home to Steve Jobs and Muhammad Ali. Of jazz and Motown. Twice-over savior of Europe. Enabler of the first man to step on the moon.

And then came Alex. He met her at a friend's dinner party in London. She embodied, from the moment they started dating, his own exclusive slice of that golden land of promise and opportunity. He fell in love with her generous and easygoing nature, with her curvy, plump body and over-abundant breasts. Even her midwestern accent when she said "dahd" and "cahlege" instead of *dad* and *college* enchanted him. And he fell in love with her blue-blooded family, too. Clifton and Bitsy accepted him, a lad from the middle of the middle of the social order, with open arms.

When he began his career in the City, America's hold on his imagination gripped him ever more tightly. During his years at the bank, what he witnessed was America's seemingly unstoppable dominance, which, in turn, fed his belief in her infallibility. The disaster of September 11 did nothing to shake his convictions. He had no doubt the American economy would bounce back stronger than ever, as would the almighty greenback, symbol of its might.

But then came the shock of Cleveland, where he finally woke up to the enormity of his folly. As a trader living in an insulated world governed by numbers, Simon had rarely given thought to the individuals behind them. But now, conversations with local businessmen at Clifton's party, his father-in-law's speech, the subsequent showdown in the dining room, all irrevocably broke the spell, pointing to one thing only: his wrong-headed misreading of America's economic realities. If such a wealthy, respectable family could be going to pot, then all his previous assumptions about the direction of the world's finances were dead wrong, and the dollar was done for. He would never look at numbers, he vowed to himself, in the same way again.

• • •

Yes, he was finished.

The American ship was sinking—and she was going to take him down with her.

If he hadn't been found out until now, it was only because he had doctored the numbers—by entering fictitious option hedges in the booking system that appeared to offset his losses. His computer science degree, and the knowledge gained over a year in the back office verifying trades, had given him the skills to exploit the weaknesses of the bank's outdated risk-management system and cover his tracks. But it would take no time for Andrew to uncover his manipulations by going through his transactional records. It would be all over in a few hours.

A scrutiny of the po-faced clock revealed the hour to be nearly four. What would happen to him? Nick Leeson had gotten six and a half years for bankrupting Barings Bank. Given that his own losses of $50 million were only a fraction of the losses of that rogue trader, might he not get a shorter sentence? He should have told all to Andrew and pleaded for leniency when he had had a chance to do so a few hours ago. But it was too late. Getting a grip on himself, he swallowed hard.

Was there any way out? He felt nauseous, as if he had a sewer in his throat. No, there wasn't any way out, reason was telling him. What about legging it? *Run, run*—a tiny voice screamed somewhere inside him. But where would he go? He couldn't possibly hide forever.

• • •

This time he heard the patter of Alexandra's bare feet trotting down the stairs. She sat herself on the barstool beside him. Cheeks cupped in the palms of her hands, elbows on the counter, she glanced at him softly, and said in her musical voice, "I'm worried about you."

"It's nothing, Alex. Just the bloody jetlag," he lied, his head hanging low. "I expect I shall be going directly to the office."

Simon was about to be found out, and he still couldn't bring himself to make a clean breast of it to his wife. At first, he didn't bother to tell her when he still had hopes of recouping his losses. When things got stickier, he hadn't wanted her to fret. And now, he simply hadn't the stomach to face her.

"You seem so tense. Is everything all right at work?" she asked, massaging his shoulders.

"Of course. Everything's all right. Why would you think otherwise?"

"Take a few deep slow breaths like we learned in yoga class. You'll feel better," she suggested, lifting her arms above her head in a graceful stretch.

Yoga, yogurt. Whatever. He despised them both. He drew the line at American faddishness. But he loved his wife. He obediently inhaled deeply a couple of times, noisily sucking a lot of air into his belly.

He flashed a drawn smile at her. "Worked like a charm." It did have a slight calming effect, at least on the tightness in his chest.

"This might also work." Alex took his hand and, with a humorous come-hither glint in her eye, guided it under her nightgown.

Her breast was exquisitely soft and pneumatic to his touch. But what would normally have been a surefire turn-on stirred no part of his body into action.

When she sank slowly to her knees, in a familiar and well-beloved prelude to their lovemaking, he pressed her head and lips hard against his crotch—still nothing.

She looked up at him with a quizzical gaze.

But overcome by his inadequacy, by the embarrassing shame of having to thwart her desire, Simon couldn't meet it.

He was no good. No good at anything.

He had never before, ever, refused her advances. He watched on helplessly as Alexandra scrambled back to her feet and fled back to the bedroom.

Alone again, Simon wallowed in his frustration. His secret was unmanning him. Surely, it was time to confess to Alex. Tell her the truth. But how, exactly, would he go about it? Look deeply into her trusting amber-brown eyes and say, "Hullo darling, I'm a cheat, a liar, a fraud…"? Alex adored him. Admired him. She had left everything behind to build a new life with him in England, for God's sake. How could he do this to her? He could just see her cute face—cheeks still plump as a little girl's—trembling with shock at his betrayal, could just see the tears welling up in her eyes.

But tell her he must. He couldn't avoid it any longer. *Tonight, perhaps, after work. Tonight, yes.* It was not—he recoiled at the image of his eventual fate—as if they would slap handcuffs on his wrists right away.

Alex. The love of his life. The beautiful, sexy American girl who had made him the happiest man in the world. What a fool he was for putting her love for him at risk. Allowing his hubris to jeopardize it all. *Vanity of vanities.* She *would* forgive him, wouldn't she? She *would* wait, wouldn't she? Would he lose her too? His entire being shaking, he could hardly begin to grapple with that terrifying possibility.

But he had no right to expect anything from her after what he had done, and he wouldn't stand in her way if she wanted out. If she sold their place in Kensington and their country cottage, she should be able to clear at least half a million pounds after paying off the mortgages. And he would let her keep it all.

He stared miserably at the pristine kitchen floor. The very notion that he was forced to make such calculations made him want to burst out crying, all his confidence in their future life together dissolving into a puddle at his feet.

His eyes wandered up to the clock again. Jesus! It was past five. Time to get cracking. He rose reluctantly from the barstool and tiptoed up the stairs to his dressing room, careful not to wake Alex. His eyes swept over his wardrobe with its dozens of shirts neatly stacked on the shelves and the rows of trousers folded on hangers—the casual uniform of traders. But by the end of the afternoon he wouldn't be a trader anymore. So, no. This morning he would wear a suit and tie in honor of his last day in the City. *Sort of like the way,* he thought darkly, *one wears a suit out of respect at a funeral.*

• • •

There remained one last farewell. He'd have to give up his beloved car, the silver Aston Martin DB7 sitting in his garage. She was the shining badge of his success. He caressed her flanks, admiring her beauty—there was nary a scratch on her perfect body. He opened the car door, got inside and sat very still, his hands on the steering wheel. The leather felt warm to his touch, and the temptation to drive her was strong. But there was no question of taking her into the City this morning. He got out of the car, his heart heavy with regret, and shut the garage doors. Walking down the quiet lane from their house, his footsteps resounding loudly on the cobblestones, he didn't look back. Turning onto Gloucester Road, he hailed a taxi, just as it began to drizzle.

London looked peaceful as the black cab sped through the streets, the pale-yellow rays of early sunlight that glanced off the waters of the Thames refracting through the pearly greys of misty clouds and scattered raindrops.

There was scarcely any traffic, and he arrived at the bank at precisely seven. Flashing his ID card to the guard, he took the elevator to the second floor. He swiped his card again and pushed open the glass door to the trading floor.

• • •

His heart in his throat, Simon went directly to Andrew's office at the edge of the trading floor. He wasn't there. It was unusually quiet even for a Monday morning, but Simon knew that the lethargic hum of rustling newspapers and people nattering in low voices could change at any instant. Andrew was nowhere to be seen.

His eyes roamed over the huge open space, almost as large as a football pitch. God, how he would miss this place. The loud din on the days of frenzy and adrenaline highs. The rows and rows of desks with their black telephones, the flickering computer screens. But most of all, the traders, young hunters, most of them, getting ready for the kill when the markets opened.

Where was Andrew? Simon stood outside Andrew's office for so long that he was starting to attract attention.

"Hi, Simon. What gives?" called out Paresh, the Japanese yen trader who was sitting close by.

"Not much going on, I see," Simon remarked.

"You wouldn't be saying that if you were here on Friday. We had a roller-coaster ride. The market's just run out of steam."

Friday...when he and Alexandra had only just arrived in Cleveland. And Alex had made him give up his BlackBerry for the day of the party.

"Really? What happened?" Simon asked, feigning interest.

"More appropriately, what didn't happen? The yen went into a tailspin after the Japanese threatened massive currency interventions. Then oil spiked again after the Iraqis rejected the American demand for the unconditional return of UN weapons inspectors. We were dodging bullets all day."

"Wow. Guess I missed all the fun." Simon nodded, starting to walk away, a low-pitched throb beginning in his head. Where *was* Andrew?

"Hey, chum," Paresh called out, raising his voice at his receding back. "Did you drink all the way back to London, or what? You look like a drowned kitten!"

Simon pirouetted around and managed a weak smile, palms up in the air in a gesture of mock helplessness.

"Seen Andrew by any chance?"

Paresh shook his head.

It wasn't like his boss to be late. Simon glanced up at the digital clock behind him on the wall—the one that announced the times, in bright red numerals, in New York, Tokyo, Hong Kong, Singapore, and Sydney. It was a quarter past seven in London.

Still no sign of Andrew. His head throbbing, he made his way to the small refreshment room to get some coffee. Nick, the sterling trader, leaned forward and tugged playfully at the hem of his jacket as he passed by.

"What's with the suit and tie? Who are you trying to impress? Interviewing for another job?"

Simon was in no mood for banter.

"Seen Andrew?"

"Nope."

Almost half past already, he noted, his eye on his watch. Where the hell was he?

As he headed back to his desk, Rodney—a tall, beefy, twenty-four-year-old commodity trader from Down Under—came over with a big smile to say hello.

"Just bought a thousand contracts of December Brent futures. I'm going all in. I think this baby is going to forty bucks. What do you think?"

Simon, miles away, his head still aching despite having ingested coffee, two candy bars, and three Advil, took a moment to return to the present. Like many of the young traders, the friendly, outgoing Aussie looked up to him. And now that he was leaving it all behind, he wondered, would he, popular bloke that he was, be at least a little bit missed?

"I don't know." Simon took his time to answer. "A thousand contracts is a pretty big bet on oil considering the size of the move we've already had."

"I'm telling you, matey, you're wrong. The invasion of Iraq is coming very soon. It might even have begun already. Yesterday US warplanes struck an air defense communications post. The Saudis have finally agreed to allow the Americans to launch the attack from their territory. All the pieces are falling into place."

"You're underestimating the time it would take Bush to get a UN resolution." This came from Grant, a salesperson who covered hedge funds. A health nut who biked to the bank every day, he had materialized at their side, uninvited, his muscular thighs bulging through the fabric as he bent over to remove the clips from his trousers. "Nothing will happen until January or even February at the earliest. In the meantime, I think OPEC will boost production this week."

"Who's asking you for your opinion?" Rod snapped back. "For your information, at least six OPEC members have said publicly they're against an increase in quotas. The OPEC secretary just said this morning the world has enough oil. I'll bet you anything they don't increase production this week."

"Suit yourself. Don't say I didn't warn you," said Grant, shrugging his shoulders.

Simon stared ahead vacantly. He had no heart for the debate. Why in the hell should he? He'd be out of this place in a couple of hours.

Forever.

Chewing furiously on his gum, he asked for the umpteenth time, "Where the fuck is Andrew?"

Finally, he got his answer.

"I saw him going into Nigel's office and then storming out," said Rod. "He didn't look too happy to me."

Andrew had come to work after all; so where was he? And what in the hell had happened between him and Nigel? Nothing good—of that, Simon was sure. His despair mounting, he tried reaching Andrew on his mobile, but the call went right to his voicemail.

The phone on Simon's desk was ringing. It had been ringing for some time now, apparently. Resurfacing from his self-absorption, he listlessly picked up the receiver, and said, "Yes?"

It was Nigel. Simon jumped to attention.

"Please step into my office right away."

Nigel King, head of trading and Andrew's direct boss, was a remote figure. Nigel had never communicated with Simon directly before—not ever. What reason could there be for this unusual summons from the big boss, other than the pronouncement of his death sentence? There was no question that he had been found out. And where in the hell was Andrew? He had been counting on him holding his hand. *Bugger it.* He was screwed, all right.

Simon's eyes lighted on the image of the silently moving lips of the Bloomberg anchor on the muted TV screen that hung on the pillar opposite his desk. The image seemed to stare back at him mockingly, accusingly.

Screwdriver in his skull, his teeth chomping frenetically on the dry, squeezed-out wad of gum in his mouth, Simon slowly got up and started walking—no, dragging himself, legs like jelly—to Nigel's office.

• • •

Through the glass wall of Nigel's office on the periphery of the trading floor, he could see him, an intimidating figure in his pinstripe Savile Row suit and perfectly double-knotted lavender silk tie, talking into the phone. But Nigel caught his eye and with his free hand beckoned him to enter. Simon pushed open the door and stepped in.

Nigel was an impressive man in his early fifties who prior to his present exalted position had been a big-time cowboy trader—so Simon had heard—raking in millions in the go-go days of the eighties. Simon tried to deduce his present disposition from his face, but all he found was Nigel's customary well-mannered and impenetrable expression.

Nigel motioned him to take a seat, and he flopped into it gratefully, his chest in knots.

Slamming down the phone and sinking into the large leather office chair behind his desk, Nigel began without any preliminaries.

"I have some rather bad news for you, I'm afraid," he announced in his refined upper-class accent.

Nothing could save him now. *Quick. Just make it quick,* Simon willed silently to himself.

"We've decided to let Andrew go."

"Go? Go where?" Simon blurted out stupidly, his wits a salad of confusion.

Nigel raised an eyebrow. "Why, we fired him, of course."

Fired? It took all of Simon's willpower not to gasp aloud. This was not the way it was supposed to play out. The bank must have decided to hold Andrew responsible for his misdeeds. He, Simon, was the next in line to get the chop. He closed his eyes.

But the axe didn't fall.

"Andrew's revenue has been below budget two years in a row, and management has run out of patience. He's been too slow to adjust to the changing market environment. Perhaps it's his age. I know he's well-liked by his traders but then, we're not running a popularity contest."

Simon's eyes were wide open now. *What?* Andrew was sacked but for reasons that had nothing to do with him? Then maybe—

"Now for the good news," said Nigel, tilting back in his chair. He paused. "We've decided to give you his job."

Had he heard right? It seemed to Simon that the words floated in from somewhere far away beyond the room and its glass walls. Yet he had heard them, all right. They had actually knocked on his eardrums. But, at first, they bounced off as mere sounds and carried no meaning; it took a while for them to reach his brain. *Andrew's job? Impossible—it makes no sense!*

"We've always had high hopes for you, Simon."

Did they really? The bank had high hopes! The bank—that abstract power with such a hold on his life, personified at this moment by Nigel—had high hopes!

"This is the time for you to step up. With customer flows slowing down, the bank is looking for proprietary trading to make a more significant contribution to revenue. We need someone who has got both the appetite for risk and the market savvy to take us to the next level. And we believe you're the right man for the job. That the chaps on the desk like you is an added plus."

"I-I-," Simon stuttered, at a loss for words, shaking his head. He couldn't even look up at the man, instead fixing his attention, as if his life depended on it, on the heavy crystal paperweight on Nigel's desk.

"Surprised? No need to say anything at all. You're our best trader. Just don't squander the opportunity. We're counting on you."

The phone on Nigel's desk was ringing. It was Simon's cue to exit. But before picking up the receiver, Nigel had one more thing to add. "By the way, I just doubled your trading limit. I want you to swing the bat. Don't worry about losses. You have to be prepared to lose money if you want to make it. I want you to set an example for the other traders. Understood?"

"Yes, sir. Understood."

He understood better than Nigel would ever know.

In a daze, Simon got up and turned to leave. Like a condemned prisoner facing a firing squad, he had been miraculously reprieved at the last minute.

"And Simon."

"Yes?"

"I'll be away in New York for a few days. There's an audit coming up next month. Start getting your team ready. Management wants to tighten risk control."

• • •

As in a dream, Simon staggered back across the trading floor. And then, unable to contain himself any longer, he made a mad dash to the men's room. He leaned back against the white-tiled wall, barely able to hold himself upright.

He burst into wild, helpless laughter. *A promotion! What an unbelievable joke!* On him. On the bank. Wave after wave of hysterical snorts and hiccups convulsed his body, his eyes filling with tears, his knees crumbling as he slid against the wall to the floor. A promotion instead of a kick in the arse! Was fortune smiling upon him?

Some good fortune. He had considered himself to be a good trader once, with three straight years of $10 million in trading profits. He used to think that trading was the archetypal meritocratic profession: You made money yourself only if you made money for your paymasters. But it was all bollocks. Economics, technicals, sentiment—all bollocks. Trading was just dumb luck, being in the right place at the right time. No more than sitting at a roulette table: The lucky ones got paid and the unlucky ones got fired. Like poor Andrew. Worse yet, it was roulette with the modifier "Russian" added to it.

The promotion gave him no joy, nor did it bring him any peace of mind. It didn't make him feel better about himself, either, not even by one jot. As his hysteria subsided, his thoughts grew more focused. He had gained some time, for sure, but it solved nothing. The audit was just around the corner, for fuck's sake. Only a question of weeks before they discovered his losses, and when they did, the claim that he had intentionally defrauded the bank would be even stronger, now that he had—*Jesus*, and why on earth had he?—accepted the job. Managers were supposed to know better and were held to a higher standard. And he was a manager now, whether he liked it or not.

He breathed deeply a number of times, sucking air deep into his stomach as Alex had taught him. Calmer now, he rose to his feet. He took a leak and then went over to the row of sinks and splashed cold water over his face.

Somehow, he had to find a way out of this fix.

• • •

"A toast! Cheers, Simon," Rod boomed. Paresh and Nick and Grant raised their champagne glasses. "You deserve this, mate. If anyone was going to land this job, I'm glad it's you."

The boys were treating him to a dinner to celebrate his promotion. Grant had invited everyone for pre-dinner drinks at the Met Bar, one of the hottest venues in London. How Grant had wrangled a membership in this private club, nobody ever succeeded in getting out of him.

"Thanks a bunch. I'll do my best," Simon responded limply.

"Sure, you will. Don't worry about it. Come on, mate, you'll do great, just buck up," Rod declared, placing a meaty hand on Simon's shoulder. He then proceeded to down his champagne in several gulps.

"Great stuff," he said. "Must've cost big bikkies."

"Louis Roederer Cristal, three hundred quid," Grant noted briefly, before promptly ordering another bottle.

Was it good fortune?

Ensconced in the semi-privacy of a circular red leather booth with the question spinning like a top in his head, Simon was paying scant attention to his mates, celebration the furthest thing from his mind. He needed to come up with a strategy, and fast, before the audit.

Tuning in again, he realized that his colleagues were back to talking shop.

"Amazing, the dollar's up again today," said Nick, who was the spot jockey on the desk and never without his FXAlert and its live currency market quotes. "It's now up seven days of the last nine. It feels like the market can't buy enough of it."

"I think Friday's strong US retail sales numbers really got people thinking. Maybe the US isn't doing that badly after all," volunteered Paresh.

Grant was on his mobile. When he got off he added, "Been hearing all day that Soros is rebuilding his long dollar positions again. The rumor is that he's short three yards of euros already and is still adding."

Say again? A €3 billion short? Good Lord. Such a large number gave even Simon a jolt.

"More appropriately, what do you think Soros knows that no one else does?" Paresh asked.

"No idea, but I can tell you that some of my clients are banking on a strong US industrial production number tomorrow. If it comes in stronger than expected, I think we're going to see dollar bears running for the hills. Once the ninety-five level on Eurodollar breaks, there's nothing to stop a quick move towards ninety," Grant said with all the smooth-tongued assurance of a practiced salesperson.

Everyone wanted to believe the story.

Everyone except for Simon. Something didn't make sense to him. He ought to have been delighted, what with his position and the talk of the dollar's recovery. But he didn't believe a word of it, no matter what the likes of Soros might think. Not after the epiphany he had had in Cleveland.

• • •

Optimism was clearly the consensus in the City. When they went up to the restaurant that was two floors up from the bar in the Metropolitan Hotel, they found the place buzzing with activity. It was so crowded that, despite their reservations, they were made to wait half an hour for a table. Nobu, the fashionista haven, was the best barometer of market sentiment in the City. Earlier in the year when the stock market was plunging, Nobu was often half empty.

As they waited to be seated, Simon stood apart from the others, looking out the bank of windows along the dining room that gave on to Hyde Park. The sun was setting beyond the trees, flooding the restaurant with a reddish-orange light. It lent warmth to the white walls of the minimalist space and yet intensified Simon's mood of melancholy. *The end of the day,* he thought—*the end of a long, crazy day.*

When they finally sat down, they switched to sake as the waiters covered their bare wooden table with plates of yellowtail ceviche, toro tuna tartare, and rock shrimp tempura. Everyone wolfed down these delicacies as if they were fish and chips, but Simon hardly touched a thing.

"Check out your nine o'clock," Rod, leaning forward, whispered to the rest of the group.

It was Guy. Sporting a fashionably slim-cut three-buttoned suit, he entered the restaurant with a flamboyant swagger, accompanied by two catwalk-thin females in high heels, towering over him like flagpoles on either side.

Simon and Guy had joined the bank at the same time and gone through the same training program. But while Simon had started in the back office, Guy had begun trading straight away. Quickly making a name for himself as a smart trader with good instincts, he had been bid away by Goldman Sachs six months before. Not that anyone had been sorry to see him go, though Simon rubbed along with him well enough.

Guy caught his eye. With a wide grin and not a single ash-colored hair out of place, he sauntered over to say hello. A huge IWC Portugieser watch, one of those expensive pieces with a perpetual calendar, nestled under the cuff of his purple suit jacket. He just managed to flash it so that everybody'd notice before his hands disappeared into his trouser pockets.

"Gentlemen, haven't seen you for yonks," Guy said, rocking slightly on his heels. He looked at everyone from under raised eyebrows. He was well aware how he stood with the present company. His only interest, however, was Simon, whom he deemed as his equal.

"So, Simon, a little bird told me you've been promoted. Congrats."

"Word travels fast. Thanks," Simon replied.

"I can't say I'm surprised. You're the best they've got."

"I don't know about that." Not after all those losses he had amassed on his dollar trade. Not after losing the equivalent of all he had ever made for the bank.

"How's the market treating you lately, old boy?"

Discussing his trading performance was the last thing Simon wanted to do. Nevertheless, he had to say something, seeing that everyone at the table was looking at him expectantly, waiting for him to put the cheeky sod in his place. But all he managed to squeeze out, almost inaudibly, was, "The market's been difficult."

Deflated by the defeatism of his response, Simon's chums went back to munching on their food, their faces in their plates.

"And how has it been treating you?" Simon belatedly went on, trying to shift the spotlight away from himself.

"Brilliant. The mind boggles. I had a great August. Went long the S&P at eight hundred. With the market so oversold, it felt like the most obvious trade ever. Rode all the way up to nine fifty, at which point I thought the market had gone too far too fast, so I started to lighten up. Before I left for vacation I unwound all my positions. A good thing, too. Before I could even unpack my swimming trunks, the market started to tank again."

Even Simon, who usually took Guy's boastfulness in his stride, thought he was going too far this time, bragging about his exploits in an almost pornographic way, as though he was reveling in how he had bedded some bird everyone else was drooling over.

Grant, however, the eternal salesperson, always on the lookout for trades that he could flog to his hedge-fund clients, couldn't resist this opportunity for fishing. "So, which way do you think the market will go now?" he asked.

"No clue. But now that the stock market is back down, I rather think about going long again. All this talk about the invasion of Iraq and a US double-dip recession seems a bit overdone to me." Guy then leaned over the table, lowering his voice as though he were the sole possessor of an exclusive bit of information. "Our boys in New York seem to think that the US economy is doing better than the market is giving it credit for."

"Hmm…interesting…right." Guy definitely had Grant's attention. Whether deservedly or not, Goldman Sachs's reputation on the street for being ahead of the curve was second to none.

"Well," Guy said, "got to get back to my girlfriends…. And by the way, Simon, Alexandra called me today to enlist me for her charity tennis tournament, and I've agreed to play. I assume you'll be playing too. Bring your best game. You'll need it. Toodle-oo."

Everybody around the table knew that Guy was a former junior tennis champion who had played in the first round at Wimbledon.

As soon as Guy was out of earshot, Rod broke out furiously, upset for Simon and for all of them. "That fucking cheeky wanker. That self-important twat. Always mouthing off. Somebody ought to teach him a lesson."

Simon's mind, however, was already elsewhere. So, Guy was cheerleading for America as well! But anyone who could believe that the American economy was improving was either a fool, uninformed, or misinformed. And if so many punters were talking up the US, it could only mean one thing—that the market didn't quite get just how bad things were, hadn't cottoned on yet to what he had found out in Cleveland. Could it be that the market was wrong? That markets were way behind the curve and mispricing the true state of the American economy?

The question shook Simon out of his funk. Like a seasoned hunter, he could sense prey on the horizon, the smell of quarry—in the shape of a mispriced market—pungent in his nostrils. For all great traders, identifying mispricings and exploiting them was the recipe for making money. Sometimes big money. Simon found his heart beating a little faster.

"Holy shit! Listen up, mates! There's news," Nick yelled out suddenly, looking up from his FXAlert. "Saddam Hussein just agreed to allow the return of the UN inspectors to Iraq. Unconditionally. Equity futures and the dollar jumped. Oil is getting clobbered! So are Treasury futures!"

As other traders among the diners got the same news, many were in a state of near panic. Even Guy, a few tables away, was shouting frantically into his mobile. Paresh's chair scraped the floor. Rod jumped up, his broad red face turning a sickly shade of green. He had so much riding on oil.

"Sorry to break up the party, mates," Rod announced breathlessly. "Got to get cracking. Have some positions I need to clean up." Within seconds, everybody had decamped.

Simon found himself summarily abandoned, alone at the table. In the now quiet restaurant, he was able to concentrate on his thoughts. He had no idea whether Saddam was bluffing or whether the return of the weapons inspectors would be enough to placate the Americans, but his experience told him that the news was of a kind very likely to create havoc—that is, extreme volatility, over-shooting, and dislocations—in the market. Dislocation for one trader was an opening for another. His heart beating even faster, his gut instinct told him that an opportunity could be presenting itself.

Right. He knew what to do. Time to go treasure hunting in the wreckage of the markets.

The bill had been taken care of by his mates. He got up, walked downstairs, and hopped into a taxi back home.

• • •

Bounding up to the first floor two steps at a time, straight to the oak and chrome desk in his study off the bedroom, Simon punched in the code to his computer and brought up the Reuters spreadsheets on his two screens. His eyes pored over the news, the graphs, the market data—the tables with the hundreds of tiny numbers that are inscrutable and meaningless to the untrained eye. Though it was almost eleven at night, and the stock markets were closed in London and New York, the futures and foreign exchange markets, open around the clock, were still kicking, though at a less frantic pace.

He stood bent over his desk, too agitated to sit down, peering at the sea of numbers representing currencies, bond yields, and futures that make up the universe of the trader. Each number laden with significance. And then suddenly, his gaze was drawn to a digit that, though small and in black face like the rest of them, seemed to leap out at him as if pulsing in violent, blazing red. He zoomed into the Eurodollar futures table indicating the latest prices, the highs and lows of the day, the price changes from the day before.

Alexandra wandered into the study. "What are you up to?"

"Looking for buried treasure," Simon mumbled, without lifting his head from the screen. He couldn't face Alex now.

"Eurodollar futures. Contracts on the price of dollar deposits outside the US. Plain old dollars to you, love."

"Oh?"

He tried to drown his embarrassment at his morning failure in market palaver.

"They are not only the largest source of global financing, they're also the most direct expression of the market's view on the state of the US economy. When the economy grows, the Fed is likely to raise interest rates to keep inflation in check, and the price of Eurodollar futures falls. And when the economy contracts, the Fed will often cut interest rates to reduce the cost of borrowing for consumers and businesses, and the price of Eurodollar futures rises."

"I see. Have fun, then," she said, cutting him short.

The disappointed sarcasm in her tone didn't escape his notice. But he didn't allow himself to be distracted. As she slipped out of the room, he immediately focused back on the screen.

His eyes found the magic number again, of the November Eurodollar futures, which had sold off nearly 10 basis points—one tenth of a percent—after the Iraq news broke. A considerable drop.

He now sank slowly down into his chair, trying to understand the implications. Before the Iraq news came out, Eurodollar contracts were pricing in a 40 percent chance of an interest rate cut of a quarter of a percent by the Fed at its next two meetings. But remarkably, in less than an hour, the market had swung in the opposite direction and was no longer pricing any reduction at all. This was a massive shift in the market's assessment of the American economy, its outlook swinging to a distinctly positive one. Why positive? What had changed exactly? Nothing! But the market had overreacted and being caught off guard by the news, had pushed down the prices of the futures contracts too far. In so doing, it overshot.

Simon couldn't believe his luck.

What he was staring at was the rarest of bargains. An opening so small, a crack so miniscule, a blip on the screen so tiny, that it could present itself for only a few minutes before disappearing in the blink of an eye.

But Simon blinked. And blinked again. This was no hallucination. The numbers were still there. The numbers were real.

Not only was this a bargain, it was as close to a free option as he was ever going to get. The payoffs of most trades are symmetrical: You make money if you are right, and you lose money if you are wrong. But in the case of a free option, the payoffs are asymmetrical. You either make money, which is great, or you don't lose any money at all. A free option is a free pass to making money without any risk. A win–don't lose situation.

If only all of life were so risk-free!

In the case of the November Eurodollar futures, if the Fed cut interest rates, he would make money. If they didn't, he wouldn't lose a dime. In short, it was as if the price of betting on a rate cut had gone to zero. Suddenly Simon was faced with this incredible, once-in-a-lifetime chance. He would never forgive himself if he missed out on this baby.

Good hunter that he was, he pounced.

It was a few minutes past midnight already, but the markets do not stop for either the moon or the sun.

He picked up his phone and called up Eddie, his interbank broker in Chicago, to place a buy order. Eddie thought he was crazy. Why should he be buying this stuff when everybody else was dumping it?

"Are you sure about this? Eighty thousand contracts are a huge position."

"I know. Just execute the order," Simon barked without hesitation, even though this was by far the largest trade he had ever bet on.

Eddie resisted a bit more: "It's late. Liquidity is poor. I can't guarantee you a good price. Sure you don't want to wait until tomorrow morning?"

"No! I don't care. I'm sure. Get on with it. Just bloody do it."

Just bloody do it. Because, with eighty thousand contracts, a 1 basis point increase in the price—a mere hundredth of a percent—would net him a cool $2 million! And if the Fed were to cut a quarter of a percent, 25 basis points, at one of its next two meetings, he could make back all the money he had lost on the dollar.

To Simon, the Iraq news did not change the fundamental fact that the US economy was in bad shape. He was sure that as the reality of its deterioration became clearer, the Fed would have no choice but to slash interest rates. All Simon had to do now was to wait for the Fed to act. And the beauty of it was, he had found a low-risk way of betting that this would happen.

He then made another call and proceeded to exit his long dollar trade. Even with the dollar's rise in the past couple of hours, his total loss still amounted to $45 million. But his luck, he was certain of it, was finally turning.

The small home office was quiet. He turned off the light and sat in the darkness for a few minutes. This was it. He had made his gamble for resurrection—the biggest gamble of his life.

He went upstairs to bed, snuggling up next to Alexandra who, snoring faintly, was already asleep. Despite a slight stirring of life in his boxers, he felt tired. Oh, so tired.

He closed his eyes in preparation for the first restorative sleep since his arrival back in London. As he heaved a long, protracted sigh of relief, the lyrics of an old nursery rhyme bubbled up from some long-disused recess of childhood memories, went round and round in his head:

> "Simple Simon met a pieman,
> Going to the fair;
> Says Simple Simon to the pieman,
> Let me taste your ware.
> Says the pieman to Simple Simon,
> Show me first your penny;
> Says Simple Simon to the pieman,
> Indeed I have not any."

He knew he'd have his penny now. He wrapped himself in that comforting thought as in a soft warm blanket. And just as he nodded off, the words went round again, this time with a subtle tweak:

> "Says the pieman to Simple Simon,
> Show me first your penny;
> Says Simple Simon to the pieman,
> Indeed, I'll soon have many."

• • •

A trader is not much different from a rodeo cowboy holding on to the reins with only one hand, trying not to be thrown by the bucking bronco. When Simon arrived on the trading floor the next morning at seven o'clock, all hell greeted him. The floor was roaring, full of frantic traders waving their arms and yelling into their receivers and at each other. Salespeople screamed out client orders at the top of their lungs, phones ringing without stop.

There would be no war! Crude oil had plunged overnight. At one point, it was down as much as 5 percent. Nikkei, the Japanese stock-market index, had rocketed up 3 percent, and futures suggested European and US shares were set to open at least 2 percent higher.

And then came the news that there might be a war after all! The Americans had released a statement. Inspection alone in Iraq did not satisfy them. Inevitably, oil came storming back.

In the midst of this chaos, Simon was an oasis of calm. He felt strangely detached, as though he was observing the distress all around him from a mile up in the sky. Because all he had to do now was wait. Because he had a game plan, whereas these other wankers did not.

"Fucking Saddam! Fucking fuckwit! Fucking wimp!"

Simon heard Rod's bellow of pain all the way across the floor.

"Fuck, fuck, fuck!" Rod yelled out again. "That wanker Saddam cost me a million dollars!"

Rod slammed down the receiver so hard it split in two. As if this didn't satisfy him enough, he then picked up the base of the phone and smashed it onto the floor. As luck, or misjudgment, would have it, Rod had closed out his long oil positions at a big loss the previous night after leaving Nobu, erasing all the money he had made over the entire year. And now, oil prices moved above the price at which he had sold his oil contracts.

Poor sod, thought Simon. He felt sorry for him, but there was nothing he could do for him now. In any case, his own moment of truth was fast approaching.

• • •

By early afternoon, order had been restored. The trading floor was perfectly silent in anticipation of the release of the US industrial production data for August. It was a crucial number. Economists were expecting a healthy uptick of 0.2 percent. Given the strong retail sales number from the previous week, another strong number could ease any concerns that the economic recovery was faltering. Holding their breath, all present stared at their computer screens.

The number came out—and what a shocker it was. A minus! At -0.3 percent, it was the first decline in nine months. The production of automobiles, that bellwether of the American economy, had fallen by 1.4 percent.

The trading floor went wild. It was even more chaotic than in the morning. The bad news just kept piling up. The dollar and equities quickly gave up their gains from earlier in the day, while bonds staged a furious rally. McDonald's issued a warning that weak sales would hurt profit this quarter, and the Dow tanked by 2.1 percent. After regular trading ended, banking titan J.P. Morgan Chase also warned that its results this quarter would fall short of expectations amid rising bad loans.

Everywhere on the trading floor there was anger, frustration, and pain. Having bought into the story that the US economy was on an upswing, many had gone long the dollar. It was now going down, and hard—the bucking bronco throwing traders mercilessly to the ground and leaving them with losses of a million here or two million there, wounded and limping in the arena.

By the end of the day, the November Eurodollar futures had risen by 10 basis points. Renewed pessimism about the US economy led the market to bet on the Fed having to cut interest rates soon, for the second time in less than twenty-four hours.

And who was the only winner on the floor? Simon! He was up $20 million! A whopping number. Never had he made this much money in a year, let alone in a day.

He clenched his hand into a fist: "*Yes*!" He had placed his bet and hit the jackpot. Sweet, sweet triumph. And it wasn't just the money. It was the knowledge that he had been right while everybody else was wrong.

But he couldn't jump up and sing and dance for joy. Not yet. He was still $25 million in the red. And he didn't have the heart. If this was the best day in Simon's trading life, it was a tough one for the others, many of whom were Simon's friends. He was the winner indeed, but a lonely winner.

• • •

At five o'clock he called it a day and went home.

Alexandra was in the kitchen preparing dinner. Simon grabbed her by the shoulders and slammed her body against his. "I hit the jackpot, love!" he said, looking into her eyes for approval. Alex responded with a smile. "An absolutely brilliant day!" His enthusiasm boiled over. Alex's smile grew wider. He then kissed her on the lips with an urgency he hadn't felt in quite a while. And she kissed him back. His body had sprung back to life. He was hard as a rock. Unbuckling his belt, he hoisted her up onto the island counter and roughly pulled down her pantyhose and pushed up the miniskirt she was wearing, though in the excitement of the moment he didn't forget to grab a kitchen towel to cushion her head. For Alex, it might have been uncomfortable, but for Simon, shuddering with the release, the sex proved to be a liberation. The frustrations, the tension, the fears of the past few months flushed out of his mind and body all at once.

• • •

Over the next two weeks, until the end of September, the sky kept falling. A torrent of bad corporate and economic news kept pouring in. OPEC decided not to increase oil production. Consumer confidence slid. Housing starts showed signs of wobbling. The Fed did not cut interest rates at their September meeting. The stock market tumbled with the Dow closing at its lowest finish in four years.

Investors were beginning to seriously worry that the Fed was behind the curve.

Simon, for his part, wasn't too concerned by the Fed's inaction. He was sure the falling stock market was bound to force the Fed's hand at its next meeting in November. Even Greenspan, the old fox, couldn't watch the stock market go down every day without losing sleep. And he, Simon, held the fox by the tail.

The November Eurodollar futures continued their rise and by the start of October, their price went up by 20 whole basis points, yielding Simon a total profit of a cool $60 million. The relief he felt was overwhelming. The money covered all his losses—and then some.

• • •

But despite his windfall he still could not exult in his victory.

In the moments when Simon the trader retreated and the essential decency of Simon the human being regained the upper hand, he would ruminate sadly on the passing of his American dream. America was going down and nothing could save her. The money he had made was somehow unclean. He felt like a hunter taking advantage of a fierce but wounded animal. It was the weakness of the prey, not the hunter's prowess, that had led to the kill.

• • •

It was a quiet Saturday morning. Alexandra was in the living room when the phone rang. Moments later, her desperate, heart-rending wail penetrated the walls, wound along the corridors, and shrieked like a whistling wind up the stairs, where it reached Simon, who was sitting in front of his computer screens in the study. Fearing the worst, Simon catapulted downstairs.

He picked Alexandra up from her half swoon on the floor. "It's Daddy," she said through barely moving lips between gasps for air. She flung the receiver from her hand as if it were a deadly, poisonous thing. "He's dead!"

Simon rocked his wife in his arms, comforting her as best he could. They stood silently interlocked, marooned in their grief.

• • •

Simon stared at the row of empty shot glasses of vodka he had downed one after the other. He had spent the entire Sunday evening mourning his father-in-law at his local pub. Alex had flown back to Cleveland the previous night. He wanted to go with her, but he couldn't. Not in the middle of the biggest trade of his life. And besides, the preparations for the upcoming audit were in full swing. They agreed that he would join her later, for the funeral the following weekend.

Suicide. He repeated the word to himself and it sounded unreal. He just couldn't get his head around it. Only seventy-five, with plenty of life left in him yet. He hadn't known his father-in-law well, but he knew that Clifton had always been a fighter.

He had been looking forward to getting to know him better one day. And now it was too late.

Too late! And the worst thing was the timing of it. The dreadful, cosmic timing of it. No amount of vodka could wash away the feeling that Clifton's death was the price of his own financial salvation.

He laughed out loud. In the infernal game of Russian roulette, Clifton took the bullet that was meant for him.

The next vodka burned like fire as it slid down his throat.

It was as if he had killed the old man and the old man's world with his own bare hands. In his irrational, drunken state, he searched the place where his soul should have been. And he couldn't find it.

• • •

On Monday, Simon woke up with a whopping hangover and in a repentant state of mind. How could he have abandoned Alexandra? He should never have let her travel to Cleveland by herself. His priorities were all screwed up. He'd close out his positions, he vowed, and fly out to join her that very evening.

But once he was back on the trading floor and the markets had opened, the overpowering rush of adrenaline took hold of him again and his headache and heartache vanished. He just couldn't bring himself to close out his positions and leave all that money on the table.

The stock-market meltdown was becoming self-fulfilling. Surely, he reasoned, the Fed would be forced to cut half—and not just a quarter—of a percent at the November meeting. And if they did, it would net him another $40 million. Who could walk away from that kind of money? Greed, that nemesis of traders, beckoned, singing its temptations like a siren over the head of his better self. By the end of the day, his mind was made up. He would let the trade run until the end of the week or until it made another 10 basis points. But what about the vow he had made this very morning? He struggled with his conscience for the best part of an hour. In the end, he decided, Cleveland would just have to wait. No way he could leave London now. Alex would understand. Anyway, he was doing this for the both of them. He would make it up to her, he promised himself.

The falling market can only take so much battering. Before the weekend arrived market psychology began to change again. After General Electric announced a 25 percent increase in net income on October 11, S&P 500 catapulted up 4 percent.

The markets, a giant force field of millions of individual decisions—a noisy circus full of bulls, bears, hawks, doves, cats that bounce, and dogs that underperform—know only the extremes of fear and greed. In the space of just four days, the S&P 500 rose by nearly 15 percent, the biggest gain over a four-day period since 1974, a quarter of a century. The rally was as violent as the sell-off had been. No one cared that it could be no more than a dead-cat bounce—the picturesque Wall Street lingo for a short-term recovery that is unlikely to last—rather than the start of a sustained rally. No one cared because no one wanted to be left behind.

And what did this mean for Simon? The market, its confidence restored, no longer thought an interest rate cut was necessary.

Whoosh! Out the window went all the profit Simon had made, vanishing into thin air in the space of four days.

• • •

Though physically present at Clifton's funeral, Simon's mind was not. He went through the motions of extending condolences like an automaton. What cruel twist of fate had given him such a chance at redemption only to snatch it away? He was beyond angry with himself. He should have closed out his positions while he was still ahead. How could he have been such a greedy dumbass as to put his life in jeopardy a second time? He grieved, not only for his father-in-law, but for himself. He could have kicked a thousand dead cats. He could have throttled a thousand live ones.

• • •

The audit, looming like a gallows erected in the town square, was just two weeks away, and Simon was still sitting on his original losses of $45 million.

Then—

Ready for some tennis on Sunday? read the text message from Guy.

Bloody hell! The tournament had completely slipped his mind. He paced around the bedroom in his boxers, his ginger hair wild. It was too much. He was in no state for exertion, for sports, or for Guy. Even the tone of the text grated on his nerves. But there was no getting out of it. He couldn't let Alex down; she'd given her heart and soul to the charity tournament, plunging herself headlong into the preparations after their return to London.

Despite Simon's fervent prayers for rain, Sunday turned out to be a spectacular October day. He dragged himself out of bed. He and Guy were the top two seeds in the draw, likely to face each other in the final.

Alexandra had chosen a tennis club on the south side of Hyde Park, a ten-minute walk from their mews house. The tournament was set to begin at nine o'clock. By a quarter to, guests were already filling the stone entrance pavilion that housed the club's offices and a small café.

The turnout was huge, and it was not because of any sudden interest in equine welfare. It was the anticipated duel between him and Guy that was the magnet. Half of his trading floor had shown up: There were Paresh and Rod and Nick and Grant, already guzzling beer at this early hour of the morning. He waved to them, trying to look jaunty. He couldn't let them down, no matter how disinclined he was to play. He would do his best to represent the bank and his mates with honor against Guy and at the very least give them a good show.

The morning session breezed by quickly and uneventfully. Both he and Guy won all their matches in straight sets.

The final was scheduled for three o'clock in the afternoon. By then, the crowd had grown pretty rowdy, waiting, drinks in hand, for the face-off between the two players left standing: Simon and Guy.

Guy won the first set easily, 6–1.

In the second set, Simon found his game and went on the attack. After splitting the first four games with Guy, he held serve in the fifth and broke Guy in the sixth. Guy broke back, but Simon went up 5–4 with a stunning backhand down-the-line return.

Simon played as if his life depended on it. He dashed ferociously after every ball, going for winners on every shot, his do-or-die energy compelling Guy to play defense. Guy's unforced errors mounted.

In the next game, Simon served for the set. The crowd watched with bated breath. He aced his first serve! Fifteen–love! But then, to moans from the crowd, he double-faulted on the next. Fifteen–all. Guy's returns on Simon's next two serves went wide. Forty–fifteen! For the set point, Simon hit a huge forehand that tunneled past Guy to fall on the baseline. The crowd erupted in cheers.

Simon's confidence soared, though Guy might have been the better player. *I can do this.*

In the third set, Simon went on playing like a man possessed. Nothing mattered anymore. Channeling his anger at the world, at himself, he gave everything he had to the match. He had eyes only for Guy and the ball, the entire universe—the bank, his trade, his pending doom—disappeared, collapsed into the intensity of his concentration on the current moment.

His tenacity paid off. He broke Guy in the seventh game to go up 4–3.

In the next game, he aced his first serve. The sound of crisp clapping rose from the rows of spectators pressed against the fence.

With his second serve, Simon bounced the ball a couple of times before reaching up sky-high to aim, his toes barely touching the ground, stretching his arm up to its maximum capacity, slamming a serve straight down the middle of the court, the ball clipping the line, and then rushed up to the net.

Guy returned the kick serve with a block.

Simon hit a crisp forehand volley cross-court to Guy's right.

Guy just managed to slide to the ball, his tennis shoes skidding on the hard surface of the court, and he lobbed it back over Simon's head.

But Simon's racquet caught the ball in midair, smashing it hard but only just clearing the net, giving Guy the chance to stay in the point.

Heads swiveled from right to left and right again, in thrall to the thwacks of the balls bouncing off the racquets.

Guy swung hard, and with a loud grunt aimed directly at Simon, who was still standing in front of the net.

The speed of Guy's ball was terrifying. It smashed smack into Simon's temple. An audible gasp of "oh no" rose up in the air. Simon toppled over backward like a tree, his head coming down hard on the ground. He felt an intense nausea and then—nothing.

• • •

"A concussion," the doctor at Cromwell Hospital told Alex. "A freak accident. Very bad luck. I'm a tennis player myself. Who would've thought tennis could be a dangerous sport?"

Simon lay unconscious. The doctors were puzzled. The fall couldn't have been that hard, but somehow, the angle at which his head had struck the ground caused a hair-line fracture that ran across his skull almost from ear to ear. All the test results were positive, and there was nothing for it but to wait.

His family from up north came bearing flowers. His trading buddies came and went. Guy showed up, contrite, with the trophy and a big check for the horses in hand. Even Nigel popped over for a courtesy visit. Alexandra, naturally, was constantly at his bedside.

One day, two days, three days passed, and then, on the fourth day, Simon opened his eyes, waking to the sound of Alexandra's musical voice.

"Welcome back, my love," she said, squeezing his hand.

He was released before the weekend and he prepared himself to go back to work on Monday.

• • •

The markets, however, are never comatose. On the very same day Simon got out of hospital, the bucking bronco kicked again. The market bounce that had driven Simon to despair proved to be a very dead cat indeed.

On that Friday, October 25, the September data for durable-goods orders were released. They were much weaker than expected, falling 5.9 percent in the biggest drop in nearly a year. A report on consumer confidence added to the concern that the economy was losing momentum. The University of Michigan's index of consumer sentiment for October sank to the lowest level since September 1993, a ten-year low.

On November 6, the first day Simon was back at the office, the Fed, responding to the alarming deterioration of the American economy, enacted an emergency interest rate cut of half a percentage point. The overnight bank lending rate fell to 1.25 percent, the lowest rate since July 1961, the lowest rate in more than a generation. Eurodollar futures shot up to dizzying heights.

Simon's bet had finally paid off. He immediately realized a profit of $100 million. A staggering amount, even for those habituated to the obscenely large numbers that change hands in the financial markets. After subtracting his dollar loss, he was still left with $55 million. A tidy sum.

Lucky Simon. Lucky, lucky Simon. The freak accident? Pure, unadulterated luck. Who knows what kind of stupid action he might have taken while the dead cat was still bouncing? He would have sold his Eurodollar contracts, that's what, he kept repeating, horrified, to himself. What a debt he owed Alexandra. If it hadn't been for the tennis tournament…or her frigging love of horses…or that tennis ball.

It was better to be lucky than be right. Yes. He was the luckiest trader in the world.

And that night, in bed with Alexandra, his body made it known to her as much.

• • •

Now that he had made his packet, what should his next move be? Simon could have rested on his laurels and waited for bonus time to come around. But the itch to trade was too strong. Having almost lost his pants by betting on the dollar's appreciation, he had sworn to never touch the dollar ever again. But after the Fed's interest rate cut triggered a sharp decline of the dollar, he didn't hesitate to get an early jump on the wave. He immediately established a short dollar position, betting the dollar would go down even more, by selling $500 million against the Japanese yen. Why the Japanese yen? Because Simon reasoned that interest rates in Japan, being already near zero, had no room to decline further to absorb the dollar's fall.

• • •

Spinning the giant roulette wheel once again, with God knew what repercussions worldwide, with no second thought of or even awareness of the outcomes, Simon executed the trade in five consecutive clips, or lots, with the last $100 million done with the New York branch of Fuji Bank.

And where did the $100 million acquired by Fuji Bank end up? With Nippon Oil, which needed $50 million to pay for crude-oil imports; with Sumitomo Trust, which needed $25 million to acquire some Microsoft shares; and, finally, with Nike, which needed $20 million to repatriate its earnings in Japan back to the US. As for the remaining $5 million, these were exchanged for yen the same day for hundreds of Fuji Bank's commercial and retail customers in Japan.

Among those customers, half a world away, was a Mrs. Tomoko Watanabe, a small, pudgy, middle-aged housewife. She walked into the Kashiwa branch in Tokyo the following afternoon to buy the $300 that she needed to wire to her daughter studying for her PhD in anthropology at the University of California, Los Angeles. After this was done, she exited the bank, mounted her rusty old bike, and pedaled back home through the narrow streets to make dinner for her husband and son.

Chapter 4

TOMOKO WATANABE

Tokyo, Japan, January–July 2005

"Low interest rates punish savers."

—Bill Gross

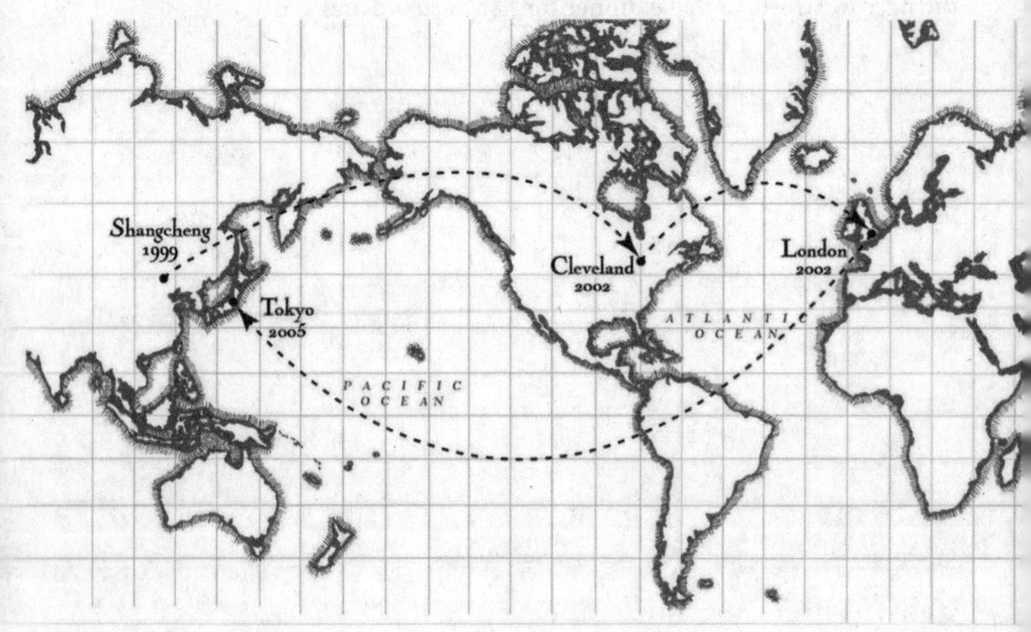

THE HOUSE IN KASHIWA, CHIBA Prefecture, southeast of Tokyo, was a two-storied box with aluminum windows and clad in white mosaics. It had a grey-tiled roof and a tiny front garden. The wind was howling outside as Tomoko struggled to get up from her bed. It was six o'clock in the morning and still dark, and everybody in the house was asleep. She was loath to abandon the warmth of the heavy duvet, but today was her husband Akihiro Watanabe's birthday, and she wanted to surprise him with a special breakfast.

Tomoko shivered as her feet, encased in thick white socks, trod silently on the tatami mat covering the floor. It was cold, even for January, and this was one time she wished there was heating in the bedroom upstairs. She put on her slippers, pulled on a heavy cardigan over her fleece pajamas, and went down to the kitchen.

The kitchen, Tomoko's kingdom, was small, but she ran it like a tight ship, every utensil and small appliance kept in its assigned place.

She began to prepare her husband's favorite menu: clam miso soup and omelet rolls. There was smoked fish left over from the previous night, as well as cooked rice.

After turning on the small heater and quickly swallowing a cup of hot tea, she put on her old blue-checked apron and set to work.

Poor Aki, she was thinking, as she removed from the fridge the asari clams she had bought the previous afternoon; he really deserved some cheering up. Only eight months ago he had lost his lifelong employment, the first serious crisis in their marriage of twenty-two years. The electronics company he had given his all to for over thirty years had gone bankrupt after its main customer decided to outsource to China.

She rinsed the clams in cold water, rubbed them clean with a dish-cloth, and set them aside to soak in salt water. She then filled a pot with water from the sink and blanched a leaf of kelp. When it had softened, she removed it with chopsticks and then put it back in the pot to boil for a minute or two before taking it out again.

Though Aki had found a new job quickly enough, Tomoko was worried. It not only paid a third less than his previous salary, it was a temporary job, with a contract that had to be renewed every six months. While Tomoko was, by nature, someone who took life's setbacks with a pragmatic optimism, she felt helpless in the face of the loss of their financial security. As she added dried bonito flakes to the boiling water, she shook her head and pursed her lips at the injustice of it.

When the fish was cooked, she passed the broth through a fine sieve lined with a cloth. Discarding the scum, she sieved it again. And again. Inspecting the liquid for any telltale specks, she repeated the process until she was satisfied the broth was perfectly clear. She now reached out for the clams, soaking in their bath of brine.

Usually, Tomoko loved the ritual fuss of birthdays, especially her husband's—the shopping for presents, the paper decorations and cards, the candles on the cake—but this year there wasn't much cause for celebration.

She rinsed the clams and tipped them into the broth. Bringing the liquid to a boil, she skimmed it patiently. Once the clams had opened, she mixed in the miso paste, squeezing it through a small sieve with a spoon. The soup was ready.

Now for the omelets. What was more worrying, she thought, breaking eggs into a bowl with a deft flick of her wrist, was that his pension was gone. And the new job offered no pension at all. The bleakness of their future agitated her as she whisked the eggs with more vigor than necessary and poured them into the frying pan.

The omelets were done. When they had cooled a bit, she rolled them up into narrow, finger-shaped wraps and put them aside. Then she arranged the fillets of cold smoked fish in the middle of a long rectangular plate, which she decorated in one corner with a dollop of daikon radish infused with ponzu sauce. Finally, she heated up the rice and took out some nattō, fermented soybeans, everyone's favorite.

She looked out the window above the sink. The heavy night darkness was lifting, and she could make out the falling snowflakes and the leafless branches of the cherry tree in their garden bending in the wind. A cold grey light was beginning to infiltrate the kitchen. She switched off the overhead lamp, figuring she could do without it now.

A brown Formica-top table with six chairs stood in a nook just off the kitchen. *Poor Aki,* she repeated to herself as she began to set it. At the age of fifty-three, there was little chance of his finding steady employment again. Although they never talked about it, she knew that, ashamed and frustrated, her husband was unraveling. His drinking binges had become more frequent, and he had taken to coming home at all hours. He was also becoming moody and short-tempered.

Only last week he had flown off the handle when she told him she was thinking about looking for a part-time job. He wouldn't hear of it, he had responded angrily. Their son was still at school and needed her. Besides, what would their neighbors think? It was out of the question.

Though Tomoko knew his objections had more to do with his pride, she didn't bring up the subject again. She vowed to herself she would find another way to help. But how?

Tomoko put down a small flower arrangement, teacups, bowls, and chopstick supports on the table. She had to find a way to help Aki. Whereas she could still take comfort in little things, he had just lost his entire world. She took a moment to align the chopsticks just so. Taking a step back from the table, she viewed the result with satisfaction.

Tomoko glanced at the kitchen clock squeezed between the toaster oven and a shelf. It was seven-thirty and all was ready. Plenty of time left for a leisurely meal before Aki left for the office and their son, Nishio, left for school. What a pity her daughter, Keiko, wasn't there.

Tomoko brushed that regret away, together with a lock of her permed black hair that had strayed onto her forehead, and stood meekly at the entrance of the kitchen, waiting. She could hear her family coming down the narrow wooden stairs.

She bowed to her husband and her mother-in-law as they appeared, her face faintly flushed from her efforts, her shoulders hunched forward ever so slightly. "*Ohayō gozaimasu*," she said, with the politest of greetings.

But Aki only grunted a barely discernible thank-you as he viewed the mini-feast she had prepared and sat down, noisily pushing back his chair.

Then he buried his face in the morning newspaper that Tomoko had laid, neatly folded, to the right of his chopsticks.

He was followed by Nishio. At fifteen, he was a tall and gawky youth, with a few wisps of dark downy hair on his upper lip and chin. He advanced towards the table and sat down in silence. He sat there sullenly, looking down under lowered eyelids, not once making eye contact with his mother. He consumed his soup in a few rapid gulps and hurriedly shoved some rice into his mouth. Then with a curt, barely mumbled good-bye, he got up and was gone.

"Don't forget your bento box," Tomoko's voice rang out after him, "you must eat lunch!"

The third person at the table was Mishimo, Tomoko's mother-in-law. It was she who owned the house, and after the death of Akihiro's father some ten years before had given over most of the space to her son's family, keeping only one room for herself. It was a situation not without friction. She had never liked Tomoko and was of the opinion that her handsome son could have found a better match than the daughter of a taxi driver. Or, at the very least, a prettier one. Though their exchanges were invariably on the right side of civil, Mishimo inevitably found fault with everything Tomoko did. But this morning was different. She spooned down the soup slowly, savoring every sip. "Excellent, Tomoko," she remarked loudly. "Well done." A compliment! Tomoko was touched to the bottom of her heart.

She then turned to her husband.

"*Anata*," he said, using a Japanese term of endearment. "I hope you'll be home on time for dinner. I bought a cake for tonight. And there will be eel as a main course."

Aki didn't shift his eyes from the newspaper. "No. I'm eating out. Client dinner. Don't wait up for me. I'll be back late."

If Tomoko was disappointed, she showed no sign of it.

"Akihiro-san. I also bought you a small gift," she announced timidly. She had bought it out of her personal savings and had hoped to give it to him at the evening meal. She would have to give it to him now instead.

She went to the living room where she had hidden it. Coming back, she bowed respectfully and held out the package in her two open palms like an offering, saying "Happy birthday" in English.

Aki finally deigned to lower the newspaper and stared at the box wrapped in delicately folded bright blue paper, tied with a slender red-and-gold string. He reached out to take it. But instead of opening it, he put it in the pocket of his suit jacket.

"Have to rush now," he said dismissively.

"It's the lighter you always wanted," said Tomoko. But Aki responded with a dead gaze of bitterness at the wall behind her. Suddenly, he jumped up from his chair with such violence that it crashed to the floor.

"*Baka*! You stupid woman! *Kono ama*, you bitch!" He exploded in an inexplicable fit of rage.

Tomoko shrank back.

"How many times do I have to tell you not to waste money?" he yelled. "Don't you see the situation we're in?"

Without warning, he grabbed the cast-iron teapot from the table. He seemed ready to hurl it straight at her. Tomoko raised her arm to defend herself. He had hit her before, and she thought she knew what to expect.

At the last moment, however, perhaps in response to a whispered word from Mishimo that never reached Tomoko's ears, he changed the direction of his aim and the heavy pot went flying toward the kitchen. Spurting tea, it smashed loudly into one of the kitchen cabinets.

In the silence that followed, Tomoko couldn't move. Her heart beat wildly in her chest. But she didn't say a word. Out of the corner of her eye, she was just in time to catch the expression of icy disapproval on Mishimo's face.

• • •

Tomoko shuffled after her husband to the *genkan*, the lowered area where one takes off one's shoes before entering the house and puts them on again before leaving. She handed him his bento box, as well as a brown envelope. In charge of the family's finances, it was she who meted out the monthly spending allowances to each member of the family. Every month, on payday, when Aki's salary would come into the bank, she'd deposit 10 percent in their savings account and withdraw the rest in cash for household expenses.

"I've added something extra for your birthday," she said gently, trying to look cheery, pretending the tantrum in the dining room was behind them. She then helped him with his overcoat and wrapped a muffler around his neck. "Take care. It's going to be very cold today."

Aki grunted a gruff, barely audible "*arigato gozaimasu*" and stepped outside, slamming the door behind him. It was not an auspicious start to the day.

• • •

Tomoko was well trained in the roles of dutiful wife, dedicated mother, and deferential daughter-in-law. With Mishimo settled in front of the TV in the living room, she went back to the kitchen to clean up.

Though they owned a dishwasher, she almost never used it now, preferring to save on electricity. So she washed the dishes and pots and pans by hand. She then rinsed out a couple of plastic bags and carefully smoothed out a sheet of aluminum-foil wrapping for later reuse. Tomoko had adapted to their changed circumstances with a sense of thrift that was second nature to her. If before she ran her house as a model of efficiency, now with the budget shrinking, she had become frugality personified.

After having read that an average household could spend ¥10,000 a year on paper towels alone, she never touched them again. Articles in the popular magazine *Sutekina Okusan* such as "98 Recipes Under 100 Yen a Serving" became the kind of item she stored in her memory whenever she went out shopping.

• • •

After Tomoko had finished in the kitchen, she continued with her morning chores. When they were done, she went upstairs to her daughter's room.

She opened the door and stood at the threshold, hesitating for a moment as if she were about to enter a sacred shrine. She closed the door quietly behind her. It was two years since Keiko had left on a scholarship for California. She inhaled deeply from the air of the small room, fancying she could detect Keiko's lingering scent.

She was very close to her daughter. They were good friends, and she missed her dreadfully.

Tomoko went over to the untouched bed and plumped up the pillows, brushing away some specks of dust and then wiping away the dampness on her lashes. Once upon a time she had had a modest career of her own, as an assistant to an accountant, but following Japanese custom, she had to give up her job once she was married and dedicate herself to the running of her household. All her hope for the future, all her unrealized ambitions, she projected onto her academically brilliant daughter.

She adjusted the floral fabric of the curtains that she and Keiko had chosen together and sat down at the desk by the window.

Keiko had taught her before leaving how to surf the internet on the old PC, and Tomoko had been a quick learner. She now switched on the power and clicked on the inbox. Happily, there was a new message waiting for her. Tomoko paused for a few moments before opening the email. She savored this precious time to herself and wanted it to last as long as possible. Keiko rarely failed to send her daily reports, news about her life from all the way over there, beyond the ocean. Today she included a few photos from her latest trip to Mexico, with a snapshot of her sitting on top of a pyramid in a place with the strange name of Chichén Itzá. As far as Tomoko was concerned, it was as if her daughter had been abducted by aliens and spirited off to another planet.

Though Keiko had never directly asked for help, Tomoko knew her daughter was always in need of extra cash. Whenever she could, she would wire her small sums from her own savings without telling Aki. Keiko didn't know her father had lost his job, as Tomoko hadn't wanted to worry her. But how was she going to continue helping her when money was so tight? When they were already digging into the family's meager savings?

• • •

Tomoko went to the bathroom to wash up. In the bathroom mirror she caught the reflection of her face. How plain and pudgy her features were. Her eyes were small and round, and her flat nose was too wide. She should count herself lucky to have landed a husband at all, she thought. Yet she had, and an attractive one at that. She should be grateful.

She looked more closely into the mirror. She presented one cheek to the glass and then the other, examining them as intensely as she had examined the broth before. All clear. Tomoko's one vanity was her smooth, milk-white skin. She never failed, even in the palest sunshine, to protect it. Some sunny days of summer could find her dressed as if for battle—long sleeves covering her arms, huge dark glasses, a broad-brimmed hat, and, as an additional measure, a parasol. And she never forgot to slap multiple layers of sunscreen on any exposed patch of skin. Despite these precautions, she was still concerned. At forty-six she had nothing but the faintest lines on her forehead. But the bogeyman of aging indiscriminately stalks all women. What she feared most was the appearance of brown or black spots that would inevitably mar her complexion and make her even more unlovely in her husband's eyes. So, she religiously applied whitening cream from the rows of tubes and jars accumulated in the bathroom cupboard. She owned every product she could lay her hands on: There was nothing she wouldn't do to avoid that sorry fate.

A few days before, browsing through *Very*, her favorite women's magazine, she had noticed an ad for a new whitening cream claiming to be more powerful than any other on the market. It would be sold as an introductory offer at a 50 percent discount for one day only at the main branch of Mitsukoshi department store in Nihonbashi.

The sale was today. For half a week her vanity had struggled with her sense of thrift. Her vanity won. But to assuage her guilt, she promised herself to forego the pair of shoes she would've been saving up for.

• • •

"*Okaa-san*, I'm going out."

Mishimo's eyes didn't move from the TV screen. "In this weather?"

"It has cleared up. Look, Mother, it isn't snowing anymore!" Tomoko pointed at the living room window. But her mother-in-law, flicking through the channels with the remote, didn't turn her head. "I've made you lunch. Don't worry, I won't be long," Tomoko said, not daring to tell her she meant to go all the way into central Tokyo.

"Just mind not to waste any more money. Remember what Aki said."

"I'll be back in time to serve dinner."

And she left.

• • •

She emerged from her house bundled up in her warmest clothes: her tan puffer coat, a knitted hat, and her old rabbit-fur-lined boots that unfortunately she could not quite zip up to the top of her plump calves. She shut the low iron gate of her front garden behind her and, adjusting her sunglasses on her nose, began walking down the snowy street. Tomoko was happy to be outside under the blue sky and shining sun. She waved cheerily to her next-door neighbor, who was carrying out a large pile of newspapers tied up with string.

The thin layer of snow that had accumulated during the night dressed up the roofs, the balcony parapets, and the garden walls of houses like a new coat of paint. Though Tomoko knew the snow wouldn't last beyond a couple of days, she reveled in the white icing that had transformed the ugly jungle of exposed telephone wires and electric power lines, running in bundles and loops along the street, into festive garlands; in the starlike glistening of the powder of snowflakes on the leaves of shrubs and ginkgo trees.

Little traffic penetrated this section of their neighborhood. Other than the occasional muffled thundering of the train that ran across a nearby bridge, it was silent, almost village-like. The street was so narrow it was wide enough for only one car, and there were no sidewalks. The train station was about twenty minutes away from her house. She had plenty of time. The evening meal was mostly prepared, and Aki would be home late.

At Kashiwa Station, Tomoko took the JR train to Ueno. She gazed out the window at the endless suburbs that radiated out from central Tokyo, excited by her brazenness; she so rarely travelled into the heart of the city, and never on her own. She was looking forward to the adventure. She had planned her little outing down to the smallest detail, which was not too difficult considering that the rapid trains ran precisely to the minute and were never late. It was now noon. She would return on the 5:17 and be back home in ample time to serve Mishimo and Nishio dinner. She exited at Ueno and took the Tokyo Metro Ginza line to Mitsukoshimae Station. The entire journey took her forty-five minutes.

• • •

Mitsukoshi is the oldest Western-style department store in Japan, with roots dating back to the seventeenth century. As a symbol of Japanese capitalism, it holds a special place in Tokyo's history. Its prestige, at some point spreading throughout all of Asia, is equivalent to the famous Harrods of London, the kind of place where people go not necessarily to shop, but to sightsee and gawk.

The main building, erected in 1936 and taking up an entire city block, is a large, rather stodgy mass of dull grey, relieved only by the march of red awnings along the street façade and some gilded ornamentation. A golden statue of Mercury, the classical patron god of commerce, naked but for a fig leaf, balances itself on one foot above the entrance canopy. With one hand holding the caduceus and his other with its forefinger pointing skywards, he seems to hail all who enter.

Not that Tomoko, advancing from the station along the façade of the store, took any notice nor knew anything of these architectural details. But as she approached the main entrance elevated above the street, the two large bronze lions crouching on stone plinths on either side of the steps, as if keeping guard at a great temple, were impossible to ignore. Their presence filled Tomoko with a degree of awed trepidation as she hesitated at the threshold. When she timidly pushed open the doors, however, she felt instantly reassured as two uniformed ushers bowed deeply in a show of respect. It was as if she, Tomoko, was their most valued customer.

Such was her welcome as everywoman. And the assault on her body and senses, once she entered, was as gratifying as it was immediate, wrapping her in a gentle breeze of toasty warmth, of mellifluous notes of an organ playing Pachelbel in the background, of softly glowing buttery lights, and mingling scents of perfumes wafting through the air.

Tomoko stared up the soaring height of the vaulted ceiling and the grand staircase sweeping up the four tiers of galleries. At the center stood a statue of the goddess of fortune, which rose like a huge coral formation from the sea. For a long moment Tomoko stood gaping in wonder at the skylit space. This department store was nothing like the one in Kashiwa where she usually shopped. It was not like a temple but rather like a great cathedral.

But the huge space, far from overpowering, on the contrary, uplifted her and made her feel free. Free to float through the galleries to her heart's content, to admire the displays of all that her heart could possibly desire.

For desire, she thought, was on display everywhere—tempting her, seducing her. The traditional kimonos cut from the richest cloths, their long sleeves spread out on bamboo poles set against wood-paneled walls to show off their artful patterns of twigs of budding flowers or jewel-colored birds; the silk sashes of every hue and design cascading down display stands; the porcelain cups and jars and vases announcing their fragility in glass cabinets. And she marveled at the chopsticks. They came in every size and shape hewn from the most precious and rare woods imaginable. And the glossy lacquered rice bowls and boxes, the expensive pens, and wallets, and keychains. And how the desire only grew at the sight of jewelry, scarves, hats, and gloves. And handbags. Belts. Shoes.

Tomoko had never seen such luxurious abundance before. And a wondrous thought struck her: All this stuff was for sale! She was walking in beauty; never mind that she couldn't afford any of it.

• • •

Eventually, she did purchase the whitening cream, sold, as advertised, at half price in the cosmetics section. Tomoko, clutching her prettily wrapped prize and consulting her wristwatch, found she still had plenty of time. The nice saleslady serving her had informed her there was a new wing to the store that had opened only a couple of months before.

"It's very modern. Everyone falls in love with it. Go and see for yourself. You'll enjoy it."

"*Arigato gozaimasu*," said Tomoko, thanking her for her suggestion. She decided to act upon her current spirit of adventure and check out the new wing.

After several twists and turns through the labyrinth of the old department store, Tomoko found the bridge connecting it to the new wing. She took the escalator from floor to floor, making a quick tour of each department. But when the escalator steps melted into the ninth floor, the business of selling abruptly ended. According to a large sign, she had arrived at the Cultural Salon.

The entire floor was devoted to classrooms on either side of a long parquet corridor. At the far end, it opened up into a waiting room in which a large group of women was gathered, some standing patiently in an orderly line.

Curious, Tomoko ventured down the corridor. On the right wall was a bulletin board with notices announcing the day's various activities: a flower arrangement class, a reading from a new book on Zen Buddhism, a lecture for new mothers. Tomoko instantly recognized Machiko Yamamoto's face from TV talk shows smiling out at her from one of the notices.

"Good afternoon." A voice came from behind her back.

Startled, Tomoko looked over her shoulder. The voice belonged to a young woman in a store uniform holding a clipboard.

"Pardon me. I didn't mean to disturb you. Can I interest you in our investment seminar, perhaps? It's very popular. Yamamoto-san is one of our best speakers. She's going to give a lecture on getting the most out of your savings and achieving financial security. It's starting in fifteen minutes, and there is still space left."

"Is there a fee to pay?" she asked, looking shyly down at her feet.

"No, it's free," was the reassuring reply.

Maybe she could learn something. Besides, she still had an hour to kill. So, Tomoko put her name down.

At five minutes to two, everyone was shepherded into a large classroom.

Neon-lit and spartan, Tomoko thought it looked like Nishio's school. The tables had been pushed into two rows in a large horseshoe shape, and after some scraping of chairs and shuffling around, everyone was seated. Tomoko found herself in the front, directly opposite the small podium.

At precisely two o'clock, Machiko Yamamoto swept in with purposeful strides. She cut a theatrical figure, idiosyncratically dressed in a tight-fitting red jacket, matching red lipstick, and a long, voluminous black skirt. All eyes turned to her with a palpable thrill. She was a minor TV celebrity, after all. Tomoko opened her purse, took out her glasses, and peered more closely at the slender woman, in her forties like herself. She was perfect, with her gamine haircut and her straight glossy black hair topped by a perky red hat.

And her skin was perfect, too. *Money,* Tomoko couldn't help thinking. It took money to look like that. She pushed her feet in their shabby boots deeper under the chair. Then she quickly removed her glasses and put them back in her purse.

"Thank you all for coming today," Machiko said, bowing low to the company. "I am Machiko Yamamoto, and I have come here today with an important message for the women of Japan," she announced in a powerful voice, spurning the microphone. "I am here to share my experiences with you so that you may profit from them and improve your lives.

"But, before I begin, I would like to ask everyone here a question. If you're here today because you're worried about the financial future of your family, please raise your hand. Don't be shy. We're all among friends here."

Almost everyone raised their hands. Tomoko, finding courage in numbers, eventually raised hers, too.

"Thank you for your honesty. Regardless of your financial situation today, you are right to be worried about the future. The Japanese economy is sick. It has been sick for a long time. Our economy grew by an average of just one percent over the last ten years. Pitiful! And this year isn't going to be much better."

She paused.

"Do you know what one percent growth means? That's almost nothing. Allow me to illustrate."

She pressed a wireless clicker and a large chart appeared on the screen behind her.

"See that tall red column? It represents the value of our entire economy last year. Now see the large blue column next to it? It represents the forecast for our economy this year. It should be standing taller. But you can't tell the difference in height—because it's taller by only one percent. Japanese economic growth is practically invisible."

A low buzz spread through the classroom as everyone digested this information.

"Now I'll let you in on another little secret, though many of you may already know it from firsthand experience. The lifetime security of employment that our parents took for granted is slowly dying. Salaries have been flat or are declining. If, that is, you have a salary at all. These days we are told that we should consider ourselves lucky if we, or our husbands, still have a job."

A number of women in the audience exchanged glances and murmured their assent.

"Even though income is not going up and even going down, prices, on the other hand, have not stopped rising. They're shooting up and up."

Another click brought up a blue flat horizontal line, representing income, which intersected with a bright red arrow pointing upwards, representing prices.

"My friends, food, heating, travel—everything, in short—is getting more expensive all the time. The government keeps telling us there's no inflation, but we know this isn't true. We all know it's a fairy tale."

Everyone in the room reacted by vigorously nodding their heads. A couple of women clapped their hands briefly. Machiko's words had struck a chord with all present. Not least with Tomoko, who was more than familiar with the painful effect of rising prices, especially of food at the local supermarket, which had forced her to go ever further afield in search of bargains. *What a woman*, Tomoko thought admiringly. She had the guts to tell things as they really were.

Machiko approached the circle of tables.

"The picture I've just painted isn't pretty, is it? But there's something far worse. Can anyone guess what that may be?" she asked, almost seductively, her voice dropping a register.

She looked around enquiringly, her smiling eyes resting on every woman present, inviting their participation. Then they fell on Tomoko. Tomoko, too petrified to utter a word, cast her eyes down, her eyelashes fluttering. In the end no one dared volunteer an answer, too afraid of the embarrassment should they turn out to be wrong.

Machiko marched back to the podium and turned around to face her audience. She thundered like a fiery preacher predicting the end of days. "Zero-interest rates! Zero-interest rates, my friends, is the enemy that is destroying our future! And with your permission I'd like to show you why."

With a colorful sweep of her red lacquered fingernails, she beckoned to a man waiting discreetly at the open door to the hallway. In he came, half hidden behind a tall bundle of banknotes tied up with twine that he dropped on the middle of the floor.

"Don't get too excited, this money isn't real," Machiko remarked flippantly with a saucy toss of her short black hair and a small smile. "Now imagine," she continued, "that this pile represents your entire savings. And this—"

She reached into the small black shoulder bag that hung across her body, took out a few notes of real yen, and held them up in her hand so that all could see. She then bent her knees and set the real banknotes down beside the pile of fake ones, the hem of her full skirt fanning out gracefully around her ankles as it grazed the floor.

"There," she said, straightening up again and adjusting her hat. "At today's interest rates of zero-point-one percent, that's about how much your deposits at the bank make you in a year. Not very impressive, is it? Assuming interest rates remain at this level, it would take a hundred years—by which time some of our grandchildren will be in their graves—to increase by ten percent. That is, to a level that would actually make a difference."

Silence now reigned in the classroom. Everyone followed her every word, her every gesture with bated breath.

"This means that you must save more and more to be able to achieve your target for a modest, let alone comfortable, retirement. Millions of Japanese have yet to fully recognize this impossible predicament. But the day of reckoning is already here for those who are about to retire or are retired already. People are forced to dig deeper and deeper into their savings to make ends meet. The statistics indicate that many retirees are giving up on necessities just to survive. In fact, growing poverty among elderly people is now a sad reality in Japan."

As if on cue, everyone covered their mouths with the palms of their hands, the collective inhalation of breath resonating like the sound of air pumping up a giant balloon.

Machiko had them just where she wanted.

"My friends. I don't mean to alarm you. But you can no longer sit back on your hands and pretend that everything will work out somehow. You must be proactive. If you don't start looking after your financial health, nobody else will. If you don't start looking after your own financial health today, it will be too late.

"And I've come to present you with a way out. It does exist, but you have to be prepared to be brave. Doing nothing and sitting on your savings at the bank is simply not an option anymore."

"But how can you expect us to do anything about it?" a woman wearing a yellow scarf sitting behind Tomoko burst out. "I'm just an ordinary housewife. I know nothing about finance…or making money. Only managing it. Or," she added in an afterthought, "spending it."

Everybody smiled at this public admission of helplessness, but in their hearts, they felt the same way.

"This is what my seminar is about. To teach you how to invest so you can get higher returns than at the bank. To help you step out into a new world of stocks, bonds, and currencies. Once upon a time we were told that wise money management meant putting every yen in time deposits. But these don't yield any return anymore, and because of inflation, money is worth less and less. Your husbands bring home the money, it's true, but it's your responsibility to safeguard its value. You must take control and change your way of thinking.

"Today, wisdom means seeking higher returns. Times have changed. You must do this. For yourselves. For your families." She halted abruptly, as if a new tactic had just struck her, and after a moment she asked, "How many of you are housewives?"

All but a half dozen younger women raised their hands.

"Let me tell you something about myself. I was in your exact position once. I was a housewife too, until my divorce five years ago. I have two children that I had to raise on my own. I couldn't find a full-time job, and part-time work, as you know, pays badly. Like you, I knew nothing about investing. I took to trading out of necessity. I made mistakes, but I learned. After I acquired the skills, I was able to multiply one million yen to fifty million yen over a four-year period. Today I've achieved financial security and independence. I bought my own house, sent both of my sons to the best cram schools in Tokyo, and now they attend the best universities."

This time the collective gasp was one of pure admiration. The women in the room rose to their feet, clapping like mad. Tomoko was bowled over. She, too, jumped up. She had never met anyone like Yamamoto-san before. So independent-minded and courageous! To think she even had the audacity to admit her divorce to a bunch of strangers! She went on clapping until her hands were as red as her face.

• • •

Glasses of white wine were passed around after the lecture. Tomoko was sipping hers, though she knew it took very little alcohol to make her head spin even faster than it was spinning already. She hadn't had such an inspirational time in years. It felt good being among women like herself: supported and welcome. And despite the expense, she bought one of Yamamoto-san's signed books. It was entitled *A Beginner's Guide to Investing for Housewives.*

It was dark outside when Tomoko rushed out of Mitsukoshi, worried about the train she had missed.

But passing by the main entrance on her way back to the station, a familiar figure called out to her, "Quite an impressive lecture, wouldn't you agree?"

Tomoko stopped in her tracks. It was the woman who had been sitting behind her at the seminar, the one with the yellow scarf. She was standing under one of the red awnings of the department store front, quietly smoking.

"Cigarette?" the woman offered boldly, holding out an open pack and a lighter.

Tomoko didn't smoke. She shrugged inwardly. This was the day for out-of-the-ordinary experiences. She took one.

"Do you intend to follow Yamamoto-san's advice?" The woman articulated out loud the same question that Tomoko was asking silently of herself, as she bent her head down and lit the cigarette, cupping the flame with one hand against the cold breeze that had begun to blow. Straightening up, she inhaled deeply, coughing slightly.

"I have no idea. I might. There's a lot to think about."

They both stood there smoking and watching the threads of smoke spiraling from the ends of their cigarettes.

Tomoko's thoughts swirled in her head, upward and onward like the smoke. She and Aki had never really talked about their future. What was in store for them when he retired? She had always diligently scrimped and saved and had assumed it would be enough. But as Yamamoto-san explained, it wasn't enough and, worse, might never be enough. Yamamoto-san was right. It was her responsibility to do more for her family. And now a new door had opened. Perhaps she should walk through it.

"Investing is a high-risk game."

"It most definitely is," Tomoko assented, dragging on the cigarette, enjoying the nicotine buzz, the newfound exhilaration of freedom she felt in every puff. She would have loved to linger. But it was really getting late. She mashed her cigarette in the tall public ashtray standing on the sidewalk, reality intruding, rough-shouldered, interrupting the impromptu camaraderie.

• • •

For the first time in her life, Tomoko was almost two hours late. Her mother-in-law was waiting in ambush, scowling down furiously at her as she entered the *genkan*.

"Where on earth have you been?" Mishimo hissed.

"I'm so very sorry. I lost track of time," Tomoko stammered lamely.

"How dare you disappear like that? Is this what you call being a good mother? Do you even care about Nishio?"

Tomoko was used to her scolding, but this was surely too much.

Not so, it transpired.

"You needn't bother to remove your boots. The police just called. Nishio was caught stealing. Shoplifting, if you want to know."

Tomoko shook her head in disbelief, her eyes fixed on the floor, blinking uncontrollably. Guilt washed over her like a cold shower.

"They said you're needed at the station right away. Can you begin to imagine my humiliation when I had to explain you weren't home? With such an irresponsible mother, no wonder Nishio is turning into a criminal! It's your fault." Mishimo's voice rose to hysterical heights. "I warned Aki about you when he married you. I warned him you would bring a stain upon our family!"

Without a word, Tomoko spun around on her heels and shot straight out of the house. Despite the clunking discomfort of her half-pulled-off boots, she practically flew on her bike all the way to the local police station.

At the station, the officer on duty informed her that Nishio had been caught walking out of a music store with two CDs. Given that this was his first offense, the store had decided not to press charges. He would be let go with a caution and his record would remain clean. But—of this she must be aware—if caught a second time, there would be no show of leniency.

Tomoko signed the release form with trembling hands. She could barely lift her eyes from the shame.

When Nishio was released from the holding cell, he looked so frightened that she didn't have the heart to scold him. Clearly, he had been punished enough.

"What kind of CDs were they?" she asked gently, pushing her bike by his side.

"Coldplay," Nishio uttered in a barely audible voice.

"I see."

Though the name of the band meant nothing to her, Tomoko did recognize her son's cry for help. Nishio was a good kid despite his bouts of adolescent mulishness. He was crazy about music, and it had been her decision to end the guitar lessons they could no longer afford. His transgression would never have happened if she had provided him with an outlet for his passion. It was her fault, she beat herself mercilessly, all the way home.

Yet, as she walked at Nishio's side, a steely glint gradually began to appear in her small black eyes. It was an outward expression of what she was really made of inside, despite years of put-downs and abuse. The time had come to redress the wrong she had done to her son.

• • •

It was past midnight. With the household retired for the night and Aki—who had come home drunk for the third time that week—safely in bed, Tomoko tip-toed into Keiko's room, Yamamoto-san's book under her arm.

She switched on the bedside lamp, propped a cushion under her head, and settled down on the twin bed. Yamamoto-san's smiling face stared out at her from the book cover, beckoning, encouraging her to open it. She skipped the short introduction and turned to page one. And so she began to read, if reading can describe the way she swallowed up the contents like a scholar hungry for enlightenment.

The book was essentially a beginner's guide to investment. With colorful graphs and charts, every step in the investment process was clearly indicated and explained. Nevertheless, and despite her hunger, Tomoko found the going difficult. It took her nearly two hours just to get through the first five pages. After all, the only decision she had ever made where money was concerned was whether to keep their savings in a checking account or a fixed-term deposit. Doggedly, she went on.

Whenever she felt the pages beginning to blur, she dug her nails into her cheek to keep herself from falling asleep. By three in the morning, she had come away with her first crucial lesson: that financial markets are as complex as they are volatile. She also learned that, just like in Mitsukoshi department store, there are an infinite variety of products for sale. There is the stock market. There is the bond market. There is the foreign exchange market. And the commodity market. And each market has its own special attributes and dynamics.

She shut the book and stared out from the small pool of light cast by the lamp into the shadowed room beyond, chewing on her thoughts. A good investor was very much like a good housewife, able to discern quality in what she buys—and to sniff out good value. She knew she had a lot to learn, a mountain of concepts and information to digest that in her initial reading she only barely understood. The world of investment was foreign and exotic, but she wasn't discouraged. After all, she had no fear of numbers. Her core training had been in accounting, and she had been a good student in high school and junior college. She was a quick learner, too. She would rise to the challenge. She had to.

And with the happy thought that she might improve her family's lot, she went to bed and crept under the covers next to her open-mouthed, snoring husband.

• • •

Over the next few weeks, she read and reread every paragraph in Yamamoto-san's book, stealing every moment she could spare from her housework. She never relented, not even while sitting on the heated seat of the toilet under the stairs. She kept her activities well hidden, lest anyone should discover what she was up to. Keiko's room became her secret base of operations, where her daughter's computer gave her round-the-clock access to the global financial markets.

Within a few days, she joined Yamamoto-san's online investment club. For ¥1,000 a month, she received a weekly newsletter and gained access to her blog. And when her nose wasn't in the book or her eyes on the PC screen, she would repeat to herself while cooking or ironing, or sorting the laundry, the four golden rules of investment preached by Yamamoto-san until she knew them by heart like a catechism:

Don't be afraid. To make money, you must be prepared to lose some money at first.

Do your homework. Focus on only a few investments that you will become an expert at.

Never keep all your eggs in one basket. Diversification will help you sleep at night.

Use your head but also listen to your heart.

With each passing day, and with the aid of market assessments and investment tips on her mentor's blog, Tomoko grew more confident that she was starting to develop a feel for the market. She forged ahead with a sense of purpose she hadn't felt since her children were small. Her days were full and so was her heart.

• • •

The time for action arrived at last. Armed with her newfound knowledge, Tomoko rode her bicycle to a brokerage firm on the main street in Kashiwa. Once inside, she found herself sitting at a desk opposite a well-mannered, well-dressed young man. She looked at him with an unwavering eye. In a steady voice, she overrode his glib sales talk and asked to open an account. She knew exactly what she wanted, and she was out to get it.

She deposited ¥1 million, about $10,000, a third of their total savings, and bought three funds recommended by Yamamoto-san's newsletter: a US corporate high-yield fund, an Australia dollar fund, and an emerging-market fixed-income fund. Not that she knew much about these funds, but she trusted Yamamoto-san's recommendations. What she did know was that that they offered an average yield of 6 percent. This meant that with her investment of ¥1 million, she would be receiving a monthly income of ¥5,000, enough to pay for one guitar lesson a month for Nishio. A baby step, but one in the right direction.

She became a familiar fixture at the brokerage. Soon everyone working there knew her by name. Like a committed gardener, every day on her way back from her shopping she tended her garden with assiduous care, looking out for dangerous weeds and new growth. And to her delight, she discovered that the value of the funds she had bought, on top of the interest they paid out every month, started to rise almost immediately. The emerging-market fixed-income fund went up 10 percent in the space of just four weeks.

When she found out how much she had made, Tomoko kept it to herself. It wasn't the moment to celebrate just yet. On the contrary, she transferred yet another ¥1 million of their savings to her brokerage account and bought the same three funds.

That evening, she announced to Nishio that he could resume his guitar lessons.

Nishio was so overjoyed that, forgetting his rebellious teenager attitude, he thanked her profusely. He hopped about like a child and went whistling to his room to do his homework. It was one of the happiest days Tomoko could remember in a very long time.

• • •

It was the beginning of April. Nishio was the first to notice the change in her. "*Okaa-san*," he told her one afternoon, "your new haircut is really cool. I hated those stupid curls you wore. They made you look old."

Tomoko gave him a big hug.

Three months had passed since she had opened her first investment account, and it was time, Tomoko decided, to inform her family about what she'd been up to. The occasion she chose for the revelation was Sunday lunch.

As she busied herself in the kitchen, Tomoko happened to look out the window. The buds had come out on their cherry tree. Very soon it would be a cloud of white. How fast time had flown since winter, she thought.

When the whole family was seated around the table, she made her move. "Please pay attention, everybody. I have something to say that concerns all of us," she announced after serving dishes of hot udon. Aki looked up from his newspaper, mildly surprised at the firm intonation of her voice. Mishimo produced her best dead-fish stare. Nishio fiddled with his earphones.

"I've taken it upon myself to look after the financial security of this family. I'm happy to let you know that the investments I've made have achieved some very nice returns."

No one said a word. Aki's eyes opened wide with bafflement and incredulity.

"What did you say?" he asked at last, his narrow nostrils beginning to quiver with hostility.

"I've made money, *Anata*," Tomoko replied softly. "About two hundred thousand yen over the past three months. Not bad for a beginner."

Not bad? It was a lot of money. Almost two-thirds of what Aki brought home every month.

Aki's tone changed abruptly. He was actually on the verge of being polite when, addressing his wife again, he asked, "But how? How on earth did you manage—" he sputtered. "How did you know what to do?"

In less than a minute, Aki had said more to her than he usually did over the course of an entire day.

Tomoko proceeded to recount the whole story—her chance attendance of the seminar, her encounter with Yamamoto-san, and all that followed. Incredibly, even Mishimo had the grace to listen to her without interruption, feeling compelled to begrudgingly say, "Well done," when Tomoko had finished. But she couldn't refrain from adding, "It was about time you did something good for this family."

As for Nishio, he immediately picked up, with the sharp senses of a child, that a big change was transpiring. "Wow, *Okaa-san*. Does this mean you can buy me a new guitar?"

Tomoko laughed and walked off to her bedroom. She came back with a huge box wrapped in gift paper. "Here, Nishio. I was told at the store that this guitar is top of the line."

• • •

As Tomoko became more knowledgeable, she started to look deeper and deeper into the riskier waters of the world of finance, such as margin trading: using borrowed money to invest. One day she made the final leap, and she opened an online foreign exchange margin-trading account that would allow her to borrow up to ten times the value of her capital. By transferring the remaining ¥1 million of their savings, she now had the purchasing power of ¥10 million.

Again she followed Yamamoto-san's recommendations and began to accumulate long positions in the Brazilian real, the Turkish lira, and the New Zealand dollar. These currencies offered an average yield of 15 percent. This meant that after paying the interest on her borrowed money, and even if these currencies did not appreciate, she could make ¥1.5 million a year: more than ¥100,000 a month. With that money, not only could she grow their savings at a more rapid pace, but she would have more than enough money to increase the allowance she sent to Keiko every month.

Leaping into this particular pond, little did Tomoko know there were many Tomokos in Japan. With hundreds of thousands of housewives pouring their savings into high-yielding currencies like the Brazilian real, the real began to appreciate rapidly against the yen. In the space of six months, Tomoko made one million yen—a stunning 100 percent profit on her original capital. She had taken a big risk. It had paid off.

• • •

It was Tomoko's birthday. This year, with all the money pouring in, there was cause for celebration. Not at home but at a trendy Italian place in Ginza. It would be a special treat, for it was rare for the family to eat out, let alone at a foreign restaurant. Though Mishimo tried to kick up a fuss when she found out Tomoko had reserved a table for the four of them, she stood her ground.

They arrived at the restaurant decked out in their best clothes and in a splendid mood. Tomoko was wearing a new jacket. It was bright vermilion like Yamamoto-san's. Aki was in the new pale-blue shirt she had bought him. Nishio was wearing a new sweatshirt. Even Mishimo, who seldom left the house at all, had stepped out in her kimono.

Everyone looked happy, noted Tomoko contentedly. Aki seemed a changed person. He was drinking less and coming home earlier. He had even helped Nishio with his homework this week. Now he was almost sunny, grateful that Tomoko had found a way of augmenting the family income without having to go out and get a job. The loss of face had his wife been seen going to work outside would have been unbearable.

As for Mishimo, to Tomoko's astonishment, she had complimented her on her culinary skills at dinner the other day.

With everyone gathered around platefuls of pizza and pasta, Tomoko dropped her latest bombshell. "I've decided to go to visit Keiko in America. It's been two years, and I miss her."

Aki's spoon clattered onto the table.

"There's no need to make a fuss. I'm sure you can get along without me for a couple of weeks," Tomoko said sweetly.

Aki was about to protest. Tomoko thought he looked rather silly with his open, gaping mouth. She countered with a defiant look, her eyes unblinking, her head tilted impishly to one side.

"My mind is made up, *Anata*. It's no use trying to dissuade me."

Yes. Her mind was quite made up. Lately she had been considering investing some of her trading profits in safe American government bonds. So, besides her longing to see Keiko, she had an additional incentive to go. Nothing could be better, she thought, than gauging the strength of the US economy firsthand, with her own eyes.

But she divulged none of her thoughts. Instead, she surreptitiously reached out for Aki's hand under the table. And Aki, fully tamed, squeezed her hand back.

• • •

What a whirlwind of first impressions! The immense scale of affluence—the roads wider, the bridges longer, the houses bigger, the traffic denser, the level of noise in the streets a full-out assault on her ears—all of it was foreign but thrilling. A vibrant energy seemed to course through the very air of California. The crowds in the shopping malls, in the restaurants, the hotels, in the downtown areas of the cities and towns, and, not least, the presence of building cranes everywhere all showcased an economy which, in sharp contrast to Japan's, was riding high. All this activity was a manifestation, Tomoko concluded, of the American animal spirits that Yamamoto-san had spoken about. Even the giant Sequoia trees that Keiko had taken her to see inspired confidence. Within two weeks she had made up her mind and ordered her broker to put half of the balance of her account into American bond funds, convinced she was making the right choice in securing the family's finances for good years to come.

• • •

Tomoko bolted upright, instinctively grabbing on to Keiko, who was sitting beside her in the aisle seat. She had been admiring the new leather purse with its trendy brass studs that she had just bought when the deafening blare of an alarm went off.

"What's happening?" asked Tomoko in a loud, nervous voice as wave after wave of shrieking sirens almost drowned out her speech.

"I'm not sure," Keiko answered, leaning over to get a better view from the window. "It sounds like a lockdown."

Tomoko pressed her face against the windowpane. A mud-splattered van was careening wildly across the vast plaza of multiple lanes filled with cars slowing down for the border crossing. Another van, some distance behind it, was driving at breakneck speed, weaving in and out of the traffic. The police were chasing after them, and there were uniformed border agents everywhere.

The first van got stuck in traffic and stopped in its tracks. Two men jumped out and began to run. The second van crashed into a sedan and was quickly surrounded by border agents.

Then shots rang out, fired in rapid succession. Tomoko turned, wide-eyed, to her daughter. She had never heard the sound of live gunshots before, and she tried valiantly to fend off the terrifying scenarios that began to tumble through her mind.

"Don't worry, *Okaa-san*. We should be safe right here where we are, inside the bus," Keiko reassured her.

She had barely finished the sentence when a bullet ricocheted off the windshield, leaving in its wake a star pattern of shattered glass.

The crowded bus exploded into a jumble of arms and legs as people jumped up from their seats and tried to get away from the windows, shoving each other as they jostled to get into the aisle. "Keep calm, folks. Return to your seats," bellowed the driver.

Keiko's smooth forehead puckered up with worry, her eyebrows arching downward in a frown. Her pretty, childlike face looked scared, tears ready to fall. Tomoko clasped her hand tightly.

Ten minutes passed. They heard no more gunshots. Calm slowly returned to the bus. It seemed that the incident was over, and that there was nothing for it but to wait for the all clear. *It might take hours,* thought Tomoko. Their shopping spree to Tijuana, Mexico, the bargain-hunter mecca a couple of hours' drive over the border from Los Angeles, was turning into a nightmare. It was supposed to be the perfect finale to her two-week stay. Overcome by regret, she kicked herself hard. It was all her fault. She should have resisted her urge to find bargains and never have insisted on coming.

She imagined Mishimo's sharp, thin voice screeching in her ear: "You're such a bad mother, putting Keiko at risk."

A loud pounding on the closed door of the bus jolted her from her thoughts.

Tomoko peered out of the window, and from her angle could just glimpse a man in dusty jeans, his hair matted, shouting at the top of his voice, "Open up! Open up!"

Oh my god!

He was holding a gun!

"Get down, Keiko. Now!" she exclaimed, shoving her daughter down onto the floor of the narrow space in between the rows of seats. Tomoko shrank herself into a ball and lowered her head.

The pounding didn't cease.

"Open up! Open up!" the man shouted at the driver.

A shot in the air was enough to convince the driver to give in, and the door opened with a loud hydraulic shudder.

Tomoko bobbed up to peek above the backrest of the seat in front of her.

The gunman was on the bus and pointing his weapon straight at the driver's head.

She ducked her head down again.

"Drive! Drive!" the gunman spat.

Tomoko and Keiko were sitting about two-thirds of the way back. A couple of rows ahead of them a young girl suddenly began screeching uncontrollably.

"Shut your mouth, you stupid bitch!" yelled the gunman.

The bus lurched forward and then stalled. "*Idiota*! *Puta*! Steer left! Left, I told you!" he cried out, amidst the girl's renewed screaming.

Abruptly, he turned around and lunged down the aisle to her seat and slapped her hard on both cheeks. But this only made her scream louder. Enraged, the gunman grabbed the girl by her blonde hair and yanked her into the aisle. "Up, *puta*, to where I can see you, you crazy cunt," he grunted, dragging her toward the front of the bus and then dropping her down on the floor.

As if she were a sack of rice, Tomoko thought. She had been looking on with mounting anger. The girl was about Keiko's age. It could have been Keiko being pawed by this *chikushou*, this *monsuta* bully. The temptation to do something was irresistible. She sat up. The gunman had his back to the passengers, barking orders to the driver. This was her chance. She got up, her eyes on the gunman, and clambered over Keiko, who was still cowering on the floor. She stepped cautiously and silently down the aisle—then—*Whack!* And then another whack, and another and another. "*Monsuta! Chikushou!*" With curses ringing out in Japanese, she pummeled him furiously with her heavy leather bag. Caught off guard, the gunman spun around, his features contorted by surprise and pain. The bag's weight and the brass studs were evidently effective. He gestured furiously with his gun. But Tomoko didn't flinch. The driver seized his chance. He disengaged from his seat and overpowered the gunman from behind, wresting the firearm from his grip.

Within a few seconds, it was over: The would-be hijacker lay prostrate in the aisle.

What a feat! The entire bus cheered.

When, at last, the border agents entered the bus, they were greeted by a most improbable sight: that of a small middle-aged Asian woman standing like a big-game hunter over her kill, her foot firmly planted on her trophy's neck.

• • •

Everyone was talking about Tomoko's heroic exploit, and some passengers came up to shake her hand. They were safe now and well on their way back home. Tomoko, for her part, felt good, and she basked in the glow of Keiko's adulation.

When the bus stopped for a brief lunch break at a gas station, Tomoko made a quick dash for the restrooms. Exiting, she noticed that in her rush she had forgotten her hat on the bus. There was no chance that she'd expose herself to the ferocious sun for a moment longer than absolutely necessary, so she went back to fetch it.

As she approached the empty bus, she saw a trousered leg emerging from the baggage hold on the side. Another leg quickly followed. They belonged to a young man who then nimbly jumped down onto the asphalt. A stowaway! Their eyes interlocked and he froze. Tomoko didn't know what to think. He looked harmless enough, she told herself. But it was none of her business. The young man threw her a cautious smile before slinking off into the jungle of closely parked cars.

• • •

As he stole across the parking lot, Ernesto was feeling anything but brave. He was late for his rendezvous with the coyote who would take him onward, and he had heard too many stories about people being caught and sent back. Crouching low, his shoulders hunched, he darted about as stealthily as a cat. His heart racing as he scanned the rows of parked cars until he spotted a grey van. He reached for the handle, eased the door open, and crept inside.

Chapter 5

ERNESTO HERNANDEZ

Los Angeles, USA, July–October 2005

"When interest rates are low we have conditions for asset bubbles to develop."

—George Soros

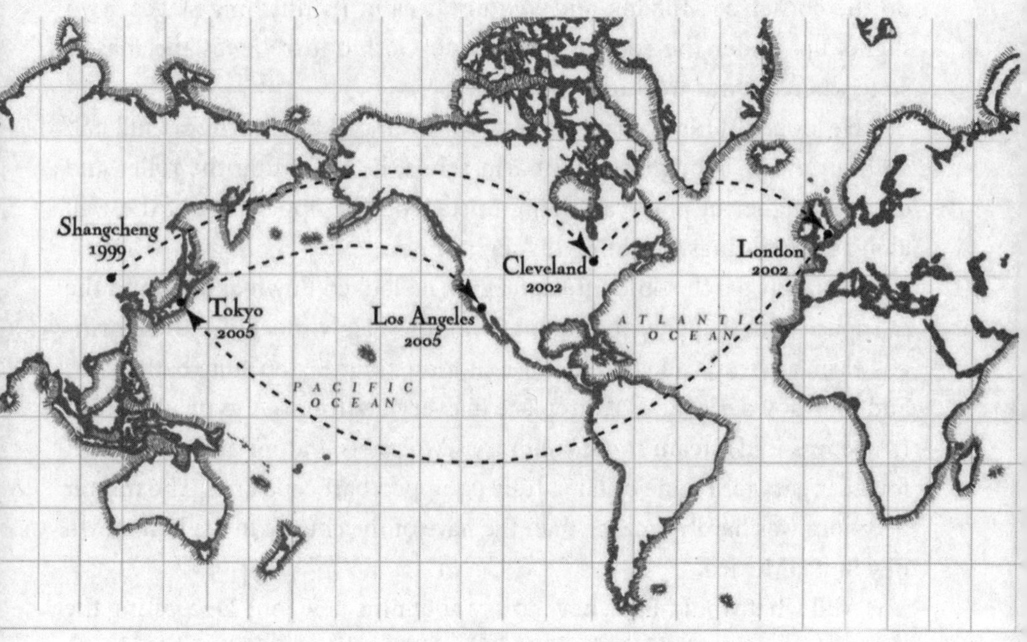

ERNESTO HERNANDEZ, HIS THICK BLACK ponytail tucked under a cap, stood high up on the scaffolding.

He set the paint roller down in the pan and wiped the sweat off his forehead with a red bandana. It was the end of August, and the Santa Ana winds blew hot through the open windows.

He stepped back for a moment on the wooden platform and studied the wall with a critical eye. His brushwork was smooth and even, every drop of paint exactly where it belonged. But the satisfaction lasted only for a fleeting moment. What was the point of all this work? He seethed. What was the point of his achieving perfection when the object of his attention was so insignificant and mundane? All he had ever wanted was to be an artist. And now he was stuck in this hell. House painting! A continuous reminder of what he had given up, an affront to his talents and ambition.

But he had a duty to fulfill. Though working here, in this monster of a house, was a particular slap in the face to his sensibilities.

The eight-thousand-square-foot mansion in Montecito, California, on the corner of Milbank and Ventura, was in its finishing stages. Two flights up, under the roof of the pseudo-Gothic turret, was the master suite where he was working.

He looked at his watch. He was getting hungry, but lunch was still half an hour away. Though his right arm ached, he picked up the roller and climbed higher up the scaffolding to start on the upper part of the wall along the moldings, straining his slight frame.

From his perch some fifteen feet up, he looked down and around the tall space with its generous bank of windows. How much did these gringos earn, anyway, to live in a house fit for a king? Six en suite bathrooms and four powder rooms. A fireplace in every bedroom. A gym, a Swedish (so he was told) steam room, a library. Two pools, indoor and outdoor. A four-car garage, a wine cellar, a fully equipped barbecue area. The master bedroom was hardly smaller than the nave of the church in his hometown of Cibuta, Mexico.

And what would Papa have to say about his new job? Decorating the palace of some capitalist gringo pig? His father, the socialist and card-carrying member of the Partido de la Revolución Democrática, who had worked in a shoe factory all his life, and who liked to repeat in his gravelly voice, over and over: "Too many shoes for too few, too few shoes for too many"?

He'd probably have a stroke and drop dead on the spot.

The paint roller sloshed up and down the wall as the words of his father echoed in his head.

An average American consumes a hundred and fifty gallons of water a day versus just five gallons used by an African family. Americans guzzle twenty-five percent of the world's oil even though they are only five percent of the world's population.

These sermons about the injustices of the world were a daily ritual when the family gathered for dinner.

But it was not until Ernesto had left home and gone to university in Sonora that his father's angst began to make sense. There Ernesto fell in with a band of socially conscious students who shaped the way he looked at the world. Night after night, they huddled in smoke-hazed dorm rooms, arguing over how best to purge society of its ills.

And then one night, late into the small hours, he met Juan for the first time. Tall with flashing eyes, he strode into the room: "Waste, too much waste, *camaradas*! You can feed eighty million people just with the food the gringos throw away each year," he pronounced. Words just like those of his father. Ernesto was seduced by his charisma at once.

Maldición!

Even though it had been only a week since he arrived in the US, his life in Mexico already seemed like a faraway dream. He slapped the roller on the wall with such anger and frustration that it snapped in two, spattering his face all over with paint. He would be reprimanded, but he didn't care.

He was happy at university, but misfortune struck the family when his father lost his job. The shoe factory in Nogales where he had toiled for years had been forced into bankruptcy. The maquiladoras—American-owned plants along the border—were shutting down all over Sonora because of Chinese competition. And Apá was too old to find a new job. Besides, he had been drinking far too much.

Ernesto's five siblings were all still in school. With the letter from his cousin Carlos assuring them that "California—all of *el otro lado*—is in the middle of a crazy building boom," and after repeated pleas from his mother, he had finally relented and agreed to go find work in the United States. The family came first, no matter the sacrifice. He dropped out of Universidad de Sonora despite the art scholarship he had won and despite knowing he had it in him to become a good artist.

But Carlos had been right about opportunities in California. Ernesto was immediately offered a job that paid $100 a day, a small fortune. Ernesto quickly made the calculations in his head again, for the hundredth time. Working six days a week: $600. Working for an entire month: $2,500, more than he could earn slaving away in Mexico for an entire year.

His mind raced on. Even after deducting living expenses—and they were so damn high in America—he was still left with $1,700 a month in his pocket.

And he could earn even more if he worked Sundays: He wasn't afraid of hard work, pushing the roller up and down against the wall with ever more gusto.

But on second thought, no work on Sundays. His mother had made him promise never to skip Mass. As they said their good-byes, she pressed a small amulet with the Lady of Guadalupe's portrait into his palm. It was now hanging on a chain around his neck. Reaching out with his free hand, he lifted it up to his lips and kissed it. Not that he was religious anymore—not after committing with Juan the sin that could never be confessed. But he was grateful that Our Lady, generous and forgiving, had seen him through the dangerous journey over the border.

There was still that debt of $2,000 to the coyote to pay off, he reminded himself sternly. But the repayments wouldn't last forever, and he'd still have some $500 to send back to his family each month.

Though his stomach was growling with hunger, the calculator in his head continued to whiz. The reality was that even with all his expenses, sending money home, and paying back his debt, he would be able to save $1,200 a month. He went through the numbers in his head again. There was no mistaking it: $1,200 a month. Over $14,000 a year.

In three years he could save enough money to allow his brothers and sisters to finish high school, and for Mamá and Apá not to worry anymore. He would only be giving up three years before returning to Juan, to his studies and his art. Surely, he could endure a bit of misery and loneliness in the meantime, he thought, mentally squaring his shoulders in determination. All he had to do was stay the course.

• • •

The doorbell was ringing. Emerging from the fog of sleep, Ernesto had the feeling the bell had been ringing for a long time. In his underwear, he staggered to the door and pressed an eye to the peephole. A man with curly brown hair and sunglasses stood on the doorstep in the morning sun, a briefcase in hand.

Ernesto was alone in the house. Carlos had gone fishing at Echo Park Lake, as he did every Sunday. *Never let any stranger in*, he had warned him. Fastening the safety latch, Ernesto opened the door a crack.

"Can I help you?"

"My name is Sebastian Aguilar. May I trouble you for a few minutes?"

Dressed in a pale-cream linen suit with a yellow silk tie and a matching handkerchief triangle sticking out of the breast pocket, the man was too classy looking for *la migra*, thought Ernesto. Besides, the man had a bright and full-toothed smile.

"One moment." Ernesto shut the door, retreating to pull on his jeans. He then lifted the latch and opened the door.

"Hello, there. What a beautiful day!" Aguilar said, beaming.

"What do you want? Am not buying nothing."

Aguilar laughed and switched to Spanish: "*Hablas Español?* Don't worry, I'm not here to sell you junk. Like I said, it's just for a few moments. May I come in?"

Against his better judgement Ernesto let Aguilar inside.

Aguilar took off his sunglasses, quickly assessing his surroundings with an experienced eye. He pointed to the two peeling leatherette chairs by the small dining table, the only seats in the room.

"Mind if I sit down?"

"OK," Ernesto said, and then, remembering his manners, "Do you want a drink?"

Aguilar shook his head and handed him a business card. It looked expensive, with an embossed gilded logo of a sun on its face.

"Let me introduce myself. I am a senior broker at Sun Valley Financing. We specialize in securing home financing for new immigrants. You're a recent immigrant, I take it?"

Ernesto nodded. It wasn't strictly an untruthful answer. The man hadn't asked if he was legal.

"We like to think of ourselves as a company that helps people. That's why we call ourselves Sun Valley. 'Hope and Help' is our motto and our mission. Hope for new immigrants."

Ernesto scowled.

"You look surprised! This truly is the land of freedom and opportunity. My parents were green once, just like you. Arrived with only the shirts on their backs. And look at me now! I provide for Mamá and Apá, I have a good job, a car, and a nice house. My only wish is to facilitate my newer *compatriotas*' journey, to help accomplish their dreams, as I have done. All we do is help our brothers buy their first car, their first house."

Ernesto didn't respond.

"It's hot in here," he said. "Maybe I should help you get an air conditioner?" he joked lamely.

This brought a small smile to Ernesto's face.

"I'm guessing you don't own this place."

"No. I just live here with my cousin."

"Now tell me, how would you like to own your own house someday?"

"Why would I need a house?"

"Doesn't everyone need a house?" Aguilar chuckled, his eyes crinkling at the corners in a perfect imitation of merriment. "You strike me as a bright young man. Think of it as an investment. And we at Sun Valley can help you."

"I told you. Not interested. Maybe my cousin. But he has no money."

"It doesn't matter. You don't need money."

"What?" Ernesto was immediately on his guard again. "You can't get something for nothing!"

"It's very simple, hombre. We can help you, or your cousin, get a mortgage." Seeing Ernesto's perplexed look, he clarified, "A loan from the bank. Naturally." Aguilar quickly added, "We would take care of all the paperwork. Walk you through the process. Home ownership is the backbone of the American dream, and we believe everyone should have a fair chance at getting on the housing ladder. Do you understand?"

Aguilar pulled his handkerchief from his breast pocket to wipe his sunglasses. "You don't need any money," he said emphatically. "None at all. Nada. The down payment is zero in some of the loan packages we offer."

Zero money? A house with no money? Did he take Ernesto for a fool?

Standing up, he said angrily, "I don't know what you want, but I'm not as naïve as I might look. Nothing is free in this world. Not even in America. Not interested."

And in English: "Please leave."

"OK. OK. I didn't say 'free.' All I'm saying is that there are ways for a person of modest means not to have to wait to buy his first house," Aguilar replied with a quick smile. "But buying a house is a big decision. Take your time and think it over. If you change your mind, give us a call. Any time, come rain or shine, I'm at your service."

He slapped his thighs and rose from his chair with a sigh of defeat.

What a load of bullshit, Ernesto told himself when Aguilar was out the door. *Jesus*. What was his game? And he sure didn't need a house even if they were giving it away for free. He wasn't planning to stay in this foreign country one minute longer than necessary.

Aguilar's visit made him miss Juan and his family even more. Though Los Angeles was merely an eight-hour drive from Cibuta, it could as well be on the other side of the moon as far as he was concerned. Those warm evenings drinking beer. The political and philosophical debates. The singing and the playing of guitars. Juan's caresses. He felt listless, sapped of all energy. So what if they had no money or possessions? Mexico was his home and there was nowhere else in the world he'd rather be. In Mexico everything—the dust, the cacti, the sky—resonated with meaning, and he, like a tuning fork, never failed to resonate sympathetically back.

• • •

By the afternoon, Ernesto felt better and decided to venture outside. He had never seen the sea! That's where he would go.

When he arrived in Santa Monica, the first thing that struck him was the immensity of the stretch of sand and the sweep of the horizon. Even in the desert, the sky never seemed as expansive as it appeared to him now, rising above the flatness of the ocean. Exhilarated, Ernesto kicked off his flip-flops and rolled up his jeans. The warm grains of sand felt good between his toes. After wading up to his knees in the saltwater, he sat down on the beach. He always carried a sketchbook with pencils and colored chalks in his knapsack, and he began to sketch the half-empty beach, aiming to capture the pier and the Ferris wheel outlined against the canvas of the sky.

Not bad, he thought, examining the result when he was done. Sketching was what he excelled at. Even in grade school, his talent had drawn the attention of his teachers and gained him entry into art school. He could render almost anything on a two-dimensional surface, from landscapes and buildings to the human figure. It was as if he were born with the laws of geometric perspective preinstalled in his brain—as if he had a camera in his eye.

When he had filled up half the pages, Ernesto got up, brushed the sand from the seat of his pants, and made his way slowly toward the pier.

He couldn't have wished for a better spectacle. Crowds of people in pairs and in groups—children holding onto colorful balloons, dogs straining on leashes—ambled along toward the reds and yellows and blues of the Ferris wheel and roller coaster that beckoned at the end of the pier. Hoisting himself up onto the iron railing midway down the pier, Ernesto took out his pad and began to sketch again.

A gaggle of girls in their teens strolled his way. One of them, a lanky brunette with bright blue streaks in her hair, was holding a small white terrier in her arms, its leash trailing on the ground. Suddenly, the dog broke free and, barking furiously, shot away from her like a little missile. The girl ran after it but couldn't keep up. All this Ernesto observed from his perch on the railing. The little dog veered toward him. He jumped down, ran after it, and scooped it up, holding the squirming mass of fur close to his chest.

The girl was not far behind.

"Thanks a million!" she cried breathlessly, taking her pet back into her arms. Burying her face in its fur, she scolded in mock anger, "Moses, you silly dog. You could've drowned." Then, turning to Ernesto, she said, "You saved his life!"

Ernesto was embarrassed. "It was nothing, miss."

"Miss?" The girl laughed prettily and held out a hand. "I'm Kip. What's your name?"

"Ernesto." He smiled as they shook hands. She looked younger than him—sixteen maybe?

Kip looked up at him. She couldn't help noticing the sweet dimples at the corners of his smile. His thick, smooth, black hair, glancing in the sunlight, didn't escape her notice, either.

In the meantime, her girlfriends had almost caught up with her. "I'll only be a sec," she called out, signaling them to keep walking on without her.

Kip and Ernesto stood facing each other in awkward silence. Ernesto looked down at his sketchbook, lying open on the ground where it had fallen, a faint furrow between his brows. Following his eyes, Kip bent to pick it up.

"Oh, I'm so sorry. Foolish me. I interrupted your work…." She flipped through his drawings before handing them back to him.

"These sketches are really great. You're an artist?"

His first instinct was to answer no. The title of artist was sacred to him. For now, at least, he was just a lowly house painter. But on second thought—

"Yes. Yes, I am."

"Cool! I lo-o-ve art," she giggled.

He sized her up shyly. The blue streaks in her short hair matched her eyes, and the expression on her face was mischievous and friendly.

"Can you make me a sketch of Moses?"

Ernesto laughed good-naturedly.

"Plee-e-ase. It would be his very first portrait." She clasped her hands and contorted her face in a funny pantomime of supplication.

Ernesto couldn't resist.

"OK. Why not?" Kip, he would eventually find out, always got what she wanted.

For a few minutes, Ernesto busied himself drawing an impression of the wriggly mass. "Funny name for a dog," he remarked.

"Oh. I found Moses abandoned in a basket." She giggled again. "Near a river."

• • •

Half an hour later he was walking back to the beach with Kip and her friends, who had joined them. Kip hopped with delight as she showed off Ernesto's drawing of her dog. "Isn't it absolutely awesome?" she proclaimed excitedly, passing his sketchpad around. Her friends were now curious, too, and amidst cries of "cool" and "wow," Ernesto found himself the center of attention.

"Where are you from? Chile? Venezuela?" The question came from the petite blonde in the group.

"Mexico."

"Oh?" The slight upward movement of her carefully penciled eyebrows was not lost on Ernesto.

He hastily corrected himself, "Mexico City."

"So what are you doing here in California?" asked another of the girls.

What could he say? Not the truth: Having declared himself an artist, he had to think quickly, making it up as he went along.

The lies tripped out easily. "I'm an exchange student at UCLA."

It was the best that he could come up with. He knew that UCLA had a famous art program.

"Are you really? That's *so* awesome," exclaimed Kip.

"And you? What are you studying?" he asked.

"Me? Oh, I'm a high school junior. But"—her face suddenly became solemn—"I'm taking a media communication course this semester. I want to be an agent. You know, working with actors and artists and stuff. Who knows? Maybe I'll represent you one day." Ernesto smiled back. But he didn't know whether to laugh or cry at her generous, if childish, offer.

Kip abruptly stopped in her tracks.

"Hey, I've just thought of something," she said. "How about I introduce you to my dad? He collects art. He would totally love to meet you. He knows just about everybody in the art world."

Without even giving Ernesto a chance to respond, she continued, whipping out her phone, "What's your cell number? I'll fix it up and text you later."

• • •

Ernesto spent the rest of the afternoon with Kip and her friends. As they licked ice-cream cones and watched the sun slowly turn a fiery orange, it was, thought Ernesto, the perfect ending to a perfect day.

One that wouldn't repeat itself, because after they said their goodbyes, Ernesto didn't believe he would ever see Kip again.

But to his surprise, Kip was true to her word. That very evening, once he was back in East LA, he got a text message from her inviting him to a dinner party at her parents' house the following Saturday. He tried to wriggle out of it. A bit of deception on a chance encounter was one thing, but going to her house on false pretenses would make him a full-blown liar.

He came up with a million excuses, but Kip would not take no for an answer. As if she was stamping her foot repeatedly like a spoiled child, she bombarded him with texts all evening until in the end he caved. He didn't want to hurt her feelings or seem ungrateful. He promised himself that he would tell her the truth about himself when he saw her.

• • •

To reach Malibu where Kip's parents lived from East LA without a car proved to be as complicated as travelling to another country. It was only thirty-six miles, but it took Ernesto four long hours—one metro rail journey and two bus rides. It felt as though those in charge of designing and running the city's public transportation system had conspired to make it as difficult as possible for people like him to get to the place where the rich of LA lived.

Not that he was in a hurry. As much as he was curious, he was petrified. Would they—Kip's parents, the other guests—see right through him? Throw him out of the house? But it was too late to extricate himself now.

Public transportation did not suffice. For the final stretch of his long journey, he had to take a taxi from the Malibu Village bus stop up to the hills.

The taxi slowly wound up the twisting roads. *Madre de Dios*. It was a paradise. Washingtonia palms and ficus trees grew to giant heights among thick hedges and rose bushes, swaying gently in the mild California breeze. And the streets! They were so clean—with not so much as an errant gum wrapper tainting the sidewalks—that Ernesto felt he could have licked them. A paradise of houses and gardens so meticulously cared for that they appeared to have been unwrapped only moments before, like presents on Three Kings' Day. *It isn't real,* Ernesto whispered to himself.

The unreality didn't stop there. The taxi deposited him in front of a sprawling ultra-modernist house cladded in white metal tiles with an undulating, wave-like roof. It was as if the house had just alighted, like a huge sea bird, on the expanse of green lawn at the end of the long driveway.

"*Madre de Dios, Madre de Dios.*" He exhaled heavily in amazed shock. But this wasn't the house of a drug lord, he reminded himself. This was what capitalism at its mightiest looked like. *Kip's father must be a capitalist swine in chief.*

Feeling more estranged than ever, hoping against hope that the fifty-dollar white shirt and new shoes he had splurged on would make the grade, he took a deep breath and walked up determinedly toward the maw of the lion. Kip, her long lavender-and-silver dress shimmering in the light, was waiting for him in the doorway.

"You're late. The performance is about to begin," she scolded. "Come on."

Performance? What performance? Not knowing what to expect, Ernesto followed her obediently as she led him around the house to the garden.

The grounds were as massive as the house. And the setting! High up on a cliff open to the water, a series of low, descending terraces ended in a wide infinity pool spilling seamlessly into the Pacific Ocean below. Ernesto glanced back at the house. Its white-tile-and-glass façade sparkled like an orange jewel in the dying evening light.

Above the pool, on one of the terraces, the guests were already seated in rows of chairs in front of a small, elevated stage. The stage set consisted of a large open box, draped on three sides with what looked to Ernesto like strips of white cardboard. It was otherwise bare. As Kip and Ernesto slipped into the last row, Kip quipped, giggling, "Dad got into performance art after we ran out of empty walls."

By now it was almost dark outside. A floodlight was turned on, illuminating the empty stage with a bright white light. A crescendo of violins pierced the air. Everyone seemed to be alert with expectation. But for three excruciatingly long minutes nothing happened, and the stage remained deserted and silent. The only sound was the faint soughing of the wind blowing in from the ocean. Some of the guests began shifting impatiently in their seats.

Then slowly, the boards folded inward, in origami fashion, to form a small, angled, pear-shaped cavity. The light focused on the cavity as it went from white to green. A few more minutes crept by without any action. The light switched to white again and the violins exploded in grating, discordant chords. On the stage, nothing stirred.

Finally, the lights went out. There was a perceptible sigh of relief from the small crowd. The stage and audience were now shrouded in darkness. The audience made no sound, in anticipation of some action. But only after an additional excruciatingly lengthy pause did the lights switch on again. The large pieces of cardboard unfolded and opened, back to their starting position. A young woman, with long, uncombed black hair, leaped onto the stage holding up a placard, which read:

EVERYTHING IS NOTHINGNESS
NOTHINGNESS IS EVERYTHING.
AN EXERCISE IN BEING

It was over, and following a brief hesitation, the guests burst into loud applause.

¡Jesús, María! Ernesto understood the gringos less than ever. Surreptitiously, he pressed his hand against the amulet under his shirt.

• • •

Having done their bit for culture, the guests drifted, chatting, through the sliding glass doors from the terrace into the living room. Ernesto, separated from Kip, found himself in the heart of the house, in a fifteen-foot-high-ceilinged space. The floor was of dazzling white marble, and hanging lamps of elongated copper rods of various lengths swayed above him, emitting rays of amber light that pulsed in synchrony with fluctuating notes of jazz. Brown-skinned maids in little white starched hats and aprons carrying trays of canapés and drinks circulated among the guests.

Feeling faintly ridiculous and very much out of place, his new shoes pinching his feet, timidly Ernesto helped himself to a canapé. Glancing up at the severe-faced waitress who served him, he could swear he had seen her somewhere before—at the 7-Eleven in East LA maybe? She, too, showed a glimmer of recognition. But then he was overcome by a more pressing concern: Should he swallow the small morsel all at once, in one bite—or two?

Still no Kip. He shouldn't have come, Ernesto thought unhappily. He tried to focus on the walls, which were, just as Kip had described, covered with art. Andy Warhol's *Marilyn* laughed back at him from one wall. A Picasso clown looked on with a melancholy face from another. Next to it, a silently screaming pope, raging in agony inside a cage, open-mouthed, seemed to be cursing him. He, too, felt trapped. If only he could scream out; but who would hear him?

A finger tapped him on the shoulder—

"Sorry I abandoned you. I just had to get out of that awful dress Mom made me wear."

Ernesto smiled with relief. In combat boots and jeans, Kip looked more like the girl he met on the beach.

"Now let's get to work," she said. Grabbing him by the hand, she led him toward a small group of people standing in front of a pink-and-orange Rothko.

"Hi, everybody!" she announced in a loud voice. "Say hello to my new friend, Ernesto Hernandez," Kip said, pushing him forward. She introduced him in turn to her father, Josh Coen, her mother, Hanna, and to her aunt, Joanne.

"We're so glad you could join us," Hanna welcomed Ernesto graciously.

"Ernesto is an artist! An awesome one, too," Kip declared.

"Is that so?" her father, a man in his fifties with a head of springy gray curls, said, nodding at Ernesto encouragingly. "And how did you like our little artistic contribution earlier?"

"It was…ah, well, interesting. It was…" Ernesto squirmed, searching for a word that wouldn't cause offense. "Honest, I guess."

"Well said. Honesty makes for great art."

"And so does the courage to speak truth to power." This came from Joanne, Kip's gallery-owning aunt. "The image the artist created was that of the fundamental core of the female being. I found the reductive meaning of the empty womb as the signifier of the patriarchy both powerful and moving."

Puzzled, Ernesto looked up at the tall, imperious-looking woman. He hadn't understood a word she'd said. She seemed deadly serious, but when she turned her attention to him, a smile of sorts appeared, framed by a halo of bright red hair.

"Young man. What's your thing? Conceptual? Figurative?" she asked.

"I'm working on a mural at school," Ernesto answered haltingly. It was an embellishment at best. Back in Mexico he had been in the planning stages of a large composition. Before he could elaborate, Kip interrupted, "Ernesto is an exchange student at UCLA. He's from Mexico City."

"UCLA? Good for you," said Joanne. "This is such a wonderful time to be a young artist! The market for contemporary art has never been stronger. Everyone is looking for the next Basquiat or Damien Hirst."

Kip seized her chance. "Did I tell you, Aunt Joanne, that Ernesto is a direct descendant of an Aztec warrior and a Spanish aristocrat?"

Ernesto almost gagged on his second canapé. But he didn't contradict her. Kip's imagination was extraordinary. As was her boundless audacity.

But, clearly, Kip knew very well what she was doing. While Ernesto was reduced to smiling enigmatically, all the members of the group stopped sipping their cocktails and gaped at him.

Joanne, for one, reacted right on cue: "Really? How fascinating! Aztec, you say? I'm a big fan of pre-Columbian art." With her eyes fixed on Ernesto's smooth, bronze-skinned face, with the keenness of a hawk circling its prey, she added, "The Mexican art market has been red-hot lately." The large diamond on her hand shone brightly. "Especially since the biopic about Frida Kahlo came out."

"Oh, I loved that movie!" Hanna joined in enthusiastically. "Salma Hayek should really have gotten the Oscar for best actress."

"Yes. Great movie. The point is Frida Kahlo is back in the limelight and dragging up the price of Mexican art with her. I've heard that Madonna, who already owns two of her paintings, is looking to buy more." Refocusing on Ernesto, she said, "If you, young man, have some work you'd like to show me, I'd be more than happy to take a look."

"Thank you, thank you very much," Ernesto replied shyly, his lips slowly broadening in a wide, engaging smile.

"That's cool. You're the best!" Kip beamed. "Aunt Joanne, there is one more thing you should know…."

"Yes, my dear?"

"Ernesto is a true rebel. He comes from a fabulously wealthy family. His parents wanted him to take over the family business one day, but he absolutely refused. His passion is art. So he ran away and came here." And with that she blew the shocked Ernesto a small kiss of triumph over the open palm she held under her chin.

Ernesto could hardly breathe. *It isn't real. It isn't real.*

• • •

Dinner was served in the glass-walled dining room, scintillating with crystal and fine china. As the guests took their seats, each found a ceramic hen nestled in a straw-filled basket at their place. At Hanna's cue, they pressed a small lever on the side of the bird. Surprise—the hen clucked and laid an egg.

Cracking open the shell, Ernesto found not a cooked egg, but white foam sprinkled with brown flakes. "Truffle shavings," said Kip, guiding him in a low voice. Nestled inside the foam was a small yellow ball, perfumed with… "Saffron," she added.

The mushroom soup arrived in individual fur-covered terrines shaped like rabbits, a presentation that provoked no little comment.

Then came the main course, Hanna's magnum opus. Several pheasants, with brilliantly colored feathers and beaks, were held aloft so all could see and admire, before being brought to the sideboard.

Ernesto, half starved and more than a little tipsy from drinking two glasses of wine on a near-empty stomach, was looking forward to satiating his hunger with something more than breadsticks.

Getting ready to dig into the steak tartare that had coyly emerged from the innards of the fowls, he discovered with one plunge of his teeth that this, too, was not what it seemed. A concoction of minced beets, quinoa, and red paprika, and marbleized with streaks of tofu, it looked like the real thing.

The chocolate cake at the end of dinner, in the mold of a boar's head with tusks of marzipan and eyes of fruit jelly, was at last real. Ernesto devoured two slices, half a tusk, and one eye.

• • •

"Josh, we're thinking of buying a house in LA, but prices are sky-high and the Fed just hiked interest rates again. I've heard the market's cooling, too. What's your advice?" Joanne's husband, Michael, an advertising executive, boomed the question across the table once coffee had been poured.

Everybody's ears perked up at the mention of property prices. Nothing like real estate, the obsession of the hour all over the country from coast to coast, to get the party rolling.

"Pay no notice to the fearmongering out there," interjected Sheryl, a successful real-estate agent known for her house-hunting skills in the service of Hollywood stars. "I can assure you the market remains strong. Last week I sold a house in Beverly Hills that had five bidders and went for twenty percent above asking. Prices of good properties in desirable areas are still increasing. Do I have to remind you? Location, location, location."

Josh, one of the biggest property developers on the West Coast, agreed. “Yes, even if there is a dip, it won’t last very long. I just bought a piece of land in Las Vegas on which I plan to build a two-hundred-unit residential tower. With boomers starting to buy retirement homes in low-tax states, we can’t build fast enough to meet demand.”

Ernesto listened to the exchange with only half an ear. He didn’t understand the gringos’ obsession with houses—building them, selling them, or buying them. He wondered what Juan would have to say about it. He must remember to ask the next time he telephoned him. If only he could sketch everything in sight to record the capitalists in action with their snouts in the trough. Juan would have a laugh.

“Even if short-term interest rates are going up, long-term mortgage rates are still near record lows,” Felix, Sheryl’s husband and a portfolio manager at PIMCO, weighed in. “The global financial markets are flooded by a glut of savings from Asians desperately looking for returns. Japanese housewives, Asian central banks, you name it. As long as they’ve got to park their money somewhere, bond yields and mortgage rates will stay low. This will provide a big support for the real-estate market. By the way, the rich Chinese, I hear, are already starting to buy houses in California.”

“I’m not all that surprised.” Hanna, owner of a new-age spa, beamed. “My Chinese customers tell me they adore California.”

“So, hold on to this thought,” Felix continued. “If only one percent of China’s billion people bought a second home in California, that’s ten million homes.”

Everybody did indeed hold on to that thought, the sheer size of the number opening their imaginations to a new realm of possibility. It even caught Ernesto’s attention. As for Joanne, it persuaded her right then and there to make an offer on the house in Beverly Hills she had viewed that afternoon, lest the Chinese spirit it away from under her nose.

• • •

After dinner, Kip offered to drive Ernesto back to his dorm. Once in the car, he reached into his brand-new knapsack. "I have something for you," he said shyly. He took out a pastel drawing. It was of Kip.

"Oh, it's beautiful, Ernesto," she breathed. And she reached out to his face and kissed him briefly on the lips. He tried not to shrink back.

When they were out of sight of the house, she pulled onto a dirt road. The moon was rising in the sky, showering the landscape of hills with a silvery cascade of shimmery light. "We need to talk."

Ernesto's heart skipped a beat. Was it payback time? How could he convey to her gently that he didn't like girls? He shifted his body against the car door, as far away from her as he could. But he needn't have feared her advances.

"You must prepare for the showing with my aunt, you know. You need a place of your own to paint. And I have just the thing. Dad has recently evacuated a second-floor loft in downtown LA. I know I can convince him to allow you to use it as a studio for a couple of months."

Overwhelmed by Kip's generous offer, Ernesto's dark brown eyes glistened in the moonlight. He was speechless with surprise and gratitude. This stranger must be an angel descended from heaven. A warm pulsing wave washed over him, reigniting his ambition. America! Was nothing impossible in *el otro lado…*?

Later that night, on the floor of his cousin's one-bedroom rental in East LA, Ernesto took a long time falling asleep. Everything bothered him. The loud music penetrating from the neighboring houses and the stifling air in the room. Stale cooking odors wafted in from the tiny kitchen, and the acrid stench of urine from the toilet seemed to defile his nostrils more than usual. He tossed and turned, but the old mattress was lumpy and stank of mildew. Carlos was a dirtbag who never cleaned up. The net curtains on the windows were stained with the carcasses of crushed flies. How could he go on living like this? But the knowledge that he must was his last conscious thought before he dozed off.

With sleep came escape. A big, beautiful, bright yellow house appeared in his dreams. It had a swimming pool surrounded by palm trees. He was splashing around in its turquoise water with his brothers while Apá, lounging in a deck chair, a bottle of the best tequila at his side, looked on. The sky above was a miraculous green, like the mantle of Our Lady of Guadalupe. In the gleaming white marble kitchen that looked out onto the pool, which in the strange illogic of dreams was as wide as the entire façade, his dear mama was beaming at him as she prepared a mound of tortillas.

• • •

True to her promise, Kip provided Ernesto with a space in which to paint. Over the next few weeks, whenever he could snatch the time, after work or on Sundays, way into the small hours of the morning, red-eyed with lack of sleep, Ernesto labored on his canvases in the run-down loft with all the explosive energy only a twenty-year-old can muster.

It took him little time to decide what he would paint for Joanne. Inspired by the transformative poetry of the great Mexican muralists, he too wanted to use color to assault the eyes of the soul. But his vision reached further. After discovering the dreamlike surrealism of Henri Rousseau, he aspired to fuse the two traditions—doing for the sierra and desert what the Frenchman had done for the jungle.

During the breaks between work and painting, he would meet up with Kip. Sometimes he was invited to hang out with her family at their house. They were so warm and encouraging, so welcoming. It was wonderful to sit by the infinity pool with a glass of iced tea in hand and chat as if he had known them for years. Soon he began to think his prejudice against the rich was misplaced. *Was Juan wrong?* Kip's family were just regular people except, perhaps, in their appreciation for art and beauty above all else.

• • •

"*Trabajo*. Hard work. That's the only way to go. Keeping your eyes on the ball. And you know what that is, don't you? You came here to help your family. Your poor mama scraped together the last pesos she had to help you come here. You're a good boy, Ernesto. Don't squander the faith she has in you."

Carlos was only ten years older than Ernesto, but he saw himself as his cousin's guardian. This little lecture was prompted by Ernesto's request for a loan. It was the final straw for Carlos. Ernesto's strange behavior lately had not escaped his notice, but he had kept silent until now.

"Well. Will you give me a loan or not?"

But Carlos hadn't finished trying to get to the bottom of it.

"All these comings and goings of yours. Where've you been hanging out?"

"Nowhere," Ernesto answered sullenly.

"You've been skipping Sunday Mass a lot, and you didn't show up for work at least a half dozen times. And when you do show up, you sleep on the job."

Leading a double life was exhausting. All the rushing back and forth between Encino, East LA, and the studio downtown, the juggling of the short twenty-four hours in the day. Maneuvering in a maze of lies was tiring, too.

"Why do you need a loan, anyway? You earn plenty. Is it a girl, Ernesto?" Carlos was getting really frustrated. "Come on! Spit it out! Don't lie to me."

His shoulders slumped forward, his head hanging, Ernesto was staring intently at the dirty floor. His eyes landed on Carlos's overgrown and blackened toenails and then rested on the blue skulls tattooed on Carlos's calves. There was no way he could tell him. No way in hell. His own parents, though proud of their eldest son for having landed a scholarship, had never really approved of his studying art, which they didn't believe was going to lead to a real career. If anything, Carlos was even more narrow-minded. He would never understand.

"No.... No."

"Come on, *chico*. Out with it. You can confide in me," Carlos said in a softer tone.

"No. I haven't met anyone, I'm telling you!" Ernesto exploded.

"Easy, easy. I can see that something's eating you. If it's not a girl, then how do you explain the new shoes, the new clothes?"

Carlos must have been snooping through his stuff. The shame he felt for lying abruptly mutated into self-righteous anger.

"None of your damned business," he shot back, turning away.

Carlos grabbed him by the arm. "What's gotten into you?" he growled. "Where's your head? The company you keep is your own business, but it's my business to keep my promise to your mother to keep you on the straight and narrow. Have you been sending money home?"

Ernesto's initial "yes" was followed by a shamefaced, barely audible "no."

Tightening his grip on Ernesto's arm, Carlos stared at him, incredulous. "Do you mean to tell me you've been spending all your money on yourself?"

On his clothes, on a new cellphone, on taxis, on all the expensive tubes of paint, primers, thinners, brushes, easels, and other art supplies. What he earned didn't begin to cover it.

Fueled by his self-righteousness, Ernesto tore himself from Carlos's grasp. With his cousin's "I'm disappointed in you!" following him all the way to the door, he flung it open and stepped out into the night.

• • •

Hot and flushed, his heart beating in his ears, Ernesto wandered about the deserted streets of East LA, the occasional police car passing by spotlighting his silhouette as if he were a criminal on the run.

His thoughts cascaded one after the other. What right did Carlos have to lecture him like that? If he had been derelict in his duty to his family, it was no one's business but his own. He was old enough to decide what was good for him and for his family. Carlos understood nothing. Kip's aunt ran one of the largest galleries in LA. This was a once-in-a-lifetime opportunity; others would kill for it. Living with his cousin had become a liability: He needed his privacy and the freedom to make great art. As soon as he could get his hands on a place of his own, he would move out. He couldn't go back to Carlos. Not tonight. Not ever.

But his conscience smarted as if stung by a scorpion.

Who was he kidding? He knew well what his mother would say. Lying is a sin, and the only forgivable lie was a white one made in a good cause or under extraordinary circumstances. And Juan? Ernesto could feel his disapproval piercing right through him.

The only palliative was painting. Once again, Ernesto took a bus downtown.

• • •

A month went by in a heartbeat. Ernesto was working away, his hands and hair and apron splashed with paint, when Joanne showed up in the makeshift studio without warning.

Joanne began her inspection in silence, taking no notice of Ernesto's drawn, exhausted face. With the handle of a scraper held tightly in his fist, Ernesto followed the red cloud of her hair with anxious eyes. She then began commenting nonstop on the texture and composition of one canvas, on the brush strokes and color harmony of another.

She had some advice, too. "Go wild, Ernesto. Let that Aztec blood in you rage. Control is good, but use it sparingly."

After some twenty minutes she was done. His heart pumping uncontrollably, Ernesto awaited her verdict.

"All in all, you show real talent. Think you can manage half a dozen canvases for next month? I'm ready to sponsor you to participate in a group show. I'm sure you'll be a hit. Just carry on with the good work and I'll be in touch. Here." She produced a Post-it note pad from her purse. "Contact me directly if you need anything." She scribbled down her cell number and stuck the note on the iron frame of the window before leaving.

A group show! In *Los Angeles*! What a beginning to his career! Who would believe it? After Joanne had gone, Ernesto whooped with delight like an excited child, skipping and prancing around the room with wild abandon. Then sinking to his knees, he clasped his hands and cried out his thanks to the Holy Virgin.

"Thank you, thank you," he shouted at the top of his voice, certain she would hear his gratitude all the way up there in the sky. He stared at his canvases, his very own progeny, bursting with pride. Picking up his palette and brush he threw himself back into a frenzy of painting, working late into the night and forgetting to eat and drink until, exhausted, he fell asleep on the concrete floor.

• • •

The following morning, hunger and fatigue finally drove Ernesto outside to grab some coffee and a burger. He sauntered down the street, barely feeling his feet touch the ground. What might normally have taken him ten or twenty years to achieve—and most likely never—was about to happen in a few short weeks. It was as if time itself had collapsed.

Juan was so wrong about America! America was the land of opportunity after all, the land of infinite possibility, the land where dreams come true. America had just discovered his talent, given him a chance, and was now about to make him famous.

Overtaken by a wave of feelings of warmth towards everything, the entire universe took on a new cast. The grubby sidewalks, the shabby storefront windows all over downtown LA sparkled with the prospect of a bright tomorrow. People smiled at him in the street; they already considered him as one of their own.

As he floated weightlessly down the street, Ernesto's eyes happened to alight on a familiar-looking logo of a sun. Its golden rays glinted in the morning light, conspicuous in the maze of competing signs that lined the buildings along the street. Funny he hadn't noticed the sign before. Funny it should have been under his nose all along. It beckoned, in Spanish: *Zero-interest loans! Instant mortgages! Immigrants—we want your business!*

Slowly, the interlocking wheels of his mind began to whirl. He approached the entrance. Entering the stairwell, he followed the lure of the golden arrow as if mesmerized, climbed up to the second floor, and pushed open the door.

Sebastian Aguilar recognized Ernesto at once. Ignoring the paper bag with the six-pack in the crook of his arm and his dirty and disheveled appearance, he greeted him with a warm handshake. Waving him past the receptionist into his office, he sat him down at his desk.

"I've decided to buy a house," Ernesto announced, his eyes shining.

"Good decision," said Aguilar with a broad smile.

"How does it work?"

"Do you have a social security number? Tax return records?"

"No."

"We'll arrange them for you."

"Is this legal?"

"Don't worry. We do this all the time."

"I have no money."

"Not even for a down payment?"

"No."

"No worries. What's your monthly income? I'm asking because I have to figure out what kind of mortgage is right for you."

"About twenty-four hundred dollars a month."

"Fantastic." With that, Aguilar began punching numbers into his computer. Within a few minutes, a three-page report slid out of the printer. He stapled it together and handed it over to Ernesto.

"Congratulations. You've just been approved for a two-hundred-and-fifty-thousand-dollar mortgage."

"That's it?"

"Yep, that's it. And now I'm going to show you the perfect property. It's a brand-new house, priced at two hundred and seventy-five thousand dollars but I'll give you a deal because I like you. I can let you have it for two hundred and fifty thousand."

Aguilar proceeded to show him photos of the house on the computer screen.

"Really? Are you sure? Can I really afford this?" It seemed too easy.

"Of course! In the first year, you'll only have to pay five hundred dollars a month towards your mortgage. Interest will go up after the first year, but you'll have the option to refinance. Instead of paying rent, which is like throwing money out the window, you'll start building equity—value—in your own home. Trust me, you're getting a helluva deal."

Five hundred dollars? Only three hundred dollars more than the rent he was paying Carlos for sleeping on his floor. Only three hundred extra dollars would buy him his freedom. The idea of having his own place where he could come and go as he pleased proved impossible to resist.

"Where is this house?"

"It's in San Bernardino, an up-and-coming neighborhood. A lot of people are moving there. In five, ten years, it might be the next Beverly Hills."

"Really? I'd like to see it."

"I'd love to show it you, but I'm very busy at the moment. There's really not much to see beyond the photos. I can assure you that you're getting a great house at a bargain price. I advise you to close right away. Prices are going up every day and I can only guarantee you this phenomenal price until tomorrow. I've got five other potential buyers who are knocking at my door about this property."

Ernesto wavered. But Aguilar seemed to have an honest face.

"This is a surefire investment," Aguilar continued in his soothing voice. "The whole world believes in American property. You've absolutely nothing to lose and everything to gain."

This assurance clinched it for Ernesto. "I'll sign the papers now."

• • •

Ernesto staggered dizzily out of the offices of Sun Valley Financing back into the sunlight on the street. He was still penniless, but here he was, the proud owner of a house in San Bernardino. Though he hadn't even seen the place, he couldn't wait to write to his mother to let her know that he—no, they—now owned a stake in America, a stake in this great country that promised to look after him and his family.

• • •

The project in Encino was winding down. Soon it would be finished, and Ernesto would have to look for another job. Not that the prospect of losing his job worried him. Painting the last wall of the last bedroom, he was in full daydream mode, his arm pushing the roller up and down like an automaton, his mind letting loose the arabesques of his imagination. He pictured a sell-out show, the festive cocktail party afterwards, with him, Ernesto, feted by all the important art critics on the West Coast. He saw Juan, his arm hugging him tight, his initial disapproval melting into a beaming smile at his success. And not least, his parents and brothers and sisters standing under a sky raining down dollar bills, never wanting for anything ever again.

When lunchtime came around, Ernesto pulled on a windbreaker. It was late October, and the weather was turning cooler. He was heading out when all of a sudden he heard a dog barking. It was more like a yap, and it sounded familiar. Next thing he knew, a furry white ball was at his feet, aggressively baring its pointy teeth. *What on earth?* It was Moses. He lifted him up into his arms.

When Ernesto caught sight of Kip's blue Volkswagen Beetle parked outside, his heart sank. Or rather it dropped with a tremendous thud as if it were about to fall out of his body altogether.

Kip was at the wheel, her face frozen over. She swallowed hard and said, as he approached, "Aunt Joanne called me yesterday to tell me she's impressed with your work, you know. She said she believed you had a future."

Ernesto held tightly onto Moses as he leaned towards the driver's seat.

"I tried to call you on your cell. To tell you the good news."

Oh God, oh shit. Ernesto realized with horror that he had forgotten his phone in Aguilar's office. She cleared her throat.

"But I couldn't reach you. I called up the art department at UCLA to leave you a message. They said they had never heard of you. Can you imagine what I felt, Ernesto? I was sure that it was some sort of mistake, but there was no mistake…." And she started to cry softly.

Ernesto gripped the edge of the window with one free hand and didn't say a word.

"I waited outside the studio and followed you," she went on between short gulps for air.

"I saw you board a bus. And then another. I spent all night in my car in East LA. Can you imagine what I went through? And I followed you out here this morning," she said, crying some more.

"Kip, please, let me explain," Ernesto said, kicking himself. How deep into his self-absorption he must have been for her bright blue car to have escaped his notice.

"No, don't. Don't you even try," she said, brushing away her tears. "How could you deceive me like that, Ernesto? You *lied* to me! I don't give a shit who you really are, but you *lied*. After everything we've done for you? I thought we were friends. Mom says you've been using me. That you're a predator."

She looked up, meeting his eyes.

"Did you plan everything, Ernesto? From our first meeting on the beach? Tell me. Tell me!" she screamed at him hysterically.

"How can you think that? Of course not. Come on, Kip. Just calm down and get out of the car. Let me explain—" He fumbled with the door handle.

"Don't touch the door! Don't touch the door! No, no. It's over between us. Over!"

Ernesto silently handed over Moses. The sound of the car's revved-up motor preparing to leave was like a death knell.

"Kip. Listen to me," he cried out more loudly, over the noise of the engine. "You don't understand!"

But Kip pressed down hard on the gas pedal. The car shot away.

• • •

Joanne. He just had to get in touch with Joanne. She was impressed by his work. She had seen his talent shine through his Mexican skin. She understood artists and surely would be more forgiving where great art was at stake. Maybe she could talk sense into Kip. But her phone number was locked away in his cell. He begged Carlos to drive him to Sun Valley Financing. Perhaps feeling that he had treated his cousin too harshly, Carlos agreed without asking why.

Galloping up the two flights to Aguilar's office, Ernesto retrieved his cellphone and rushed right back down into the street again. Joanne. With frantic fingers, he searched for her name, called and waited as the phone rang and rang and rang. The answering machine picked up. He tried again. This time it was Joanne, her voice cold and forbidding at the other end of the line.

"We don't know who you are and what your intentions are. You're a liar. If you ever try to contact Kip or me again, I'm warning you, I'll call the police."

• • •

Devastated, Ernesto collapsed onto the curb, rocking on his heels in a keening motion, holding on tightly to the amulet of the Virgin around his neck. It was all ruined. And he had brought it upon himself. He shouldn't have kept postponing telling the truth about who he was. He should never have played along with Kip's crazy inventions that made him lose his head. Kip! He thought there was something genuine between them. In the end it was a dumb, romantic delusion, and he felt ashamed, abandoned, and lost.

But also—

Kicked out. Rejected. The anger beneath his sorrow began bubbling up, hot like molten rock. He was not a fraud! He was no cheat! Was his lie so outrageous that it warranted Kip barring him from her world forever?

So, was it his own fault? He had lied. But didn't the rich lie and cheat all the time?

Everything is pretend to them, anyway. False meat. False art. The rich picked up stray dogs easily, but apparently they just as easily threw them away. There was no justice in the world for people like him.

Everything is nothingness. He thought he now finally understood the message of that bullshit performance at Kip's house. People who have everything don't really give a damn, their stupid lives as empty as that stage. And with that understanding, his anger reached full boil.

If only he could run back to Mexico and his people right this minute. As hard as life was at home, in Mexico he was at least as good as anybody else. But he couldn't run. Now all he could do was crawl back to his cousin's house, his tail between his legs.

He would work in LA till the end of the year, no more. For the sake of his mother, he would swallow his pride for a while longer.

With this new resolve, he felt a bit better. He uncurled himself and stood up on the sidewalk. He would have to get rid of that damned house in San Bernardino. It was now a millstone around his neck as he would have to save every dollar he earned.

Shouldn't be a problem selling it, he figured. The market was so strong, everybody said. He looked up at the sign for Sun Valley Financing dangling right there in front of his eyes, its tawdry golden letters a reminder of his folly. Filled with revulsion, he hated it now. Hated himself for having succumbed to a false god. But determined to undo what he had done, he penetrated the dark hallway. Up the stairs he climbed, back to Aguilar's seedy office, back into the false god's lair.

• • •

"Come back another day," the receptionist said, her eyes on her computer. "Mr. Aguilar is out now and has appointments the rest of the afternoon."

"I'll take my chances. I'll wait," said Ernesto defiantly as he sat down in the reception area.

Half an hour went by and then a tall and impressive-looking man in an immaculate pinstripe suit walked in, talking loudly on his BlackBerry. This time the receptionist lifted her eyes from the computer. "So sorry, Mr. Creek. Mr. Aguilar has been held up. Is there anything I can get for you? A glass of water? Coffee?" she said, fawning over him. Mr. Creek waved away her offer impatiently and continued in a booming voice:

"Tell Larry we're a step ahead of Lehman. That I'm buying up every mortgage I can get my hands on. Something to remember at bonus time, yeah? Sure. Sure. Doing everything short of running naked in the streets with a sign on my back. I'll be back in New York tomorrow."

He snapped his phone shut just as Aguilar, breathing heavily, his tie askew, came in, mouthing apologies for being late. Ernesto shot out of his seat. Aguilar gave him an empty glare of non-recognition as he ushered Mr. Creek into his office, practically slamming the door in Ernesto's face.

Ernesto was not about to give up. He'd simply wait until that man, obviously important, left the office. He'd collar Aguilar if it came to it.

At last Aguilar emerged into the waiting room chatting with Mr. Creek. Ernesto accosted Aguilar with pleading eyes.

"Just two minutes of your time!"

Aguilar's amiable persona was not so amiable anymore: "OK. OK. Two minutes. I'm a busy man."

"I'm going back to Mexico. I don't need the house. I need to get out of the deal. I'm really sorry I put you through so much trouble."

Aguilar laughed, shaking his brown curly head as he inspected his new shoes. "Oh, that's impossible. That ship has sailed, baby."

Ernesto stared back at him, confused.

"Did you see the guy who just left?"

He had. How could he possibly have missed him? His leonine presence had filled up the entire room.

"Well, that was Charlie. He's just bought your mortgage, sonny," said Aguilar with a coarse chuckle. "Just bought your loan that with all the others he'll probably sell onward to some other idiot for a handsome profit."

Ernesto had no idea what he was talking about. Nor did he know that, like thousands or tens of thousands of other illegal immigrants, he had been conned into buying a house at the top of the real-estate market. Fallen prey to a subprime mortgage scam, the scam of the century, as it would turn out later. He also didn't know that the house Aguilar had sold him was worth at most $150,000. By paying the asking price of a quarter of a million, Ernesto had let himself be skimmed for a whopping $100,000. Even if eventually he did manage to sell the house, he'd never, ever, get that money back. He was now stuck with the mortgage payments, with the house, and with America.

"Run along now. Just make sure you meet those mortgage payments."

But something was horribly wrong. The blond man had just "bought" his mortgage. What on earth did that mean? Why would the man *want* to buy his mortgage? Who was he, anyway? Ernesto leaped down the stairs two steps at the time and ran like the wind down the sidewalk. He just had to catch up with him.

There he was, opening the door to a taxi. But it was too late. The man who, unbeknownst to him, would globalize his misfortune, was impervious to Ernesto's cries entreating him to "Stop! Stop!"

And the taxi took off and sped away, leaving Ernesto behind all alone on the sidewalk.

Chapter 6

CHARLIE CREEK

Norlund, Norway, October 2006

"When America sneezes, the rest of the world catches a cold."

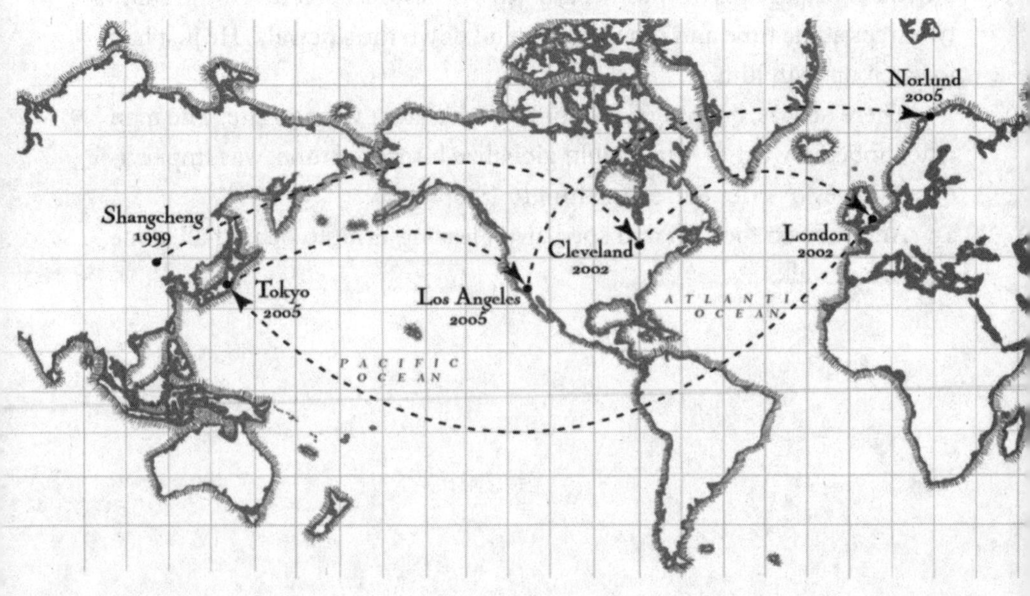

THOUGH IT WAS NOT YET noon, the low, feeble rays of October sun streaming through the windows were already casting long shadows on the floor and walls. In a few weeks, Charlie had been told, the sun would disappear altogether for the duration of the long winter months.

The space in the meeting room of the nineteenth-century town hall was spare and utilitarian, cold and bleak under the neon lights. The only decoration was a giant mosaic of muscled laborers going about their tasks and striking heroic poses as they stared vacantly, bleeding color in the neon lights, into the future space of some imagined socialist utopia.

Charlie's watery-blue eyes scanned the yellowed Formica slab of the conference table and the tarnished chrome of the tubular chairs and fell to the scuffed grey-green linoleum floor peeling away in the corners.

Who would have thought that in this shabby fishing village in a remote corner of the world in which he found himself, there was a fortune waiting to be made? But there was, without a doubt. So, projecting surefire confidence and control, Charlie Creek soldiered on:

"…the US economy has never been stronger. We believe the housing boom has at least twenty more years to go…."

He paused to let his words sink in. Taking a sip of water, he let his gaze sweep across the twelve members of the town council. A blonde on the right drifted into his consciousness. Charlie's jaded eyes lit up for a brief moment.

He sucked in his thin lips pensively while looking down at his notes. It was important, he knew, to create the impression that he was imparting his message only after the most careful consideration.

"Home ownership in the US, currently at only sixty-nine percent, is set to increase. Ownership rates tend to rise as people get older. Current demographic trends suggest demand for homes among baby boomers will increase for at least ten more years," he said, with a calm authority modulated by precisely the right measure of excited enthusiasm that he had taken years to perfect.

Aha, the blonde's lips were curling up at him, he noted, his attention momentarily deflected.

"Moreover, only fifty percent of African Americans own a home, and the percentage is even lower for Hispanics. There are many new programs to encourage minorities to get on the housing ladder."

This revelation was a home run. He could see everyone lapping up his words, busily scribbling in their notepads. Charlie pushed his spectacles more firmly back on the bridge of his nose: He had bought the expensive tortoiseshell pair just before the trip. The Norwegians were a serious people, he had been told.

"Our own survey shows that immigrant households typically buy their first homes fifteen years later than those born in the US. With about one-seventh of the US population being foreign-born—and that number is only growing—this will help support demand further.

"This is where the CDO—the letters stand for 'collateralized debt obligation'—comes in," Charlie said in his sonorous voice. "Don't panic! It's just a fancy name for a bond. It is, in fact, the simplest financial instrument in the world. CDOs are bonds collateralized by the most senior tranches—packages—of subprime mortgages. That is, the least risky. Don't be alarmed by the 'subprime' label, either. They are perfectly safe. They have triple-A ratings from Moody's, one of the most reliable credit-rating agencies in the world. The best part about these bonds is that they give you higher yields than US government bonds, even though they carry no more risk."

American bonds, which offered higher yields than European ones, were popular in Europe. It made no difference to these people what they were called: Charlie knew that all he had to do was play to their greed.

"We believe these bonds are an excellent choice given your risk tolerance and profile. We cannot recommend them more highly," he said, reaching the end of this pitch. "I'd be happy now to answer any questions you may have."

Pleased with how the presentation went, Charlie glanced at James sitting in the back of the room. James, a junior sales associate whom Larry, his boss, made him bring along on the trip, gave him a discreet thumbs-up.

As Charlie waited for reactions from the audience, he caught Blondie's eyes upon him—were they green? Charlie knew how he appeared to the opposite sex. A big, tall fellow with dirty-blond hair which, though greying, was still luxuriant and meticulously coiffed. He was proud of his aquiline looks and youthful appearance, of his broad shoulders and his straight back, of the still-flat abdomen that he took great pains to maintain. Though he was nearing the danger zone of fifty, he fancied that he had lost nothing of his irresistibility to the opposite sex. He had heard Scandinavian women were easy, and he still had the night to kill before his flight next morning.

"Any questions?" Charlie asked again, already strategizing how he'd ask Blondie for her number.

Suddenly one of the council members raised his hand and rose to his feet. He was very tall and thin, with a covering of facial hair so thick, it was as if he had grown not a beard in compensation for his shaven head, but the full, rich pelt of a woodland animal. *Must keep him warm in winter*, thought Charlie wryly.

"Mr. Creek," he said. "My name is Gunnar Johannessen. I've read that some economists believe there is a housing bubble in the United States. What is your response to their assertion?"

The bluntness of the question caught Charlie off guard. What did this hillbilly in a fisherman's sweater and with a beaver on his face know about economists? Charlie had nothing but contempt for economists. As they say on Wall Street, God created economists to make weather forecasters look good. No, he wasn't going to let their "assertions" stop him from selling his bonds.

In a voice as smooth as treacle, Charlie replied, "I can assure you, sir, there is no bubble. Ben Bernanke, the new chairman of the Federal Reserve, and one of the greatest economists in the world, has publicly stated that the price increases reflect strong economic fundamentals. Since 1929, US house prices in the aggregate—that is, national house prices—have not fallen in any given year. Translation: seventy-five consecutive years—three quarters of a century!—of rising prices.

"No other investment—let me repeat that—no other investment can boast of such a performance. Not even close. It's simply the safest investment in the world." Then he smiled his widest, warmest, most bewitching, white-toothed smile, the one he knew never failed to charm his clients.

But Gunnar would not be pacified; nor was he charmed. He shot up out of his chair again, his wiry body tense with righteous energy: "The past is no guarantee of the future! You would agree prices could fall, wouldn't you?"

Of course prices might fall, you fool. It was the sine qua non of Wall Street. As inevitable as death. And as with death, the big question, the only question, was *when*. Charlie squirmed uncomfortably for a moment.

"We-ell," he said, frowning as he hemmed and hawed, "in theory, perhaps, they can, it's always…sometimes…in the realm of possibility, but…" And he ended weakly, "They won't. Though you never know…"

He could see James in the back of the room, looking down at the floor and shaking his head.

Gunnar pressed on. "In the material you sent us, you say that as long as the default rate stays below five percent, there is no problem. However, what if the default rate were to rise above that threshold?"

Shit. Beaver-beard had done his homework. Charlie urgently needed to shut him up before the whole thing blew up in his face. And now James, the prick, was signaling that he wanted to give it a go. Charlie pretended not to see him. Who did that pup think he was? It was Charlie's battle. Nobody was going to tell him how to win it.

It was time to deploy his biggest gun: "We have several state-of-the-art models that we've been developing for years. They're telling us there is no reason for worry."

Statistical models are the last refuge of a Wall Street scoundrel. *Please don't grill me about them.* Math was not his strong suit. He was sunk if his tormentor decided to challenge him on the models.

Fortunately, no grilling. Yet Gunnar still wouldn't be silenced.

"Let me put it to you differently. Given what you know about the US housing market, would you buy these bonds for your own children?"

Ouch. This one hit him straight below the belt. Unprepared for questions of a personal nature, for once Charlie almost lost the smoothness of his tongue. It felt almost cruel of Gunnar to bring up the painful subject of his kids, the product of his failed marriage. Though he loved them with his life, they were darned expensive.

After his divorce, maintenance amounted to $100,000 a year apiece for their upkeep—and there were three of them—for private day-care and summer camps, not to mention nannies. His finances were already stretched to the limit; he had no money to invest in any bonds even if he had wanted to.

But since "all the world's a stage," he brightened and said out loudly and firmly, with a nod of his head and an open palm pressed to his heart, "Oh, yes. I most definitely would."

Taking Charlie's feigned sincerity for an honest answer, Gunnar folded his wiry body back into his chair and said no more.

There were no additional questions. The councilors began talking to each other in low voices. All Charlie could feel was a cold wind of indifference. A formless anxiety crept into his heart.

He picked up his glass and slowly downed some water. It tasted pure and clean, like newly melted mountain snow, as it washed down his parched throat all the way to the nascent conflagration in his chest.

He racked his brains for something to say that might reignite the enthusiasm he had detected before things went sour. But nothing came up. Nothing came up because he knew nothing about these people: nothing except the fact that they had recently decided to borrow against their future tax revenue to invest in high-yielding assets so that they could build an Olympic-sized hockey rink and a world-class reindeer hospital.

That it had come to this after a twenty-five-year stint on Wall Street! His fate—his career—his life—hanging on the decision of some Norwegian yokels in the fuckin' Arctic! And he had no plan B, no fallback position. How had he allowed this to happen?

A few moments passed, and the chairman of the town council, an elderly white-haired gentleman, stood up and looked around the table.

"I believe no one has anything to add at this time. Thank you very much, Mr. Creek, for your presentation," he summarized blandly, revealing not the slightest hint, much to Charlie's chagrin, as to how well his efforts had gone down.

"We will inform you of our decision," he said. And on a curt note, he added, "Expect our answer in a few days."

Charlie exhaled uneasily. Out of the corner of his eye, he imagined he saw Blondie still giving him the look. But he was past caring now.

• • •

"What the fuck, James?" Charlie asked, as he watched James typing away on his BlackBerry. He had been on it nonstop for a while now, and he was still at it as they waited to be served a late lunch in the empty restaurant of the hotel. The two of them had barely exchanged a word since the end of the presentation. "For Chrissakes. Who are you emailing?"

"Larry, of course," James answered, not lifting his head.

"What?"

"He wants to know how the presentation went," James said, still typing.

"If he wants to know, why doesn't he call me directly?" asked Charlie, the *click-click* of the BlackBerry's keys grating on his nerves.

James shrugged. "No idea."

Charlie seethed. *There is nobody else but you who can bring home this elephant,* Larry had pleaded with him. *Nobody, I tell you.* Charlie plunged the prongs of his fork into the filet of cod on his plate.

He should have known better than to trust whatever came out of his boss's mouth, but he was vain, and Larry knew how to play him. Larry also knew he was desperate for dough. *Bring back the deal and I will personally see to it that you get your million-dollar bonus,* his boss had promised.

"So what did you tell him?" asked Charlie, biting into a mouthful of fish.

"The truth," James answered.

"And what do you reckon the truth is?"

"That the presentation began well, but ended up in the toilet," said James, puckering his lips and making a loud, sucking sound.

The rude little shit.

What if it doesn't work out? he remembered asking Larry.

You worry too much. It'll be a walk in the park. Stay positive. Remember: Take no prisoners.

"Well, James, I disagree with your assessment."

"I think I can judge for myself," James snapped back, looking right past him.

It now dawned on Charlie that his boss had never intended to cut him any slack if he should fail; if he came back to New York empty-handed, Larry would have the perfect excuse to screw him over at bonus time. Or even zap him out of the bank altogether. The whole thing was a set-up, and he, clever Charlie, had walked right into the trap.

"You were floundering. You should've let me deal with the Norwegian's questions."

Floundering? Should he have let the kid speak?

"I don't think it would have made any difference, James. What else did you tell Larry?"

"That if this deal falls through it won't be because of me."

Ah, he was cunning; this kid was already getting ready to bail. The new generation on Wall Street, masters of the blame game, knew no loyalty.

"Seems you won't be buying a new Porsche this year." James smirked, finally putting down his BlackBerry.

"I don't need a fucking Porsche."

Damn the kid. What did he know what Charlie needed?

It used to be so different.

He used to be so good at his job that he could sell a dead dog. Clients loved him: Charlie, salesman extraordinaire. He knew how to pull strings to get sold-out tickets for the big games and last-minute tables at the hottest restaurants. He made them laugh, never forgot their birthdays and anniversaries, and always sent flowers or cases of wine at just the right moments in their lives. And the clients rewarded him with business—a lot of business. No one, but *no* one, and especially none of the juniors at the bank, would have dared treat him with disrespect.

Charlie pushed away the plate as his appetite fled. The fish was overcooked. Didn't these fucking fishermen even know how to cook fish properly?

• • •

The only bar still open at midnight was on the edge of the town's center. In one glance, the bartender sized up the customer still in his business suit who had just come in, shaking off snow from his dress shoes and trouser cuffs. "*God kveld.* Good evening," he called out above the loud music in thickly accented English.

Charlie mumbled a barely audible hello as he slid onto a barstool and ordered a whiskey and soda.

The bartender glided the drink over to the edge of the stained wooden counter. He smiled encouragingly, as if to tell Charlie, *how good to have some company to relieve the tedium of the late hour*.

Charlie didn't reciprocate the smile. To sulk and drown in alcohol were his only goals. His back rounded and shoulders hunched over his drink, he gripped his glass tightly with both hands. The gel no longer held back his hair from his forehead, and it fell in lank strands on his face. He made no effort to push them away. As he drank, rocked by the keening rhythms of heavy metal playing in the background, he nursed his dejection.

All he could do was think about his bonus. He ordered another whiskey, straight this time.

THE BONUS. The capital letters flashed like a garish pink neon sign in the dirty strip of mirror behind the bar, as if reflecting a projection from his frantic, obsessive mind.

He had screwed up, all right. But he had never really stood a chance, had he? He was still seething in anger at Larry for setting him up for failure by shipping him out to this nowhere place, way beyond his usual stomping ground.

He threw back his head, swallowed the rest of his whiskey in one abrupt go, and promptly ordered a third.

The *glug-glug* of the pouring liquid pulled Charlie out of his self-absorption, and he took a moment to consider the guy who was standing just two feet away from him. Not your typical Norwegian fisherman from what he could tell: the thick furry slash of eyebrows across his face, the fleshy nose, the swarthy, unshaven countenance, the dark hairs sprouting from the open collar of his checked shirt.

The bartender, friendly and open-faced, smiled at him.

"What are you looking at?" Charlie growled.

Fiddling with his glass, a dense cloud of self-pity enveloped him. Twenty-five years of single-minded and crazy devotion to turning a dime on Wall Street had left him with little time to think about anything but his clients and his bonuses.

The lyrics of the old Queen song throbbing in the bar briefly illuminated the murky reaches of Charlie's melancholy like patches of bright sunlight. Senior year in high school: They had just won the state hockey championship, and Charlie, the captain of the team, was riding on his teammates' shoulders in downtown Pittsburgh as they sang their hearts out, on top of the world. And climbing ever higher, he landed a coveted athletic scholarship to Dartmouth College, his dream school.

And then, Wall Street! At the tender age of twenty-three he, Charlie Creek, son of a small-town pastor, walked straight through to the Promised Land, ushered into the club of the chosen ones with his charm and good looks.

When Charlie grunted an order for a fourth whiskey, the bartender eyed him warily. He drank slowly, savoring the smoothness, sip by sip, as one by one he savored his memories. He had loved his job: the prestige, the glamor, not to mention the money. He had worked hard from the get-go—the first one to arrive in the morning and the last to leave. Always going the extra mile. Never complained. Not once, goddammit!

There were days when he thought his lips would crack from all the smiling. He may not have been the smartest guy on the trading floor, but he more than made up for it by being resourceful and dependable, the *numero uno* go-to guy for his bosses. By the time he reached the age of thirty, he was the highest revenue-producer on his desk and the youngest-ever managing director at the bank.

Patches of sunlight merged into an expansive horizon of cloudless days. He lingered on the memory of a time when his professional triumphs had overflowed into his private life: the partying, the parade of beautiful women, the fast cars.

Enter lovely Stephanie from Down Under right in the nick of time, when Charlie was about to hit forty.

What a feather in his cap! Stephanie had been young, and rich into the bargain. Charlie had made it to the top, all right.

Five hundred guests had come to their lavish wedding, featured on the cover of the *Hamptons* magazine. The images crowded in: the European honeymoon, the $3 million house in Westchester, the arrival of the twins, of Sophie. The object of envy among all who knew them—the elegant, picture-book family, sought out by everyone, invited everywhere.

Charlie stared with red eyes into the bottom of his empty glass. The sun was now fast fading, and clouds, dull and grey and suffocating, began closing in, shutting out the light.

All because of one mistake.

A tale told by an idiot signifying nothing.

It had been the first and only screw-up of his career.

In a moment of distraction, a large transaction he was brokering cost the bank $10 million and the loss of an important client. The excruciating humiliation of it! Down on his knees he went and begged not to be fired. The ungrateful louts kept him on in the end, but only as some kind of second-class citizen. All the good and positive things he had ever done, all the money he had ever made for those ingrates, counted for nothing. The memory of that defeat, even now, brought a curtain of tears over his eyes.

Apparently, Charlie had now ordered a fifth whiskey.

"You've had enough, sir," said the bartender.

Charlie looked up defiantly, his chest puffed up, pulsating with self-importance. Charlie Creek, the investment banker who made more money in a year than Beetle-brows would make in a lifetime, was one of the chosen ones. How dare this nobody feel sorry for him? Only he, Charlie, had the right to feel sorry for himself. It was his privilege—and his alone.

Downhill, downhill. At the ripe old age of forty-six, everybody gave up on him, including his wife, *the bitch*. Even his mom, with whom he had always been very close, had up and died.

Everyone was out to get him: his co-workers, people jealous of what he owned or had achieved, people lying in wait for him to take a wrong step. Traders, salespeople, secretaries. Especially young guys like that arrogant pup James, who could sniff out the dying buck, were ready to send him flying over the cliff.

In the bat of an eye, Charlie went from being Mister Popular to being the butt of vulgar jokes on the trading floor.

His wife joined the chorus: Charlie was losing his touch. Charlie wasn't so charming anymore. Charlie was a loser. So it went, and the climate between them turned as frigid as a Norwegian winter.

In his sorrow, he began drinking way too much, which did nothing to stop his wife from filing for divorce. Then came the restraining order. She threw him out and turned their friends against him—friends who, it transpired, had only ever been hers. He became persona non grata at all the private clubs in Manhattan and the Hamptons.

That blow really rankled.

He let out a sigh as mournful as a wind blowing across a treeless field in winter. He felt old. So old. Fear gripped at his guts with fingers of ice.

• • •

A buzz and a vibration yanked Charlie back into the present.

When he saw that the call was from Larry, he shut off his phone.

"Any kids?" he asked Beetle-brows.

The bartender nodded. "Two. A boy and a girl."

Charlie got out his wallet. "I've got three."

"This is Sophie, my youngest," he said, pushing a photo of a bright little girl across the counter.

"Bet she misses her father," said the bartender. Did she?

Thinking about the way her mother, the fucking cunt, had poisoned Sophie and the twins against him, Charlie felt like his head was about to explode. He glowered at the bartender and snapped back the photo from his hands.

He downed his whiskey in one go, balancing himself unsteadily on the stool. It was all slipping away, the twins and Sophie, too. Dearer to him than life. Stephanie, filing for sole custody on grounds of alcohol abuse and neglect, wanted to take them away from him, all the way back to her daddy in fucking Australia!

His drinking was admittedly a problem, but *neglect*? Charlie was the best father in the world!

No way he was going to let the bitch take his children away from him. He had already signed up for counseling to get sober, and he had hired the best divorce lawyer in the city.

But the best divorce lawyer in the city didn't come cheap. And with the alimony, the mortgage on two houses, not to mention the hotel bills, he was wiped clean. Broke. Not a penny left from buying and selling mortgage bonds on the back of the biggest real-estate boom in history.

If he didn't get that bonus, he was going to lose his children. Forever.

His wobble on the stool turned into a full-arched sway, and with the accompanying sound of shattering glass, Charlie found himself crumpled on the floor. Beetle-brows came out in a rush to help him up.

"I didn't ask for any help, did I?" After Beetle-brows hurriedly retreated, Charlie hoisted himself back up onto the stool again.

He had never asked anything from anyone in his entire life. But now that he needed help, although his BlackBerry address book contained hundreds and hundreds of names, there was not a single person in the world he could ask to lend him the money he needed to stay afloat.

If he had only chosen a different path. An English major at Dartmouth, he had once upon a time considered the big questions of the meaning of life, had flirted with the idea of becoming a poet. In the end, Wall Street had won out. He had promised himself that he would retire at forty to write. But as he became a slave to the next bonus and the next, his soul shrank a little more, until the poet in him died.

If he had only chosen a different path. If only.

• • •

How did Charlie Creek get back to the hotel? No recollection when he woke up the next morning with his head full of rocks. Glancing at the bedside clock—*shit!*—it was already noon. And where was James? A car was supposed to pick them up at 10:00 a.m. to take them to Tromsø Airport for their flight back to New York. He called reception. James had left with the car. Charlie slammed down the receiver.

The son of a bitch hadn't bothered to wake him! *Wait till I get back to New York, you bastard. I'll wring your neck.* At reception, Charlie found out there was no other outbound flight that day. No use crying over it: He was stranded in this one-horse town. It was no tragedy: It was Friday today and he was only due in for work on Monday.

He saw through the windows of the lobby that it was sunny outside and that the crust of snow on the sidewalk looked thin. He'd have something to eat and then go out for a walk.

He looked down at his flimsy dress shoes. Luckily, it turned out that the hotel had a reservoir of spare Wellington boots.

After two pots of coffee, his belly full of smoked salmon, Charlie set out to explore the environs with the aid of a free tourist map. It indicated the one point of interest the town had to offer the sightseer: a medieval stave church. As far as he could make out from the tiny illustration on the map, its tiered wooden roofs looked like something out of a Grimms' fairy tale. It was a bit beyond the town limits, away from the sea and inland toward the mountains, but at what seemed to be an easy walking distance. He'd be back in no more than a couple of hours, he figured.

It was about 1:00 p.m. and the sun was very low in the sky. Charlie set off at a brisk pace, but when he reached the turning, which according to the map should have led him through a wood to the church, he realized that the map's scale was way off, and that he'd have to go on for at least another kilometer. After another half hour's walk, with the snow light and crunchy under his feet, he reached higher ground. As he paused to look around, he could see that the entire valley floor, gently sloping to the sea, had turned a glowing shade of dark royal blue. Blue light! Blue snow! Like a heavenly vision, the poetry of the landscape took his breath away.

Walking on further, there was still no sign of a church.

But then—without warning—the weather suddenly turned.

As if a giant lamp had been abruptly switched off, the sky darkened menacingly above him and snowflakes began to fall in fat, feathery blobs. He had to retrace his steps—and fast.

Within a few short minutes, the wind slamming into his face was so strong, and the snow so dense, that Charlie could barely make out the contours of the road. It was already nothing more than a flat strip of greyish white, barely discernible as it wound through the snow-covered landscape. *Must get in touch with the hotel,* he thought, whipping out his BlackBerry with shaking hands. No reception.

Tying his scarf more tightly around his neck, Charlie buried his ears into the upturned collar of his overcoat and gritted his teeth. He glanced down ruefully at his rubber boots. He'd get through this, he muttered to himself.

For another five minutes, hands deep in his pockets, he braved the growing dark and the emptiness surrounding him.

The forces of the wind and snow pushing against him like some unseen beast, he struggled downhill, despite being fit, lifting one leg after the other with excruciating slowness.

The howling of the wind grew louder, baying like a pack of wolves—and it was out to get him, thought Charlie wildly, shivering uncontrollably. He could barely see anything at all now except for the rash of white snow falling in the foreground.

And then, as he stumbled on, his foot stubbed against a hard object. He slipped, arms flailing, and fell down onto his back in the snow.

"Damn the fucking weather! Curse this hell!" he cried out in the emptiness as he got back, painfully, onto his feet. Yelling and cursing, he shook an impotent fist at the freezing, indifferent air. But as he woke up to the reality of his situation, he fell abruptly silent. Tiny icicles had formed on his brows and lashes and the stubble on his chin and cheeks, and on his hat. Bit by bit, he was turning into a block of ice. He couldn't feel his feet. Even his overcoat was becoming as rigid as a board.

Then he realized that the road had vanished into the undifferentiated darkness that surrounded him. Worse, far worse, he was unable to discern the slope of the ground and had no idea which direction he had come from, nor where the town was situated.

He was lost. Hopelessly lost.

• • •

Panic set in. He was not ready to die. Sweet Lord, he wasn't even fifty yet. Overcome by the cold and snow, Charlie began to pray, though it had been years since he had gone to church. Not that he didn't believe in God—he was no atheist—it was just that he had never had any use for Him. Not until now, that was.

The day is past, and yet I saw no sun. And now I live, and now my life is done.

Ears and face burning from the cold that shot through him like tiny arrows, eyes glazed over painfully by freezing tears, Charlie sensed the end approaching.

Shivering uncontrollably, his thoughts went wild. He just had to convince God, a wrathful God who evidently had it in for him, to spare him.

So, he began a conversation in the only way he knew how: by initiating negotiations for a deal. For the deal of a lifetime in which he was prepared, in exchange for his survival, to make the payments conjured up by his feverish mind.

Dear God. I will make amends to all those I have ever hurt. I will never tell lies, stretch the truth, or tell tall stories just in order to push through a sale. Dear God, I will give twenty percent of my future earnings to charity. No, fifty. Will volunteer two days a week in the soup kitchen of St. Bartholomew's. No, five. Even better—if You get me out of this jam, I'll quit the bank and devote the rest of my life to helping others.

Lying in the snow, Charlie's lips were barely moving. His breath was shallow, his pulse weak.

I trod the earth and knew it was my tomb.

But if God, or anyone else for that matter, happened to be listening closely, it would still have been possible to make out further renunciations. *Please, please,* he pleaded. *I'll never lose my temper, ever. I'll never swear. I'll never be arrogant or self-promoting. I'll be a good father and never shout at Sophie and the twins. I'll treat everyone with dignity and respect.*

This was his last pledge before a shout, followed by a looming shape emerging out of the fog of his agony. And Charlie, eyes streaming with grateful, helpless tears and teeth chattering, felt himself being lifted by strong arms.

• • •

Charlie woke up with his ears and nose itching and his toes tingling uncomfortably under a swaddling of quilts and blankets. It was very still and quiet except for the occasional crackling of an open fire.

"Where am I?" he uttered weakly, through swollen, fissured lips.

He tried to lift his head. Immediately exhausted by the effort, he let it fall back again against the pillows.

"Stay put. And you mustn't try to talk. The doctor says you need to rest," admonished a faintly familiar voice. "You had a tough day," it continued. "You're safe now. You're in my house."

Slowly, Charlie tried to focus in the room's dim light. The voice moved to the end of the bed, and he could just make out a bearded face and the blurred pattern of a red-and-black-checked shirt. Why was this voice familiar? An angel of mercy?

The face smiled through the beard. "Thank goodness we caught you in time. You're suffering from shock and have mild frostbite. And on the bright side, your toes don't have to be amputated." He chuckled wryly.

Amputated! Jesus! And what exactly was funny about that?

"And you might have died."

The information took a moment to sink in. Yes, Charlie remembered, agitated. His walk, the fall. But what happened after that was a total blank.

"I was out with the patrol van. When the hotel contacted me that you had gone out for a walk and was worried you hadn't returned, I organized a search party. We lifted you out of the snow just a few hundred meters from the church. Don't you remember? You're very lucky, you know. The doctor at the clinic said that just another couple of hours outdoors in this freezing temperature and you wouldn't have made it."

Charlie finally managed to open his eyes. He peered at his savior—then stared disbelievingly: It was his nemesis, Beaver Face from the town hall meeting! How on earth?

"I would have died?" Charlie struggled to say in a half whisper.

"Oh, yes. Definitely," Gunnar replied calmly.

"I owe you my life! Thank you. Thank you."

"It was nothing," said Gunnar with a casual wave of dismissal, as if rescuing people were all in a day's work. "Enough talk now. All that Vaseline on your face is probably uncomfortable, but with the sedatives we've given you, you'll have no trouble falling asleep."

• • •

When Charlie opened his eyes again a few hours later, he saw a truly angelic apparition floating toward him, with a tray in her hands. Charlie recognized her at once: It was Blondie from the meeting!

"Hi! I'm Birgit, Gunnar's wife," she announced brightly. "I've brought you dinner. You must be ravenous." With the deftness of an experienced nurse, she fed him a spoonful of hot chicken soup.

Hour by hour, as Charlie got stronger, the sequence of events fell into place. His delirious negotiations with God, his desperate pleas for survival, played over and over, fresh and vivid in his mind.

He tried to grapple with the pledges he had made. For all his faults, Charlie was a man of his word. Were the commitments he had made under duress binding? Was it indeed a higher power that had answered his prayer? Had God sent Gunnar to save him? Or was his survival due to blind luck, no more than a happy coincidence? Charlie could not dismiss the possibility that if God did exist, He could very well hold him to account. And, good banker that he was, he never underestimated risks just because he couldn't quantify them.

The next morning, Charlie was well enough to get up and walk about. The Johannessens lived in a modest wooden cabin with exposed beams, two fireplaces, and no TV. An old Volvo was parked out in the small front yard, and at the back of the house the plot fanned out into an extensive area covered with rows and rows of what looked to Charlie like straggly and blackened weeds. Gunnar, his back bent over, was working among the plants.

Seeing Charlie approaching, he straightened up and called out, "Hello there! I see you're feeling better!"

"Oh, yes, much better. Thanks for asking. How can I ever thank you enough for saving my life?"

"Don't mention it."

If he had been saved by God, it was reasonable to assume that Gunnar, whether aware of it or not, had been sent as His instrument. This meant the answer to his predicament lay with Gunnar.

"What are you doing?" Charlie inquired conversationally.

"Checking on my potatoes after yesterday's snow. My wife bet me that I wouldn't be able to grow potatoes in October." Gunnar grinned boyishly. "I was determined to prove her wrong. But now it seems that she might very well win the bet," he said, scrutinizing the ground and ruefully tugging at his beard.

"You grow potatoes for a living?" Charlie asked incredulously.

"Not at all. I teach at the local school. I'm not a good enough farmer to live off the land. Not yet."

Charlie surveyed the chilly, inhospitable-looking flats that stretched out to the strip of coastline and sea beyond. Fish, maybe, could be a decent investment, but he wouldn't put his money on Gunnar's potatoes.

"I used to work for a bank too, you know. In London," Gunnar continued.

That explained why Gunnar had given him such a hard time at the presentation.

"It was after I finished university. It didn't last very long. I quit after just three years and came here."

"Quite an extreme lifestyle change."

"I hated my work. And I missed Norway. Here I breathe fresh air and wake up to birds singing on summer mornings. I get to grow my own potatoes. What more can a man want?"

Who was this nutter? A kind of hermit and hippie do-gooder rolled up into one?

"You mean you got up one morning and decided to give it all up—your career, your comfort—to grow potatoes in the snow?" Skeptical, Charlie kept pushing.

"Yes. That's pretty much it. Meeting Birgit made the decision even easier. It seemed the most natural thing to do at the time."

"Any regrets?"

"I do miss London sometimes…but I like it here." Gunnar thought for a moment and added with a bashful smile, "Even published my first collection of short poems, *Stripes of Snow.*" An homage to—"

"Walt Whitman," Charlie, who had a perfect recall of college verses, intercepted. "*Stripes of snow on the limbs of trees.* Congratulations."

"Of course, of course. I had no idea that you had an interest in poetry."

"Well, I envy you. Once upon a time I might have taken the same fork in the road. But never mind that."

After a short hesitation, Charlie ventured, "May I bother you with one more question?"

"Fire away."

"Do you believe in God?"

Gunnar was clearly disconcerted. Fingering his beard, he answered warily after a long pause.

"A difficult question. The question of questions, really. To which I have no ready answer. In all honesty, I simply don't know. Sometimes I do, sometimes I don't. There is too much suffering in the world for me to believe in a benevolent god."

Evasive response. Gunnar wasn't giving anything away. Charlie sighed inwardly. He was no more enlightened than he had been at the start of the conversation.

• • •

"*Skål*," boomed Gunnar heartily. "To only good memories of Norway!"

Birgit raised her glass.

"Cheers! I'll drink to that. And to incredible Norwegian hospitality," Charlie countered.

The three were sitting around a simple pine table laden with food. Poached cod, moist and tender, with boiled potatoes, carrots, and fried bacon. Charlie was ravenous and ate with abandon. That night Charlie slept like a baby. The next morning, he couldn't remember ever having slept so well.

In fact, Charlie felt so well that he thought, *What do I need the world outside for?* Hanging out with Gunnar and his wife was all that he wanted at the moment, and when Gunnar suggested he join in a hockey game with the schoolboys he coached at the local rink, he was more than happy to oblige.

Charlie hadn't held a hockey stick in his hands in years, but he took to the ice easily. He hopped, spun around, and jumped, celebrating his agility, his hair flying in the air. He gave the kids a few tips and showed them some tricks he remembered from his playing days, and they flocked around him clamoring for his attention. He felt happy. But most of all, as he glided on the ice he felt exhilarated, carefree, and clean, his heart, a frozen lump for so long, well on the way to a thaw.

Later, Charlie and Gunnar were mellowing out over some joints in front of the fireplace, Birgit having gone upstairs to bed.

"It was great fun today," said Charlie. He had taken a shine to this strange but likeable Norwegian.

"You know, I owe you an apology…" said Gunnar.

"Whatever for?"

Gunnar passed his hand over his shaven head. "I was wrong about you," he said pensively. "When we first met at the town hall, I assumed you were just another Wall Street type trying to take advantage of our ignorance. Now I know different. You're not like the others. I saw you with the kids."

Charlie actually blushed. He knew very well what he was really made of.

"You flatter me," he said. Deeply touched by the enveloping kindness in Gunnar's eyes, he suddenly melted inside, the thaw complete.

He felt an irrepressible urge to confess—to the countless little betrayals and weaknesses; to the whole caboodle of shallow, egotistical, and empty values that had underpinned his purposeless life and that had brought him, he could see now, to his present state of misery. Slowly and hesitantly at first, and then with increasing passion and detail, he spilled it out, purging himself, confessing all to his host.

When he had finished, Gunnar refused to sit in judgment. "My friend," he said. "You're being too harsh on yourself. We're all imperfect in our own way. To me, you are a fundamentally decent person."

Just like a priest, Charlie thought, Gunnar had absolved him.

• • •

The weekend was soon over. The arrival of Monday reminded Charlie that he still had a life somewhere else. Or did he? God or no God, couldn't he emulate Gunnar and just get up and quit his job and devote the rest of his days to a life of meaning? To the simple life, to growing potatoes and helping other people? Maybe rekindle his old dream of dabbling in verse? God or no God, Gunnar had shown him the path to greater happiness.

Gunnar. He owed him so much! The more these ideas circulated in his mind, the more excited Charlie got. He would turn over a new leaf. He would begin by going down on his knees, begging Stephanie to take him back. He pictured Stephanie in a pretty cotton dress, welcoming him with open arms, enveloping him with the sweet scent she always wore; the kids giggling, climbing all over him, hugging and kissing him. They could all move here, to Norway. Buy a farm. Support the local hockey team. Closing his eyes, he imagined Sophie running free with suntanned legs in the mountains, bathed by love and light. That last vision was achingly beautiful. He dwelt on it for a while: He had made his decision.

All that was left to be done was to break the news of his resignation to the bank and to Stephanie. He dug out his cellphone from the pocket of his coat hanging in the hallway. No juice. Impatiently, he waited for it to recharge. No reception. And when he inquired, he found out the Johannessens had no landline, either.

"If you want to make calls, you must go into town. Birgit is going to the clinic this afternoon. She can take you along if you want," said Gunnar.

In the old Volvo, he was alone with Blondie at last. No, not with "Blondie," but Birgit, Gunnar's wife. The awkwardness he felt was something of a novelty for Charlie, and for once he was at a loss for words. Birgit, too, said nothing, looking steadfastly ahead, her face distant and withdrawn. What was this ice cube doing with the friendly, outgoing Gunnar? Charlie wondered.

He nevertheless ventured, "Did you also work for a bank in London? Is that where you and Gunnar met?"

She looked at him and smiled. "We met in London but not at a bank. I'm a pediatrician."

"Is that so?" Damn. That smile again. And the cap of her short hair was a lovely buttery yellow. Was it the same come-hither signal he thought he had seen at the town hall? Appearances could be so deceptive, Charlie thought. But no more philandering, he said to himself, remembering his vow. Especially not with another man's wife. His friend's wife.

"You must love kids," Charlie said. Then he blurted out without thinking, "Yet you have none of your own."

"No, though we tried for a long time. I have lots of children, though. My patients from all over the district. And Gunnar has his hockey kids."

"That's great," Charlie said politely, as they drew up in front of the local cyber café. He looked straight into her eyes as he got out of the car. Definitely blue, not green. And he got a sense, somehow, that there was a sadness in them.

• • •

After a couple of tries, Charlie had Larry on the line.

"Where in the hell have you been? Did you expire along with your cellphone? Boy, do I have good news for you! Congratulations, buddy, the Norwegians have just confirmed their decision to buy the bonds. Well done!"

Stunned by the news, Charlie nevertheless forged ahead.

"Hey, Larry, there is something I need to tell you—"

"Is this about your bonus?" Larry interrupted. "Consider the million dollars deposited in your account. We've already forgotten your screwups. This is a turning point. I'm glad you're back in the saddle. You're on the up."

Charlie stared blankly at the receiver in his hand. The bonus—*a million-dollar bonus*—had flown completely from his mind. A million dollars! Enough to fight for and win custody of the children!

"Larry?" he whispered, cautiously, almost tremulously. *Go on now, I have to tell him I'm quitting.*

"Gotta go," Larry cut in. "Just jump on the next flight and get your ass back to New York." And the line went dead.

So he landed the deal! Elated, Charlie punched the air in excitement. He even beat out Goldman and Lehman!

Larry was right. He was getting his mojo back.

But how, given that he had bungled the presentation?

He ordered a coffee and sat down at a table to think. *It could only be Gunnar.* Gunnar knew how much he needed the money. He must have lobbied the town council and thrown in his weight behind the decision to get him the contract.

If that were the case, nobody, Charlie thought in a rush of emotion, had ever done so much for him. The man was a saint and had saved him for a second time.

But *why?*

Was it just his magnanimity, or…was Gunnar simply a vessel for God's bidding?

He had sworn, dying in the snow, that he would quit his job and devote his life to helping other people.

Maybe God was testing him. Maybe God wanted to see if he would live up to his end of the bargain.

Charlie felt a shiver down his spine.

The Lord gives and the Lord takes away.

This was not the time to waiver. He had to do the right thing. He should do the right thing.

And the right thing was to tell Gunnar the truth about the damned bonds.

The truth was that the CDOs, if not garbage exactly, were at the very least time bombs in the making, because once interest rates reset on the bonds' underlying mortgages, defaults would surely skyrocket. And if the American housing market was reduced to relying on poor Blacks and Hispanics to keep the gravy train rolling, not to mention illegals, the entire country, never mind the housing market, was doomed.

He had to warn Gunnar, tell him to back out of the deal right now, before it was too late. He owed it to Gunnar and to God. And Charlie owed it to himself.

• • •

Back at the house, a couple of hours later, Charlie found Gunnar in the kitchen, chopping up carrots for dinner.

Charlie went up to embrace him. "How can I ever thank you enough?"

Gunnar looked puzzled. "What's there to thank me for?"

"I got the deal! It was you, wasn't it? You pulled the lever, didn't you?"

Gunnar slowly laid the knife down on the kitchen counter. "Congratulations. I'm happy for you, but I had nothing to do with it."

"Of course you did. I know how much influence you have over the town council. You must have put in a good word for me. No need to deny it, my friend."

"No, Charlie. I did not. On the contrary, I tried to convince the council not to buy the bonds."

"What?" Charlie could hardly believe what he was hearing.

"Yes, I voted against these bonds. It's nothing personal. My own research says the CDOs are too risky. I like you, Charlie, but I was not going to let you endanger the town."

Speechless, Charlie's head was reeling.

Charlie's disillusionment was as rapid as it was absolute. Behind the façade of a Good Samaritan, Gunnar was all the while undermining him behind his back.

The snake! The hypocrite! And to think he had been naïve enough to consider Gunnar his friend, one who had his best interest at heart. The betrayal felt like a punch in his guts.

"But unfortunately," Gunnar continued, "my influence is not as great as you imagine it to be. I was outvoted. The council couldn't see past the hockey rink and the reindeer hospital…"

Charlie was not listening anymore. There was no God. There was only greed. And it was greed that had saved him. The greed of the townsfolk and sheer luck. Greed and luck were all there was in the world.

Charlie had had enough. He had to get out of here right away, away from Gunnar and this place of suffocating, pristine tranquility. Get back to New York, to the bustle of crowds in the jungle of the streets, to the screaming firetrucks and police cars, to the fortresses of tall buildings, to the overflowing garbage cans on the dirty sidewalks.

Get back to the battle for his children. How he missed them.

Charlie went to his bedroom to pack his things.

“Leaving already?” It was Gunnar, who, following Charlie upstairs, addressed him from the doorway.

Charlie didn’t bother to turn around. “Could you please order me a car to the airport?”

Chapter 7

BIRGIT JOHANNESSEN

Amazon, Brazil, February 2006

"The power of population is indefinitely greater than the power in the earth to produce subsistence for man."

—Thomas Malthus

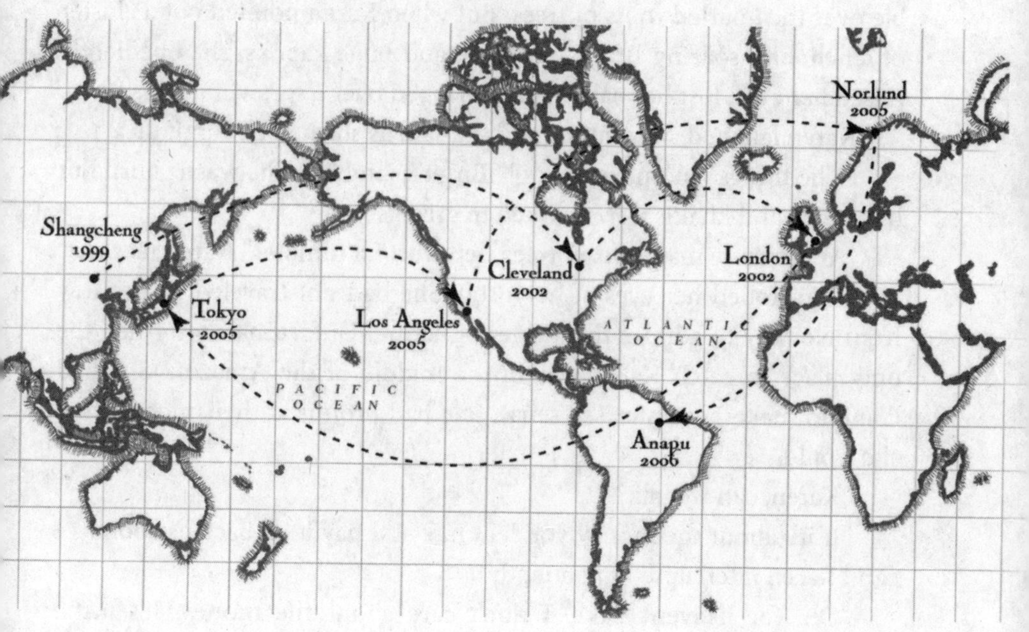

DRIP. DRIP. DRIP. COUNTLESS TINY transparent domes of water trembled on the leaves and flower petals from no perceptible movement of the air, glistening whenever a pale ray of sunlight penetrated through the dense, leafy screen of forest canopy above.

The short rain shower had come and gone, and Birgit stopped to listen to the jungle stillness. It was an eerie stillness, strangely unbroken by the cacophonic symphony of the thousands of life forms creeping and crawling and whistling unseen. It was a primeval, secret sort of stillness that had nothing to do with the absence of sound, much as it must have existed, she imagined, at the genesis of time, before the first human ears distilled meaning from chaos.

Ahead of Birgit on the trail, her sister Karen's throaty voice rang out like a bell in the forest: "It's not too far now."

Karen moved nimbly across the forest floor, but Birgit struggled to keep up, cursing her sister under her breath. Her feet slimy in her hiking boots, she fought not to slip in the muddy green lushness or to stumble over the gnarled roots of trees. But when Karen pointed out a cluster of cinchonas, soaring Brazil nut trees, and huge kapoks, she obediently raised her eyes, lost her balance, and tripped over a sprawling liana.

Karen laughed. "You all right?" she said as she helped Birgit up.

"The things you make me do!" Birgit grumbled. She wasn't hurt, but her hands and khakis were covered in green slime.

"Aren't these magnificent trees well worth a tumble?" Karen teased.

Birgit rolled her eyes at her sister. She had not traveled all the way from Norway to admire the glories of nature. Unfortunately for her, the only place to catch Karen was in the middle of the Amazon. She had come to make her sister see sense. She had promised their mother that she would.

"Karen, can we talk?"

"If it's about the money you lent me—I'll pay it all back as soon as I can," Karen interrupted impatiently.

"Oh, for heaven's sake. I don't care about the money. It's just... I'm worried."

"What about?"

"You. You're going on thirty-seven. You promised me at Mom's funeral that you'd try to…you know, settle down. It's time you found a normal job and started a family."

"Right," Karen retorted. "You want me to be like you? That's not going to happen." Her amber eyes narrowed as she pretended to be engrossed by the bark of a Brazil nut tree. "Come on. Let's go," she said impatiently, on the move again. "I'm going to show you something really special." After a little while, she called over her shoulder, "And how are things between you and Gunnar?"

Birgit didn't answer: How like her sister to try and deflect the conversation. But she was determined not to let Karen get away with it this time. She was prepared to be as patient as her sister was stubborn.

Wordlessly, the two of them continued down the trail used by the villagers in Anapu to reach the rubber trees. The atmosphere was close, and the humidity even more oppressive than before the short-lived relief from the rain.

The going got tougher as the path narrowed, and Birgit kept her eyes warily on the ground, nervously on the lookout for snakes, and tarantulas (there had been one in her cabin last night), and God only knew what other horrors lurking under the monster ferns that grew along the trail.

Karen's voice rang out again from among the mottled shadows. "I asked you a question. Are you and Gunnar OK?"

"OK, I guess," said Birgit reluctantly, obliging her sister with an answer this time. "We've been fighting a lot lately," she then admitted, battling against some creepers that looped across the path. "So, no. Not OK."

• • •

They reached a dark patch of the forest where the vines overhead grew more densely.

"Karen, I have to take a break," said Birgit, breathing heavily, propping herself up against the three-meter-tall buttress-like root of a kapok.

"You're out of shape," Karen remarked sarcastically, winding a delicate vine around her wrist.

Birgit hadn't the energy to disagree. They'd been walking for four whole hours without a break! Her shirt stuck to her back and her armpits burned, chafing from the sweat. How could her sister stand this? She thought longingly of snow and ice.

"But back to Gunnar. I have to say I'm not surprised," said Karen.

"You've never liked Gunnar. I don't understand what you have against him."

"Why, nothing," Karen said innocently. "Absolutely nothing at all, other than that he dragged you to the end of the earth and imprisoned you there. And you, my little mouse, meekly acquiesced."

"I was in love!" Birgit protested.

"In love?" Karen scoffed. "You chose him because you were dying to get married. Come on, admit it."

Her words were almost drowned out by the hollering and whooping of a troop of monkeys passing by above them, noisily jumping and swinging from branch to branch.

"You're shameless, Karen. Let me remind you, Gunnar came along only after you stole Erik from me."

"*Stole* him? He was about to dump you and hit on me instead. You should thank me for saving you from a lot of heartbreak. He was the definition of an asshole."

Birgit's pale face flushed bright pink, and it wasn't only from fatigue and the heat. Karen was treading on delicate ground. She had not completely forgiven Karen, even though the breach was ancient history and they had made up since.

But Karen persisted: "Still, don't you sometimes wonder how your life would have turned out if you had been with someone else? There are other men out there. Gunnar is a dry, virtue-signaling bore."

As usual, Karen sometimes knew her better than she knew herself, spotting in an instant the rather sizeable lump of dissatisfaction in her chest.

Birgit was about to retort when Karen suddenly crouched down and motioned to her to do the same. A column of leafcutter ants was marching across the path. Each ant was carrying a piece of leaf twice its size. It looked to Birgit like a procession of tiny umbrellas.

"Back to their home in a cecropia tree," Karen whispered, pushing back a strand of auburn hair that had escaped from the tight braids she wore wrapped around her head. "The ants live in the hollow stems of their host tree. They feed on glycogen-rich compounds secreted at the bases of the leaf petioles."

Mutualism—the evolution of synergy and symbiotic behavior across species—was the topic of Karen's doctoral dissertation at Oxford.

"In exchange, they protect the tree against encroaching vines and the invasion of other species of leafcutter ants—a win-win situation for both host and occupants."

Karen's slightly misaligned amber eyes, which Birgit had always imagined allowed her to focus on two worlds at once, glowed as she looked up at Birgit.

It was at moments like these that Birgit's love for her sister was complicated by an emotion that she always worked hard to suppress. Yet there it was, gnawing with its nasty little teeth at her heart. Envy of her sister's passion, her freedom, her brilliance, not to mention her free-wheeling love life; she even envied the uniqueness of Karen's uncanny eyes. She sometimes wished she could be more like her.

• • •

"Here we are at last! So, what do you think?" Karen twirled around in a little dance of delight, her long arms and legs loosely articulated in their sockets.

After what seemed like an interminable passage through a tunnel of unbroken greens and browns, they had emerged into a partial clearing where brightly colored orchids and philodendrons studded the surrounding trees and mosses and lichens like stars.

A perfectly tended hanging garden in the middle of the chaos of the jungle! Little marvels of symmetry and order anchored to tree trunks and sprouting in the elbows of branches in a riot of color, of blazing red and yellow heliconias, of orchids in every imaginable hue and combination of pink and purple. Birgit stood absolutely still, wide-eyed at the wonder of it.

"Evolution's answer to the poverty and thinness of the forest floor soil," Karen said solemnly. "Come. Have a look at this."

She singled out the orange bromeliads.

"Behold, a true miracle of nature. The bromeliads are a complete ecosystem in their own right. Their tightly overlapping leaves form little pools that can hold several liters of water. They provide safe environments for tree frogs, snails, salamanders, and minuscule crabs that sometimes spend their entire lives sheltered inside. Cool, isn't it?"

Karen's romantic enthusiasm was contagious. Birgit approached to take a closer look.

"When these animals die, their bodies decay and fertilize the host plants."

Birgit took a few snaps of the bright pink rosettes with her camera.

"How did you discover this place?" she asked, busily clicking away.

"Sister Dot," she said briefly, as if she didn't want to go into it.

Birgit had heard the name before from Karen. She was well aware how much Karen revered the American nun dedicated to the sustainability of the rain forest and to the poor farmers of the Amazon.

"She brought me here on my first visit to Brazil," Karen muttered.

"I would love to meet her."

Karen exhaled sharply and sank down on a toppled tree trunk, hugging her bony knees.

"I'm afraid that's quite impossible. Sister Dot's in the ground. Dead and buried."

"Oh, my god. She wasn't that old, was she?"

"No, she wasn't."

Karen shook her head despondently.

"She was shot last year."

"*Shot?*"

Karen nodded miserably. "Yes. At close range. Not far from here. The life of a kindly, harmless, and selfless woman, snuffed out…." And with an angry snap of her fingers: "Just like that."

"But why?"

"Someone decided that a little old woman clutching a Bible was too much of a threat."

Somewhere in the forest a macaw cried out.

"How awful. I'm so sorry."

"What's done is done," Karen declared flatly. "I have my own pledge to fulfill now." And flinging her arms wide open, as if willing herself to embrace the entire forest, she told her sister, "Keeping all of this safe."

• • •

Birgit contemplated the tall, slightly masculine figure so different from her own. A will of iron, that's what Karen had.

For years, Birgit had disapproved of her sister's decision to give up on a promising research career (she had published her first paper at twenty-two) to become an environmental activist. To her, it had been an impulsive act, even an irresponsible one.

But here, in the middle of the jungle, she came to the realization that it took a hell of a lot of courage to trade the safety of labs and the quiet of musty libraries for the dangers of activism.

She was glad that she had come. Finally, they would have some time to be alone together. And when Karen asked her to stay on for a few more days in Anapu, she was only too happy to delay her return to Norway.

• • •

Plunging into enormous potholes, often full of water, that scarred the open road, and then climbing out of them, the driver lurched left and then right in wide arcs in a futile attempt to avoid the worst ones.

Some thirty people, mostly women, representatives from almost every nation in Europe, were cramped together in the small bus. They were driving on the infamous BR-163, the most contentious, controversial road in Brazil and perhaps the entire world, out to assess firsthand the damage to the rainforest.

João, a local environmental activist, was their guide. Over the crackling static of the microphone, he kept up a steady stream of information and statistics, impervious to the swerving of the bus and the unventilated air fetid from body odors and diesel fumes mixed in with whiffs of industrial fertilizer coming from outside.

Birgit's buttocks ached from the seemingly endless hours bobbing up and down on the hard seat of the old bus. Karen, who was not feeling well, had fallen asleep on her shoulder. But despite the discomfort she hung on to each of the facts tripping off João's tongue in excellent English.

It was a sad tale of greed, incompetence, and corruption.

"The BR-163 runs from Mato Grosso in the south to Santarém in the north. At 1,770 kilometers long, the BR-163 is the main north–south artery of the Amazon. It was built in the 1970s to open up the jungle and develop the region. To *colonize* it, they called it!

"In the last three years the road has become the single most important accelerator of deforestation. Satellite images show that most of the deforestation has occurred within fifty kilometers of the road."

Birgit felt they must have driven half of it by now as they followed the unwavering arrow that shot straight across the landscape without a single bend or curve deflecting its devastating course. It just went on and on, the product of a planning committee far away, she imagined, with mindless bureaucrats charting a bright red line on the map with an arrogant indifference to the giant scar inflicted upon the tightest, most efficient ecosystem in nature.

"Today, the BR-163 is known as the soy highway as it provides soya farmers deep in the Amazon access to the port in Santarém and from there to the international market. Every day the forest is being cleared for new soy farms."

Birgit stared out the dirty window to her left at the green desert around them, at the unchanging and featureless carpets of soybeans growing in what used to be dense jungle growth, spreading endlessly all the way to the horizon—all that was left of a rich, teeming, three-dimensional world flattened into a gigantic pancake.

"In the time of my parents, you could see tapirs, capybaras—even jaguars—by the side of the road. They're all gone now.

"But the damage is not only ecological. It's human."

Animated now, João continued: "Large soy farms have driven off small farmers and the indigenous people who depend on the forest for their livelihood, like my own tribe."

As if to drive home his point, Birgit saw a billboard advertising American-made Deere tractors coming into view on the side of the road.

"What soy producers can't legally purchase they steal, resorting to violence and fraud, shooting people and burning down their homes. They also fabricate fake land titles. We call these predators *grileiros*, which means cricketers, because they use hungry crickets to eat away at documents to make them look old."

The typical black Kayapo geometric lines painted on João's face crunched up in a grimace of disgust.

At last, they hit a smooth stretch of asphalt. This transition seemed to trigger a wave of indignation, and somebody yelled from the back of the bus, "Why is the government not doing anything about it?"

"Government agencies use satellite technology to track illegal clearing, but they don't have the manpower to enforce the law. The Brazilian state environmental agency has only six inspectors—six!—to cover an area three times the size of the UK. This is why ninety-eight percent of deforestation is illegal. Last year, the rate of deforestation reached the equivalent of a football field every eight seconds."

He let that last number sink in for a moment.

"Every eight seconds!" João repeated. "If this goes on, in twenty-five years we'll lose another twenty percent of the rainforest. It's a total disaster."

Birgit wasn't paying attention anymore, her gaze fixed on what appeared to be smokestacks in the distance, with tall smoky plumes rising up into the greyness of the hazy sky. Her heart began to pound. What was she looking at? Soon the bus, trundling on, brought them to a new abyss of destruction.

Gone were the green soy fields, and in their place was a landscape out of the apocalypse: a graveyard that radiated for hundreds of meters from the road. Dead trees lay on the ground. Others, toppled by chain saws, were left to decay while still others were reduced to giant pillars of smoking charcoal.

Even João was speechless.

Suddenly, as if responding to their collective shock, the bus shuddered, rattled, and quaked, and then refused to go on. The driver revved the engine, scraped gears, gave full gas, but to no avail. The pothole they were mired in was too deep, and the wheels spun uselessly in the mud.

They all clambered out of the bus in silence.

Birgit had read about the plight of the rainforest but coming face-to-face with the obscenity of tree trunks smoldering like gentle beasts refusing to die, their embers glowing in a long, protracted death as they were slowly reduced to ashes, provoked an explosion of emotion in her chest. So what if trees had no voice? The doctor in her imagined she could actually hear their agony. The sheer scale of slash and burn was devastating. It was a bloody massacre.

Wandering among the debris of the ravaged forest, Birgit was reminded of old World War II photos of the carcasses of buildings in carpet-bombed cities. Houses could be quickly rebuilt, but nature, surely, was less forgiving: How fast could trees grow back to their towering heights? A hundred years? More? Perhaps never? And would the thousands of species they sheltered ever be replaced?

Half an hour had passed, perhaps longer, when Karen appeared by Birgit's side.

"Feeling better?" Birgit asked.

"Are you kidding me? No," she said, as she looked out, stricken, at the ravaged landscape. "The tauari and massaranduba trees can be as tall as forty-five to fifty meters. Their embers can glow off and on for more than two years."

Her tone was as mournful as if she was speaking of companions fallen on the battlefield.

Birgit could only manage a slow, wordless nod in response, and she reached for her sister's hand.

"God. What a hell of a price for beans."

• • •

Back in Anapu, deflated and morose, Birgit joined other members of the group who were gathered on the dimly lit veranda after a dinner of fish and manioc in the ramshackle house they had at their disposal for the duration of their visit.

The environmental activists of all stripes were talking among themselves in subdued voices, drinking warm beer, and slapping away insects. They had gathered here in Anapu to commemorate the one-year anniversary of Sister Dot's assassination.

Alma, a well-respected veteran activist from Denmark who was the coordinator for the memorial, heaved a heavy sigh. "Damn that BR-163. It's undermining all our preservation efforts. It kills me to think that in the year after Sister Dot's death the situation is actually getting worse. We're losing this battle, people."

A rustle of agreement swept through the group.

"I'm afraid I have more bad news," said João. "There's talk that the Chinese are offering to fund the paving of the rest of the road."

This revelation was greeted with a collective gasp.

"Maybe we should re-examine our strategy," said Mary, the representative from the European Environment Agency.

"Like what?" asked Alma.

"We could intensify our engagement with the Brazilian government and enhance our coordination across activist groups."

Birgit was sitting next to Karen on the railing in a corner of the veranda. She could feel the agitation of her sister rising by the minute.

"Increase the effectiveness of our lobbying," continued Mary, thinking aloud. "Do more to educate the public."

Suddenly Karen jumped down from her perch.

"Fuck this shit!" Her tall frame trembled in fury.

"You people still don't get it—the Amazon is dying. More coordination won't save it! We have to act, and we have to act now."

"What do you propose?" Mary shot back. "A hunger strike? A coup to bring down the Brazilian government?"

"No," Karen responded, "What about a good old protest where it matters. Where it'll hurt—on the BR-163. We can block it with a human chain and prevent any soy truck from getting through. And we stay put until the government agrees to a moratorium on deforestation."

Everyone began talking at once.

"And when, exactly, do we do this? Tomorrow?" Mary sneered.

"Why not? All we have to do is get off our asses."

"Do you really think that just the few of us can make an impression on these criminals, much less stop them?" Alma objected. "It could be dangerous unless we have hundreds with us."

"Which I take upon myself to supply."

All heads turned to João.

"Our local activists are itching for a fight," he said quietly. "I can guarantee you they'll jump at the opportunity and can mobilize in a few hours. I can bring my whole tribe."

Karen pounced. "So, it's settled!" she declared on the back of his words. "Those of you who are willing to join João and me, please show your hands."

A couple of young women responded enthusiastically. Birgit opened her mouth, as if poised to ask a question, but then raised her hand.

Alma spoke up again: "I hope I won't regret it, but count me in. Karen is right. It is time we put the entire world on notice that what is happening here is simply not acceptable."

Alma's vote proved to be a turning point. Slowly, one by one, more than half of the group put up their hands.

"You're all out of your minds! What can you achieve with twenty people?" Mary cried out in frustration, her voice even shriller than before.

It was João who shut her up.

"Hundreds will come, I tell you."

• • •

The ceaseless honking of cars and trucks, the loud cursing of infuriated drivers, the shouting and clapping of protestors, the intermittent blasts from megaphones, the piercing sirens of police cars, and even the cries of the piha birds, whistling their three-part song of *cri-cri-o*, *pi-pi-yo*, and *qui-qui-yo* in the sky above, engulfed Birgit in a deafening, multi-layered noise.

She had climbed up on top of one of the overturned tractors they had used to block the bridge over the river to get a better view. The Rio Aruri Grande meandered peacefully through the green jungle as far as her eye could see, but on the soy road there was utter mayhem. Traffic was at a complete standstill. Some eight trucks were stuck on the bridge, and dozens more were backed up in long lines along the BR-163. The barricades they had set up with the help of local activists using disused vehicles, chicken wire, rusting sheets of corrugated iron, and pieces of logs were obstructing the traffic in both directions on the bridge that spanned the narrowest point of the river at both its northern and southern approaches.

There was no other way to and from Santarém: It was too early to call it a success, but Karen's plan was working.

Looking over inside the barricades on the bridge, Birgit estimated that there were about sixty protestors. A paltry number, but more than compensated for by the level of energy, almost physically palpable, in the heady atmosphere. Some were holding up signs, and others chanting slogans and blowing whistles in unison. Still others sat around in rings, leaning back against their knapsacks, clapping and singing. "SAVE THE RAINFOREST! SAVE OUR PLANET!" screamed a slew of placards. And a local activist waved a large homemade flag with a peace sign hastily painted on it.

Birgit turned her gaze back to beyond the bridge. Word of their protest must have spread at electronic speed, for she could see hundreds of people on the embankments, villagers and farmers, who looked as though they had walked for hours to register their support. They had come with their children, who were playing on the muddy banks and on the jetty of the waterfront. When they waved at her, she waved back.

Closer to the bridge, she could see camera crews and reporters jostling for position among the crowds and police officers gesticulating and yelling into their megaphones as they pushed and shoved, desperately trying to restore order.

In the noonday sun it was hot and unbearably muggy, but Birgit had never felt more alive. It was as if this moment erased, at one go, all the difficult years with Gunnar and her failed efforts to get pregnant.

She felt her lips widen in a smile of exuberance at the new prospect opening up before her as she saluted Karen and the Amazon.

• • •

As evening fell and a strip of orange fire on the horizon announced the close of the second day of the demonstration, João arrived with dozens of members of his Kayapo tribe who had wormed their way through the crowds bearing fresh fish, firewood, and bananas for the protestors.

By the time the sky darkened, and the stars came out, Birgit followed the appetizing odor of grilled fish wafting in the air to the campfires where João's tribe members gathered. It felt like a village festival, with yellow flames leaping into the night sky, and spontaneous dancing and singing and clapping breaking out all around her. Beer, too, flowed freely.

But not knowing a word of Portuguese, she was no better than a mute. If she wanted to be understood—and she did—she'd have to learn a new language, one that involved moving the muscles of her face, her hands and neck and shoulders, and, at times, her entire body.

For Birgit, this mode of communication was unnatural, at odds with her upbringing, with the years of keeping the proper social distance decreed by the unspoken rules of a small Norwegian town. But she was enjoying herself immensely. She found herself smiling at perfect strangers, not only with her lips but also with her eyes, and they smiled back and sometimes awkwardly reached out to touch her silky blond hair that gleamed in the light of the fires. The proximity of so much sweaty, bare skin, and the continuous invasion of her personal space, was a new sensation, and an oddly liberating one.

She found herself dancing in not such unwanted proximity with a handsome stranger.

He pulled her closer, his fingers tapping rhythmically on her buttocks as their hips touched. But Birgit didn't mind, giving into the sensuality of his swaying movements. He ruffled her hair and she laughed. This was the adventure she had been longing for. That her very body was longing for.

The sense of release was earth-shattering. Since childhood she had believed that Karen was the wild and impulsive one. *What's happening to me?* And she continued dancing until she thought she would drop.

• • •

The next morning, a stout, middle-aged man in a gray suit, mopping his brow with a handkerchief, was let past the barricades and onto the bridge. Everyone gathered around to hear what he had to say.

"My name is Gustavo Gutierrez, director general of the forestry department for Mato Grosso," he wheezed with self-important gravitas. "I am here at the request of the governor.

"The governor would like to discuss how he could accommodate your demands in order to resolve the situation. He has asked me to invite you for a meeting."

"If that's the case, why didn't he come in person?" Karen interrupted belligerently.

"Madame," he said with a dismissive wave of his hand. "Governor Maggi is a very busy man. There are security considerations as well. He has placed his car and chauffeur at your service."

The protestors exchanged gratified glances. A concrete result at last! This was exactly what they had been hoping for—the governor, no less, was willing to listen to their demands and negotiate. It was decided right away that Karen would represent them and that Birgit would accompany her.

• • •

The air-conditioning of the luxurious interior of the Land Rover was such a relief from the heat that soon Karen and Birgit fell into a deep slumber.

They woke up with a start a couple of hours later as they sped toward a yellow mansion with a neoclassical façade, set in a clearing amidst a grove of palm trees.

"Where are we?" Karen exclaimed loudly.

"There is no reason for alarm. This is the governor's mansion—his private *fazenda*."

His private fazenda? Birgit looked at Karen uneasily.

The car came to a full stop. The chauffeur opened the door. As Birgit got out, she noticed an armed guard by the driveway. A uniformed maid greeted them and led them up a short flight of steps to the heavy wooden door of the villa. Looking back, Birgit could see the Land Rover drive off with Mr. Gutierrez inside.

They were on their own.

After being ushered into what looked like the reception room, they were greeted by a young man in a sweaty T-shirt and Bermuda shorts.

"Welcome. Thank you for coming. Please forgive my appearance. I've just come back from work," he said with a distinct American accent, holding out his hand.

Karen ignored it. "Why are we here?" she demanded, her eyes flashing. "We're supposed to meet the governor."

"I'm afraid the governor is away at present, but he will be here in a few hours. In the meantime, he has asked me to host you. Please feel at home and let me know what I can do for you."

"This is unacceptable!" Karen stormed at him. "What's the meaning of dragging us all this way to meet the governor and now you tell me he's not here?"

"Whoa, slow down. Sorry," said the young man, slightly taken aback. "I am Ricardo Maggi, the governor's son."

The sisters exchanged glances, placated somewhat.

Ricardo cleared his throat. "You're welcome to wait here, but I am going to have some lunch. I'd be most obliged if you joined me," he proposed amicably.

They ate in uncomfortable silence in the dining room. The antique dining chairs, the landscape paintings, the ornamental vases and silver bric-a-brac and other trappings of sumptuous wellbeing—the table settings, too, looked lavishly expensive—did not escape the notice of the two women. "All this money made off deforestation, I bet," Karen muttered into Birgit's ear when dessert was served.

As if he had overheard her, Ricardo, now showered and in a fresh edition of work clothes, chose this moment to break the silence.

"We're on the same side, you know. I believe in sustainable farming. Just like you," he announced quietly, with his eyes on Karen.

"Like hell you do," Karen shot back.

"You're the leader of this demonstration, aren't you? But I am the manager of this plantation, one of the largest in the Amazon, with seventy-five thousand acres under cultivation, and I know what I'm talking about."

Birgit looked at him closely for the first time. His rugged, outdoorsy looks didn't match the elegance of the dining room. His broad shoulders strained against the thin fabric of his T-shirt, and stubble covered his suntanned chin and cheeks. But his dark, delicately shaped eyes and the slenderness of his wrists belied the bluster of his muscular frame.

"You should know," Ricardo added, the corners of his lips twitching in a slight smile as he lay down his cake fork, "that I'm not one of the bad guys. So, why don't we call a moratorium on the hostilities, eh?"

Karen sniffed but Birgit smiled shyly back at him.

"Why don't I take you on a tour of the plantation?" Ricardo offered soothingly. "You might find the state-of-the-art agricultural approaches that we've adopted interesting. Do any of you have a scientific background?"

Karen almost snorted in response. "Does a doctorate in evolutionary biology count? And Birgit here is a doctor."

Ricardo laughed. "So, this tour is tailor-made for you."

They had been driving in the open jeep for some minutes, with Birgit next to the driver's seat in the front, when Ricardo remarked, "You're the quiet one, eh? Not like your fiery friend back there." He glanced in the mirror.

"My sister, actually," Birgit corrected him, with more curtness than she intended. A yearning was stirring in her again, awoken by the touch of his bare knees protruding from his shorts, which bumped against hers whenever the jeep lurched and swayed. She looked away.

"First stop is one of our soy farms," said Ricardo. They were driving on the bumpy service road that edged a field of yellow-green soy.

"This is a model farm in many ways. We believe in a progressive approach not only to the land but to our workers as well."

"A model farm? Based on whose model?" Karen interjected

When they reached a ranch-style building, they jumped out of the jeep. Set in spotless grounds, the place looked more like a community center than an outbuilding on a farm.

"We also have a recreation room and even a small library."

"A Potemkin village," Karen muttered under her breath.

Ricardo pointed out a barn for storing herbicides and pesticides. "We keep all our agro-toxins properly ventilated. I ask all the growers who want to work with me to meet three conditions: no illegally cleared land, no slave labor, no spraying of agro-toxins within five hundred meters of a stream." He counted on his fingers to emphasize each point with evident pride.

"Aren't toxins seeping into groundwater, poisoning rivers and killing fish?" Karen countered.

"I believe this claim," Ricardo said carefully, "to be somewhat exaggerated. The reality is that the soil here is very infertile. Without the right measures, it would be impossible to produce anything at all. Also, it is not true that soy degrades the soil. On the contrary, it replenishes it."

Karen riposted somewhat testily, "Oh, is what they taught you at Harvard or wherever you went?"

Ricardo refused to be taunted. "In fact, yes, I did go to Harvard. Where I got my PhD in agricultural economics. I would like you to know that everything we do here is aboveboard, within the law, and according to international guidelines."

Both handsome and an economist, thought Birgit.

"And now for a pet project of mine," said Ricardo. The wheels slithered on the un-surfaced path, muddy from a recent downpour. After a while they arrived at a stream where the banks were covered with hundreds and hundreds of saplings.

"When my father bought this property, the entire area along the stream was stripped bare. As you can see, we are in the process of a massive replanting."

"But does a good deed atone for a bad one? Does it justify bringing down the forest in the first place?" Karen protested.

Ricardo elegantly skirted her objection.

"Personally, I think it's more productive to focus on the question of the how, not the what. For instance, farmers in the Amazon basin can legally clear up to twenty percent of their land, but only if they maintain the other eighty percent as a rainforest reserve. Did you know that Brazilian producers are the only ones in the world who are obliged to maintain reserves? I would be willing to accept that cost in the interest of the environment, but the world should at least acknowledge our sacrifice, and not brand us as some kind of eco-terrorists, don't you think?"

While Karen fumed in the back seat, Birgit had to concede he had a point.

They drove on until they came across a column of tractors. "In February we start to harvest the first of our soybeans. Most of them will be travelling far, mainly to China. Have you ever been to China?

"I was there last month. What an eye-opener: the growth, the energy, the vision. China is a trailblazer, demonstrating how developing economies can catch up with rich ones."

He paused, as if to make sure his captured guests were listening.

"However, for China to maintain its rapid expansion, she needs to provide her growing workforce with a high-energy diet. The Chinese are buying our soybeans to grow pigs, poultry, and even fish. They are eating sufficient protein for the first time in their history, thanks to us."

"Interesting. I hadn't realized…" Birgit murmured.

"In fact," he went on as the jeep scrunched along the unpaved road, "over the past ten years, soybeans have become Brazil's single most important export to China, going up by ten thousand percent. This year alone, for instance, we will be selling more than two billion dollars' worth."

Ricardo's self-assurance was impressive.

"I see you have all the facts," remarked Birgit.

"Well, I ought to." He chuckled good-humoredly.

"It is not just soybeans," Ricardo continued. "We also export iron ore, timber, and beef. We are even negotiating with the Chinese for the licensing of our biofuel technology, which uses soybeans and sugarcane to produce ethanol. The real story here is that the Amazon has become both the engine of China's growth and Brazil's path to sharing China's rising prosperity."

And glancing over his shoulder at Karen, he went on, "You can't be only focused on trees and eco-habitats. There are hungry people to feed."

Karen reluctantly grunted in agreement.

But Ricardo hadn't finished. "This is why what is going on here inside the jungle is not just about the environment. It is about the aspirations of billions of people. It is about their future—the future of the world."

• • •

No Governor Maggi. When Birgit and Karen and Ricardo returned to the house, they were told the governor was held up again and would return the following morning.

Karen nearly exploded.

"The nerve! Did you bring us here under false pretenses? Did you even intend to negotiate with us?" she cried out.

Ricardo stood still, rubbing the stubble on his chin.

"I'm really sorry. I have no control over my father's coming and goings."

Birgit thought he looked miserable.

"I can offer you bedrooms for the night, supper in the reception room, and drinks."

• • •

Birgit awoke with a start. The room was dark, with two lamps washing the corners in a soft glow of amber light. After the tour of the planation, she had been exhausted and had gone upstairs to take a nap.

How long had she been asleep? It was nine o'clock already, she saw, glancing at her watch. Why in the hell hadn't Karen woken her up for dinner?

Where was everyone?

And where was Karen?

The house was silent.

In the hallway, Birgit thought she could hear soft murmurs from behind the heavy wooden door of the room next to hers. Probably Karen's room, she figured; she knocked softly. There was no response.

The door was unlocked. "Karen?" she called as she pushed the door and entered.

The shock was intense.

She caught Karen's surprised eyes—and Ricardo's. Entwined in each other's arms, they were naked.

Karen cried out, but Birgit had already retreated to her room and locked the door behind her.

• • •

Birgit threw herself on her bed and burst into tears. In her mind's eye, she saw João's stricken face among the smoldering tauari and massaranduba trees, the shrieking of the piha birds, her sweaty, intimate dance on the bridge in the light of bonfires, Ricardo's bare knees in the jeep, Karen in the jungle, leaning against the roots of a kapok, Gunnar back home among the flowered curtains, Karen's passion, Karen's dedication, Karen's brilliance. Karen, Karen, Karen. Karen sleeping with the enemy. The enemy's eyes that she, too, yearned for, though she had converted to the cause.

It was almost more than she could bear.

• • •

The following morning, breakfast was an awkward affair. No one uttered a word about the previous night.

But Birgit saw that Ricardo was stealing a bashful, doggy-eyed glance at Karen. Was he in love with her? Poor guy, he had no idea who he was dealing with: Karen would chuck him out the moment she tired of him like she had done with all her suitors.

They were on to their second coffee when the silence was shattered by the sudden appearance of Governor Maggi.

He looked supremely annoyed when he saw the two women. "So, you are still here, I see. I hope you're enjoying yourselves. Do you realize the harm you've done…?"

"Father, please…" Ricardo tried to intervene.

But Governor Maggi brushed him aside and shouted, "Do you realize the chaos you've brought upon my state?"

"Let's be clear. We're here at *your* invitation," Karen replied, not to be put out.

"Good thing you came, then," said Maggi sarcastically. "This way there will be no confusion. You have until tonight to clear the Rio Aruri Grande bridge or..."

"Or what...?" Karen retorted, her anger rising.

Birgit was trembling with a righteous fury. "But we were specifically told that you would negotiate with us!"

"Then you were wrongly informed," the governor replied in a stony voice.

Though he bore a superficial resemblance to Ricardo, his face was a coarse imitation, Birgit thought, marked by a raw and naked aggression.

"I am warning you. Clear the bridge by midnight. If not—we'll remove you by force, and I will not be responsible for the consequences."

"By force?" Birgit cried out in alarm. "What do you mean? There are villagers and children on the bridge! People will get hurt!"

"Then it'll be on your head."

And as he strode out of the room, he turned around and repeated with narrowed eyes, "This is a final warning. I will not tolerate your agitation any longer."

Everyone was stunned at this turn of events.

Ricardo, embarrassed, immediately apologized, "Karen, Birgit. I don't know what came over my father. He's usually quite reasonable."

Not this time, thought Birgit bitterly. Clearly, her sister's tryst with the enemy had borne no fruit.

"You must return to the bridge right now," said Ricardo, standing up. "Meanwhile, I'll do my best to make my father see sense."

When they were packed in the car, Ricardo came to say good-bye. "I will meet you at the bridge the moment I have news," he said, his eyes caressing Karen's face. But she looked away.

"Be careful, I beg of you. Don't do anything rash until you've heard from me."

• • •

When Birgit and Karen arrived at the bridge, they were greeted by a grim-faced Alma.

"The police have intercepted our supplies, and we'll soon be out of food and water. They also delivered an ultimatum an hour ago. So, I gather the negotiations were a total failure."

Birgit nodded. She couldn't believe how fast the governor's order had travelled.

A blast of warnings from the police megaphones, from somewhere the wailing of a siren. "No time to lose," said Alma nervously. "We have ten hours left before the brutes come charging in."

Everyone gathered in the middle of the bridge.

Alma was the first to speak.

"I think we should leave peaceably. We've made a statement; we've had our day. I am proud of what we did. Everyone here should be proud of what we did."

"You're giving up? Just like that?" Karen burst out.

"I'm sorry, Karen," Alma said, starting to walk away.

Then João said softly, so softly that the others had to strain their ears to hear him, "I'm staying. And so are the members of my tribe. This is our home, and we have no other place to go. We'll make our stand here."

• • •

Later that afternoon, Birgit heard Ricardo's voice calling out to her from beyond the barricade. She slipped through the barricade to greet him.

He smiled, as mild-mannered as ever.

"Isn't it Karen you want?" Birgit asked.

"No, I want to talk to you."

Her heart skipped a beat.

"I know Karen listens to you. You need to convince her to leave right away."

"But what would happen to the rainforest and the indigenous people?"

"Listen to me, Birgit. I don't doubt your good intentions, but isn't it a little presumptuous for you to show up here in our country claiming you know what's best for us? You know that I'm an advocate of sustainable farming. Why don't you trust our—my—judgement?"

Birgit didn't know how to respond.

"All civilizations got rich by clearing land for agriculture, including Europe."

"You're distorting the facts…" said Birgit, taking a step back.

"Not at all." The pitch of Ricardo's voice rose. "You Europeans," he sputtered. "You're all the same. You have no problem buying non-GM soybeans from us to avoid eating American GM crops. But growing soybeans to feed the Chinese suddenly becomes a sin against the environment?"

"The Amazon is not yours. It belongs to the whole world," Birgit parried.

"No, it doesn't!" said Ricardo, his anger taking over. "Damn it! The Amazon belongs to us. Find some other spot to be the lungs of the world."

He checked himself for a moment and then continued more calmly.

"I don't think you fully understand what the stakes are, Birgit. You are playing into the hands of all those who use environmental preservation as a pretext to hold us back. Is growing cheap food a crime? For a European, spending twenty percent or thirty percent less money for food makes little difference, but for a poor African or Chinese laborer, it may mean the difference between sending his children to school or not. So, you tell me. How is what we are doing wrong?"

This was an argument Birgit could not easily refute.

"You need to get yourself and Karen and the rest of your people out of here before the situation gets out of control. Karen is too hotheaded. You must make her listen to reason.

"I don't want you to get hurt. I really don't. I'm no monster, whatever you may think."

"Are you saying the crackdown is still coming?" Birgit cried. "Do you realize that there are lots of small children inside the barricade? Please, Ricardo. Can't we find a compromise? Tell your father to call it off."

Ricardo looked down at his muddy field shoes. He hemmed and hawed, obviously embarrassed by what he was about to say. At last, he cleared his throat, and said, "I tried. Believe me, Birgit, I tried. But I failed. My father didn't budge an inch. Under normal circumstances, he might have shown some flexibility."

"Normal *circumstances*?"

"You have come at a very bad time. Bad luck, I'm afraid."

"What do you mean?" Birgit asked, bewildered.

"You see, a delegation of Chinese officials is due to arrive in Mato Grosso tomorrow."

"And?"

"They are investigating the financing for a railway that will cut through the rainforest and reduce the time it takes for soybeans to get to market by seventy percent."

A railway! So João had been right!

"As far as my father is concerned, they must, at all costs, be prevented from witnessing any indication that we can't control the traffic here. The BR-163 will become more important than ever until the construction of the railway is finished."

Birgit's heart sank. They didn't stand a chance in hell.

"Birgit! Where are you?"

It was Karen, shouting from the bridge.

"I have to go, Ricardo," Birgit said in a low voice. She turned around and left.

• • •

"Where were you?" Karen gripped Birgit's arm and pulled her aside.

"I was talking to Ricardo."

"Yeah? What did he want?" snapped Karen.

"He came to warn us we should leave straight away," Birgit replied. "The governor is dead serious about the crackdown."

"Why didn't he ask for me? I hope you told him that he's wasting his time."

Birgit didn't answer. Karen certainly wasted no time climbing into bed with him, she thought.

"You don't have to stay, you know. It's not your battle," Karen said.

"You know I wouldn't leave without you."

"Well, I'm not budging. I have to make sure that João and his people are safe."

"Surely, it's easier to persuade them to leave. You're the only one who holds sway over them. In fact, it's your duty to get them to leave. Come on, there are children on the bridge. If anything happens to them, you'll never be able to forgive yourself."

"You're overestimating my powers of persuasion."

"You can't use them—or you won't?"

"What are you trying to say?" said Karen, her lips tightening.

"I think you're putting them and their children in unnecessary danger. I think you place your cause above their lives. This is an exercise in futility that will end very badly."

Then Karen said, with cutting ridicule, "I'm impressed. The little mouse has found her voice at last! *An exercise in futility*, she says? It is you, my dear, who leads a futile life, fiddling away in a remote corner of Norway with her even more futile husband and his potatoes while the world burns!"

"A futile life? I'm a doctor, for heaven's sake!" Birgit frowned, but she swallowed her anger. This was not the time to fight.

Karen walked to the edge of the bridge and looked out at the jungle beyond.

"Do you remember, Birgit, that time I went missing?"

How could she have forgotten? It had taken two days for a search party to track her down in the forest near their house. Their mother had been on the verge of a complete breakdown, and she had seen tears in her father's eyes for the first time.

"What I never told you is that while I lay there in the dark, on the cold, damp earth, I wasn't the least bit afraid, wasn't the teeniest bit lonely…"

Karen giggled suddenly. "The expressions on your faces when you found me! Daddy said it was as if I had spent the night in a pigsty, with dirt all over my face and under my nails, and my hair full of squashed beetles and twigs.

"Anyway," she went on, serious once more, "the emotion that overcame me at the time was indescribable. Still is. It was as if I had found in the forest my real home and safe harbor. I thought about death. That if I just died there and then I would have no regrets."

Karen closed her eyes, rocking herself as she cradled her arms. "Can you imagine?" she said in a hoarse whisper. "I had chosen my destiny. I was eleven years old, Birgit! *Eleven*!"

Karen looked at Birgit with her uncanny eyes from some faraway place.

Birgit was stunned. Karen had never opened up to her quite like this before.

"I've given ten years of my life to saving the forest with nothing to show for it. Every tree that's cut down is a reminder of my failure.

"So no, I can't leave. I have no choice but to see this thing through."

• • •

The crackdown was swift and violent.

Tractors crashed through the flimsy barricades, followed by armed police wearing helmets and shields and riot gear.

Birgit, Karen, João, and the members of João's tribe all joined hands, forming a human chain in a futile attempt to stop them.

Their line was broken instantly, and people were scattered everywhere.

Then a nasty game of catch began, with protestors dragged off the bridge, kicking and screaming, sometimes by the hair.

In the ensuing chaos, Birgit got separated from Karen. She looked around for her frantically.

João and his tribe were huddling together in the middle of the bridge. But Karen was not with them.

Then Birgit felt her arms being roughly pulled and pinioned behind her back. Twisting and struggling and kicking in the policeman's grasp, she watched, powerless, as a squadron of police approached the huddle, batons raised, then striking down hard.

• • •

Birgit and the members of João's tribe were taken into custody. But not Karen.

After a sleepless night alone in a cell, Birgit was released, and her confiscated passport returned to her. As persona non grata, she was given twenty-four hours to leave the country.

Of Karen there was still no sign. Nothing. Birgit didn't trust the police, but they claimed they had no idea where she was.

Birgit started to imagine the worst. She blamed herself for not having kept Karen away from danger. Karen was right: She was useless.

• • •

The flight back to Oslo was scheduled for six thirty the following day.

Birgit installed herself at the bar of the hotel Copacabana, a five-star hotel in the center of the city, to wait out the rest of the night. And she drowned her sorrows in glass after glass of white wine.

Suddenly her cell phone buzzed from deep inside her handbag. She pulled it out but didn't recognize the number.

It turned out to be Karen.

"Thank God you're safe! What on earth happened to you? I was worried sick. Are you OK?"

"I'm fine. I was worried about *you*."

"Where are you?"

"Don't be upset. I'm with Ricardo. We are at his beach house in Bahia."

"Ba—Ba—what on earth do you mean?" Birgit babbled in disbelief.

"Well, I changed my mind about Ricardo. He's not such a bad person. He found me on the bridge and saved my life."

"So what are you going to do now?"

"Ricardo has asked me to stay. I think I might. It is very beautiful here. Maybe you're right. Maybe it's time for me to settle down. Or at least, to think things over."

Birgit didn't know whether to laugh or cry.

• • •

A young man sat down next to Birgit at the bar, ordered a vodka, and threw her a come-hither look out of the corner of his eye. In a half-drunken haze, she returned the look. When he offered to buy her another glass of wine, his voice betrayed a distinct Russian accent.

"I miss the north and the snow and skiing," he said. "Do you ski?"

With a forlorn smile, Birgit hiccupped through her tears, "Do I ski? What a question! I'm from Norway. And you, where are you from?"

"From Moscow, my Snegurochka, my snow maiden," he answered flirtatiously. "My name is Arkady. And yours?"

When she had answered, he countered, "Birgit. A nice name. Has anyone ever told you how lovely you are, Birgit?"

Birgit blushed to the roots of her pale hair, disconcerted by his boldness. Arkady looked very young—way too young. He had an odd-looking face and a still odder-looking asymmetrical haircut, long on one side and short on the other. But his thick dark eyebrows and his broad smile were kind of cute, and she liked the way his light blue eyes crinkled up at the corners when he smiled.

"Are you here alone?" Arkady was wasting no time.

Birgit had always been faithful to Gunnar in deed, if not in thought. She had always believed that if she was going to cheat on him then there was no point being married to him anymore. She knew that if she yielded to Arkady's unmistaken overture, there would be no going back. Her head felt light, as if spinning in the air.

With a shrug of her shoulders, she nodded and took his lead. But once both of them had stripped off their clothes, she pushed him away.

"I'm sorry. This is a mistake. I can't."

She pulled on her skirt and silk blouse and went into the bathroom.

She looked hard in the mirror above the sink. When she saw her tired and drained reflection, she had never felt so alone.

She ignored the discreet knock at the door that came and went.

She sat down on the edge of the bathtub, feverishly twisting the wedding ring on her finger, her mind racing. Gunnar was irrelevant. Her entire former life was irrelevant. How could she go back to Norway?

The vision of millions of trees going up in smoke overcame her. Suddenly the way forward became as clear as the water of a mountain stream back home.

Chapter 8

ARKADY ANTONOV

Dubai, UAE and Havana, Cuba, January–July 2008

"The essence of globalization is a subordination of human rights, of labor rights, consumer rights, environmental rights, democracy rights, to the imperatives of global trade and investment."

—Ralph Nader

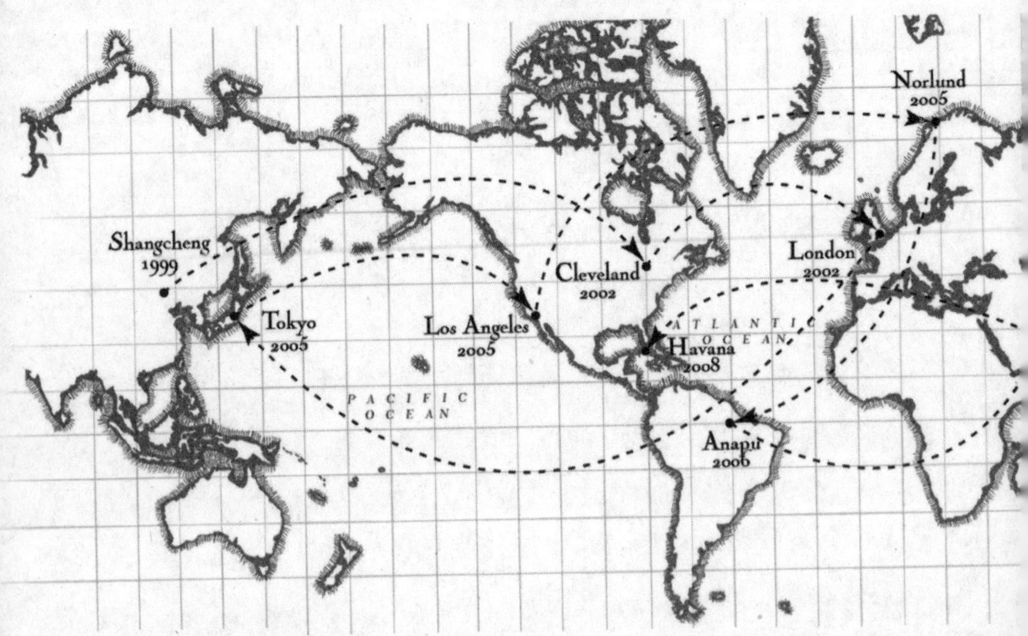

LOOKING OUT THE WINDOW OF his hotel suite, Arkady Antonov rubbed the side of his head where his ear should have been.

Arkady was born with no outer ear, and after three botched and painful attempts at reconstruction—when they came into money, his mother had dragged him to the best plastic surgeons in Moscow and St. Petersburg—he had cried out to his parents, "Enough!"

Maybe one day he'd wake up and find his ear miraculously sprouted in its rightful place, or maybe, he'd unexpectedly discover his missing organ at breakfast time, just as the barber in Gogol's story found Collegiate Assessor Kovalev's nose in a bread roll. Pristine, perfectly formed, ready to be sewn on.

The window gave on to a dark sea under the somber, moonless sky of Dubai, the new playground for the Russian rich.

He was in the foulest of moods. Forced by his father, he had come to Dubai to attend Oleg's wedding. He despised his older brother, though at this moment he despised his father, who took great satisfaction in bending him to his will, even more.

He was also exhausted, after enduring the unending wedding breakfast, lunch, and dinner in the company of his family and guests earlier in the day. The prospect of now having to attend the evening party weighed heavily on him. Reluctantly he got dressed, pulling on a pair of black jeans and a black T-shirt, calculated to annoy at this black-tie event. His movements were listless and slow, like those of an old man, though he was only twenty-four.

Should he skip the party? No. His father finally had him exactly where he wanted him, making noises about cutting off his allowance if he didn't start working for the family company.

Damn his father.

I own you. His father's deep, raspy voice burned in his head. He *owned* him? Then he was no better than a slave.

• • •

Arkady exited the private elevator to reach the $25,000-a-night Royal Suite on the twenty-fifth floor of the Burj Al Arab hotel where the party was being held.

"You're late, baby brother," Oleg yelled out as Arkady entered the suite's palatial living room. Though older than Arkady by only two years, he never missed a chance to lord it over him. "We were about to start the party without you."

Arkady didn't answer. With a shrug of his shoulders, he dropped his skinny body into an armchair at the far end of the room. His jaundiced eyes swept the room with contempt past the scantily dressed girls lolling on the furnishings: over the golden columns, pink-striped walls, pink oriental carpets, and fuchsia drapes covering the ceiling, simulating the conical shape of an Arabian tent.

A white-coated butler, one of the small army of staff that serviced the suite, rolled in a trolley laden with caviar and a pre-launch edition of Russo-Baltique vodka. The gold bottle with its diamond-encrusted stopper, a replica of the Russian Imperial Eagle, sparkled under the bright light of the crystal chandelier that hung from the ceiling.

"A million dollars a bottle," announced Arkady's father, known to all present as Vasili Mikhailovich Antonov. A lot of money, even by his standards, for a bottle of vodka. Only more reason to make sure his guests did not forget the price tag.

Arkady dashed up and grabbed a shot glass of the Russo-Baltique. He took one sip of the vodka and raised his glass. "What is this shit? Don't you have anything better to drink around here?" he said loudly.

His father threw him a killer look from across the room before returning to a heated debate with his guests over whether Roman Abramovich's Chelsea Football Club could win the Premier League title again without its legendary manager José Mourinho.

Before they could settle the question, the door opened once more. A man in a black suit walked respectfully up to Vasili and, bending forward, whispered in his ear. Twinkling with pleasure, Vasili could barely conceal his excitement as he stood up and announced to the company, "My friends. I have splendid news. A few moments ago, the price of oil hit a new record of one hundred dollars a barrel. It is the dawn of a new era!"

The announcement was greeted with enthusiastic clapping.

Arkady didn't clap. He looked askance at Vasili, wondering, not for the first time in his life, if there was anything deeper behind the vain, self-important man whom he called his father. But all he could see was the shrunken soul of a former minor government functionary who, through cunning and dubious means, had gotten hold of a lot of oil assets at a fraction of their value following the dissolution of the Soviet Union. Under Putin, he cultivated close ties with the Kremlin that further rewarded him with preferential market access and lucrative government contracts.

"One hundred dollars a barrel on the day of your son's wedding! What a gift. God is smiling on you, Vasili," gushed Nikolai Balashov, who was married to Vasili's sister. "An excellent omen. Let's toast to it!"

Everyone in the room touched glasses and tossed back a shot of vodka. Except for Arkady, who called out, "Bravo, father! Now you'll be able to drink this shit vodka for breakfast every day!"

This time, Vasili did not overlook his son's impertinence. "Arkasha, you talk too much. Nobody cares what you think," he said before turning to Nikolai, the owner of a large gold mine in Siberia.

He said to him, "You aren't doing too badly yourself, Nikolai. I believe gold also reached a new high today."

"You are too kind. Indeed, it did—thanks to you, I might add. Rising oil price is driving inflation up, up, up," poking toward the ceiling with his thumb. Nikolai smile. "And everyone knows that in times of inflation gold is where you hide." Nikolai had had many occasions to smile lately, and when he did, his tiny eyes almost disappeared under the fatty layers of his cheekbones and eyelids.

"Some are calling this an oil crisis," said Maxim Petrukhin, Vasili's old high school classmate and, after today, Oleg's new father-in-law. As the owner of several oil refineries and a chain of gas stations, rising oil prices were hurting his profit margins. "And I hear it's only a question of time before the Americans will be forced to release their strategic reserves."

"It would make no difference," Vasili snorted. "Let me tell you, Maxim, unleashing reserves may buy the Americans a few weeks or months, but nothing more. Nothing, I tell you. There's just not enough oil in the world to go around," he said, almost breathlessly.

"Did you know," Vasili continued, turning to all the guests, "that though only three percent of people in China own a car, they already consume ten percent of the world's oil? So how much oil do you think they'll need once thirty percent of them own cars? Do the math yourselves…."

"Vasili Mikhailovich, this can only mean that you'll be an even richer man than you are now," Nikolai interrupted ingratiatingly. "When that happens, I hope you won't forget who your friends are."

Vasili briefly brought his lips to the heavy gold-and-emerald signet ring he wore on the small finger of his left hand.

Arkady swung his feet up onto the delicately gilded French Empire desk opposite his chair with a deliberate thump. Everyone knew that his uncle was trying to get his father to finance the takeover of a rival gold mine. To hell with all the toadies that hung around his father all the time. *Let them rot*, he growled to himself.

Including his brother. Arkady could see he was just dying to strut his stuff before the company.

"Oleg," Vasili called out, providing his eldest, who had a degree in economics from the London School of Economics, with the coveted opening. "Any insight you want to share with our guests?"

"The American Federal Reserve is cutting interest rates again," Oleg replied with self-assurance. "The dollar is falling, and this will push oil prices even higher. What's more, the Americans can't lean on the Saudis to increase production like they used to in the past. Oil is going to two hundred a barrel, and there's nothing the Americans can do about it."

Vasili beamed proudly at his firstborn.

Arkady crossed and re-crossed his legs, barely able to contain the allergic reaction he always had to his brother's presence. He just couldn't stand him. It didn't help that Oleg, the frontrunner to take over the business one day, was tall and blond, with a commanding, high-bridged nose just like their father's, whereas he, Arkady, took after his small, dark-haired, and bookish mother.

Under the sun of his father's approval, Oleg went on, "The reality is that our planet simply does not have the resources for one-point-two billion Chinese to live like Americans. Not to mention one billion Indians."

"You're quite right about that," Vasili concurred. "Why else are the Chinese scooping up resources wherever they can find them—from Canadian oil sand to copper mines in Zambia? And now, I hear, they're looking for oil in Cuba!"

Who would have thought there might be oil in Cuba? Low whispers of surprise made the rounds among the guests.

"Human history has taught us that scarcity of resources is a recipe for war," Oleg picked up again, once the whispers had died down. "With oil reserves at an all-time low, it seems conditions are ripe for conflict."

"Yes, and a war between America and China would be very good for Russia and great for our business," Vasili remarked, in all seriousness. "We will become the kingmakers in the world."

Everyone nodded in agreement. China's rise had revived Russia's resource-based economy. Russia's time had come.

"Wishing for a war, are you now, father?" Arkady butted in. "Fifty million corpses in the last century weren't enough for you?"

"Shut up, Arkady. Don't talk about things you don't understand," Vasili thundered.

Maxim, mindful of the potentially disastrous effect of $200 oil on himself, was angling for a way out. "What if the Americans can't cope with falling house prices and rising oil simultaneously? If the American economy tanks, surely it could bring the rest of the world down with it, including oil prices!"

"I don't think you should be overly concerned, Maxim Ivanovich," said Oleg, addressing his father-in-law by his patronym. This sign of respect did not stem merely from an excess of politeness. Maxim's net worth exceeded even that of his father, and he had just presented the newlyweds with a £10 million house in London as a wedding present.

"The US is now only twenty percent of the world economy." Pressing his point, Oleg continued, "It can no longer hold the rest of the world hostage. China, India, and Brazil are the future. No, they are already the present. Their strength will more than offset any US weakness."

"Blow it all up! Blow it all up!" Arkady suddenly blurted out tipsily at the top of his voice. "Money, money, money, money. All we ever talk about is money."

"What else is there to talk about, Arkady?" Nikolai intervened soothingly, vodka glass in hand. "Money is the driver of all things, the source of all inspiration."

"Oh, my dear uncle, I beg to differ," Arkady drawled. He got up and dragged himself over to the large leopard-print divan. "There are plenty of things in life that money can't buy."

Like good taste, he thought as his eyes wandered over the ostentatious decor of the suite, as gaudy as the shiny silk shirt his uncle was wearing. He went on, "But I don't expect you, of all people, to understand."

"Please, do enlighten us," Nikolai replied affably, his good humor unruffled by Arkady's rudeness. "Give me an example of something money cannot buy in this world."

"'Cause I don't care too much for money, and money can't buy me love. Can't buy me lo-ove," Arkady crooned in English.

Vasili broke out in a huge guffaw. "What a clown you are, Arkady!" Oleg looked greatly amused, and the rest of the company broke out in raucous laughter. Even the scantily dressed gaggle of girls twittered with merriment.

"Love, Arkasha? What do *you* know about love?" Vasili inquired. "When did you ever find love without paying for it?" Vasili knew very well that Arkady had not much luck with women.

Arkady's face grew dark.

"So, Don Juan, why don't you regale us with your romantic exploits," said Oleg, piling it on.

It was one jab too far. As lithe as a lynx, Arkady shot off the divan and tackled his brother, grabbing him by the neck and wrestling him to the floor. Arkady was smaller and lighter, but Oleg was no match for his quick fury. It took some doing to pry them apart.

"You little Bakunin, you little anarchist! You're a fucking animal!" Oleg cried out, breathing heavily. "I should rip off your good ear, you prick, you worthless runt! What woman would want you then, money or no money?"

Arkady stood panting heavily for a moment, and then sat down again, a savage expression on his face. He could see the mocking scorn directed at him by everyone in the room. He twisted his lips in a wry smile. "Who among you is prepared to wager that I can find true love?"

There was a surprised silence in the room, interrupted only by the slamming of a door. Oleg had walked out.

"Come on, now," said Arkady with a swagger, goading his audience. "Are you afraid of losing the bet?"

"OK, Arkady. Let's put an end to this," Vasili interjected impatiently. "I'm prepared to give you five million dollars if you can find a woman who would be willing to marry you because she loves you. You and your twisted mind and your one-eared head. Not because of your money, which is *my* money."

Vasili slapped his thighs and got up, signaling that the party was over. "If you lose the bet, you will be working for me forever."

• • •

The aquarium offered a perfect hiding place from his family. Inside the glass tunnel beneath the giant tank, only a sheet of invisible acrylic separated him from the teeming marine life that drifted above. It was like walking on the floor of the sea, in a wonderland of suspended water in the desert.

As he emerged from the tunnel, he found himself in the towering atrium hall of the Dubai Mall, one of the largest shopping emporia in the world. Hermès, Lanvin, Chanel, Louis Vuitton, Armani, Ralph Lauren, Nike, Zara, and Mango. More than 1,200 boutiques and stores, their doors open wide, waiting to be fed. *Like the fish*, thought Arkady. Forty million shoppers a year devoured by one shop after another, imprisoned in their own aquarium, mindlessly mesmerized by the vulgar globalized glitter.

As he elbowed his way through the crowds of shoppers, Arkady's cell phone buzzed in his pocket. It was his father's secretary. He switched off the phone.

He sat down in a café, thinking darkly of his father's million-dollar vodka. The human appetite was insatiable; consumer culture had turned people into mindless and soulless maggots of greed.

He was suddenly overcome by such disgust that he thought if he could push a button right there and then and everything around him—the shops, the shoppers, the fish tank—would all explode, he wouldn't hesitate for a second. Bakunin was right. True liberty could be achieved only through anarchy—with the total abolition of the state and the rejection of all authority.

Arkady had flirted with anarchist ideas at university, but his enthusiasm never translated into action—beyond a few sporadic contributions to websites critical of Putin before they were shut down. With a strong fatalistic streak and a generous monthly allowance from his parents, he drifted through an aimless existence after university and nourished his anger. Anger at the world, anger at his father for his ill-gotten wealth, and, most of all, anger at himself for his inaction. And to drown that anger, he would drink himself into a stupor, often entangling himself in bar brawls.

If Arkady didn't exactly know what he was, or what he wanted, he was quite sure of what he rejected.

I own you now. Arkady winced at the recollection of his father's words. He and his father didn't inhabit the same universe, and the idea of having to work for him was enough to drive him insane.

There was only one way out. What if he were to find true love and win the bet? With $5 million he would be able to redeem his freedom.

The mall was a microcosm of the world. Parading in front of him were women of all colors, nationalities, shapes, and ages: tall, short, fat, slim, in saris and burkas and mini-skirts and shorts and jeans.

But were any of them capable of true love?

Arkady slumped into his chair. How would he ever find true love in such shallow waters? Did he even believe in "true love"? He had never been in a committed relationship. Would he even recognize love if it hit him in the face?

Where, in heaven's name, should he even begin his search for real love? Surely not in Moscow, London, or Paris—the big cities that were the source of the disease. No, it had to be a lost Shangri-la, uncorrupted and untouched by the forces of globalization, where people were more innocent and had meaning in their lives. But the odds that such a place did exist were as slim as his odds of winning the wager. The words *I own you now* still stung.

• • •

A day after the family's return to Moscow, it was with a heavy heart that Arkady started on his new, as yet undefined job. But hardly had he stepped through the big glass doors into the foyer of his father's company headquarters, recently relocated to the hyper-modern financial district, when he got a text message. He was wanted at an important, last-minute meeting. It was, in fact, just about to begin.

All the senior associates of the company were already in attendance, gathered around a long table in a conference room gleaming with stainless steel and polished mahogany. Arkady came in and inserted himself sloppily into one of the black-leather-and-chrome chairs at the far end with a look of studied indifference on his face.

With a nod from Vasili, the head of business development, a lean man with silver hair and a pointy chin, rose to his feet, and, with a quick bow to Vasili, began his presentation.

"We have learned from our sources that a confidential study commissioned by the Cuban government reveals that their offshore oil reserves may be as much as twenty billion barrels. If true, this would put Cuba in the top twenty reserves in the world.

"Our sources also believe that the Cuban government will soon go public with this information, setting off a race among oil companies, especially Chinese companies, to compete for drilling rights. If we move quickly, we could get to the front of what is likely to be a very long line."

Vasili waited for the presenter to sit down before taking command of the proceedings. "I hope everyone grasps the implications of this," he proclaimed, gravely looking at each one present, tugging at his pockmarked cheeks. "We have a great opportunity here. If we get it right, we can make billions. This is ours to take. After all the money we've poured into that shitty little island, it's us Russians who deserve the first pickings."

So, Cuba was next in the firing line. If Arkady's father succeeded, if Cuba indeed had oil, it would be transformed into a Dubai of the Caribbean, covered with faceless glass towers, he thought in disgust.

No one voiced any disagreement.

Vasili continued, "I want Oleg to lead this project when he returns from his honeymoon, but we need to send a team right away to start engaging with the Cuban government. Any volunteers?"

A couple of people raised their hands.

"Good. Very good. Arkady, are you with us? I want you to go along with them."

"Me? How can I be of use in Cuba?" Arkady sputtered in surprise.

"There is only one way to learn, Arkady, and that is on the job. Keep your eyes and ears open. And do what you're told."

"But, father..." Arkady protested. *Cuba? What a pain*, he thought.

Vasili put up his hand. "It has been decided, Arkady. And I expect you to keep your mouth shut and your lips away from the bottle."

Arkady folded his arms across his chest. *Cuba*, he fumed.

But suddenly his heart beat a little faster. Wasn't Cuba just the place he was looking for? Poor. Isolated. Untouched by globalization. And if

Cuba was at all like the pre-perestroika Russia of his childhood, maybe, just maybe, the very place where he could find true love. Find a girl who would love him for who he was and not for what he was worth. *Warts and all*, he thought, wriggling the misshapen lobe of flesh of his ear under the curtain of hair that he wore long to hide it.

Cuba! Why hadn't he thought about it before? His father, unwittingly, had given him a gift. His excitement mounted: Now Arkady had a real crack at turning the tables on him and winning that damned wager.

• • •

Now that his heart was set on traveling to Cuba, Arkady couldn't leave Moscow fast enough, and he made his preparations with atypical efficiency and gusto. A friend of a friend put him in touch with Miguel, a retired Russian-speaking physician in Havana: a combination facilitator, guide, and translator and, most importantly for Arkady, a matchmaker. He booked him for a month, and within a couple of days, all was ready for his departure.

By the time Arkady arrived in Havana, Miguel had arranged everything for him, including a place to stay. Since by government law hotels were off-limits to Cuban women, Miguel had found him a house in Nuevo Vedado, in what used to be an upscale neighborhood for the Cuban rich before it was taken over by Castro military elites after the revolution. It was owned by a former minister who rented it out to tourists to finance his retirement.

Miguel was polite and self-effacing, with an obliging smile always ready to emerge from behind a huge, droopy mustache. Arkady had hardly finished unpacking when Miguel whipped out a catalog full of photographs of semi-nude women—white women, Black women, blondes, brunettes, and every color in between—that he kept in his briefcase. But he had misunderstood Arkady's requirements for matchmaking.

"No, no, no. Not interested," said Arkady angrily.

Miguel, the old fox, understood the implication straight away. It was more than sex that Arkady was after. "Cuban women are crazy about Russian men. They think they are all either cosmonauts or concert pianists!"

Somewhat encouraged by that thought, Arkady dispensed with Miguel's services for the rest of the day and set out to explore Old Havana on his own.

• • •

The weather was glorious, and Havana was more beautiful than Arkady imagined. In the distance, along the avenue of Paseo de Marti, the sea shimmered with blues and golds in the setting sun of the late afternoon. Arkady walked along the wide, tree-lined nineteenth-century boulevards and shady piazzas. In the sunlight his blue eyes shone like pale lamps under his dark and heavy brows.

Bathed in pastel hues, the stately Baroque and neoclassical buildings fronting the avenues, richly detailed and ornate, looked magical.

But the city was also magnificently decrepit, its crumbling façades ravaged and defaced by the salt air, by hurricane-force winds, and by decades of disrepair and neglect. Arkady caught glimpses of yawning, empty spaces behind peeling paint and crumbling stucco. Balconies, doors, iron gratings, and window shutters had fallen off in their entirety or were hanging on for dear life at drunken angles.

Yet, in this tragic place, where people had reached the brink of starvation after the collapse of the Soviet Union, where people lived on the edge of existence, queuing for hours to exchange vouchers for meager rations of coffee, toothpaste, and beans, people did not look unhappy. Perhaps here, where there were hardly any stores and there was nothing to buy, was the evidence that you didn't need to shop to be content, thought Arkady.

Small bands and solo musicians played on almost every street corner and in every bar and café, and the streets were a kaleidoscope of red and yellow jeans, of gay fuchsia and purple and blue T-shirts. It was as if the ubiquitous music and the bright hues were a proxy for wealth, a colorful and lyrical solace for the all-encompassing poverty and deprivation.

Ambling about in his oldest, shabbiest clothes and the cheap flip-flops he had found in his shower, Arkady felt that that he blended right in with this lopsided city. Did it matter if he had a stump for an ear and his smile was asymmetrical? Everything and everybody looked scarred in some way, yet people were warm and friendly. They even smiled at him in the street. Spontaneous smiles from strangers were unfamiliar to him but he reciprocated readily. He even felt an unusual exuberance. Perhaps here was a place where he wouldn't be judged, where he would be taken for who he truly was.

Or so he deluded himself, as he rambled through this lost city disconnected from the outside world, a self-styled down-and-outer, walking loose-limbed and carefree for the first time in his adult life.

• • •

That night Arkady dreamt of Havana, of the city of destroyed memory, where the future has no place.

Music caresses his missing ear and wafts through the streets and boulevards and esplanades, in a rhythmic, plaintive salsa, never stopping, like a heartbeat, and Havana, the lady by the sea, answers with a seductive movement of her hips. A beautiful, nubile girl with honey-colored skin and enormous black eyes smiles timidly at him, and then slowly receding, waving her hand, her tight pants fade away until they become a yellow dot on an orange horizon. Moments later, black clouds appear from nowhere, and it begins to rain, the rain falling down in torrents. Arkady finds himself in a room with a partially caved-in ceiling. The wind blows in with increasingly strong, wild gusts, and the floor floods with water. Cracks appear on the façade of the brick wall and, the cracks slowly spreading, bits of wall crumble and bricks begin to fall out. Suddenly, the entire façade collapses, crashing onto the street eight floors below. High up, Arkady is unafraid. He teeters for a moment at the edge of the abyss, and then jumps into the void.

In the morning, Arkady remembered nothing of his dream. But he felt strangely happy, as if a door had opened and he was free to reinvent himself as he wished. He went to a barbershop and had his hair shorn off. So what if the miserable stump that was his ear was exposed? He would wear it as a badge of his new self. He liked his new look. He looked tough. And cool.

• • •

For the first week, Arkady spent the days at meetings with the company team and the evenings in search of his true love. Guided by Miguel, he poked his nose into every bar, club, and discotheque in town.

Their hunt began in central Havana, but it soon fanned out to the suburbs, to university campuses, and even to Miramar, the most affluent area of the city.

Girls, girls, women, women. Cuban women were hot, with smooth mocha skin and bodies as curvaceous as violins. They were everywhere, prowling the streets with bare midriffs, skin-tight jeans or micro miniskirts, teetering on their cheap platform shoes, provocatively batting their eyelids at him, or smiling, slowly licking their lips or blowing kisses. By night they hissed from among the shadows like hungry cats or swung their hips invitingly along the dark alleyways outside the bars they were forbidden to enter.

Though sex seemed to be permanently in the air, Arkady had no luck. He found no woman whose company he imagined he could bear beyond a few hours, let alone fall in love with. As soon as he got beyond the flirtation stage, they started on their sob stories, angling for cash to buy a pair of shoes, or a square meal for an elderly aunt, or in one case, textbooks.

And then came the unfortunate incident with the very pretty dark-skinned student. He had approached her on the Malecón after sunset. She spoke Russian! He believed his luck was turning at last. They hit it off immediately, and taking her back to his rental home, they had a great time. But in the morning, she was gone. And $500 was missing from his wallet.

He was forced to face up to an unpalatable truth. Poverty, he concluded in frustration, apparently focuses the mind on money just as sharply as riches.

• • •

Arkady was close to giving up. The endless meetings with Cuban officials he had to attend, without being allowed to say a word, bored him to distraction. The unproductive nights—and weekends, too—reduced him to despair. He would never win his wager.

By nightfall he was lurching unsteadily through the badly lit streets of downtown Havana. Midnight found him staggering into a bar packed with tourists. A small band was playing in the corner, and one member of the band, his arm around a foreign girl's shoulders, was teaching her the steps of Cuban salsa.

After shot after shot after shot of rum, Arkady was restless, itching for action, his brain on fire. He made a pest of himself as he rambled on incoherently, his arms flapping as he weaved in and out among the dancers. Then abruptly he sank to his knees in front of a plump brunette sitting at a table.

"Marry me!" he cried.

"Got a ring, buddy?" someone taunted him loudly. All the patrons, including the bartender, burst out laughing.

The brunette smiled indulgently, but her companion, a tough-looking guy, failed to appreciate the humor. "Get the fuck out of here! You're not as funny as you think," he growled.

"Where're your manners? I'm addressing my lady love here," Arkady replied, and he gaped at the brunette with his aquamarine eyes and inquired, in a funny tender singsong, "My lady, are you capable of true love?"

The woman giggled and smiled.

Arkady grabbed her palm resting on the table.

"Keep your paws off her!" her companion yelled, swatting his hand away.

Arkady scrambled to his feet. "You don't deserve her," he glowered and punched him in the gut.

Enraged, the man grabbed an empty beer bottle and smashed it on Arkady's head. Arkady lost his footing and fell. On the way down he grabbed wildly at the tablecloth and as he hit the terrazzo floor, accompanied by the crashing sounds of breaking crockery, all he could remember was the man's shoe crashing into his face before he passed out.

• • •

How long had he lain here? Arkady woke up, soaked in sweat. As he slowly and painfully regained his awareness, he realized he was on a stretcher in the middle of a row of patients in what could only be the ER of a hospital.

Foul odors of blood, vomit, and excrement suffocated him like a miasmic cloud, and a battery of screams and moans and sobbing sounds pounded on his eardrums. He struggled to get up. After several attempts he collapsed back on the stretcher.

Nothing had been given to him to alleviate the pain. He squinted at the clock on the peeling wall opposite. Its hands weren't moving. He raised his left arm, but his wristwatch was smashed.

Tentatively he began to examine himself. His nose was sore, but it wasn't broken. But he could hardly open his left eye. There was an open gash on the top of his head that was still bleeding, and another on his forehead. And he couldn't bend the fingers of his right hand. Most of all, he was unbearably thirsty.

With his one good eye he looked around him. Surely, he must still be in Havana, but in place of bright, sunny colors, all around him were ashen greys and dirty whites and muddy browns. The terrazzo floor on which the stretcher had been placed was cracked, and the neon tube lighting was covered with flies. There were exposed wires and rusty pipes everywhere.

So was this the vaunted Cuban public health service?

A whiff of a clean, antiseptic scent, mixed with the heavenly fragrance of wildflowers, caused him to turn his head painfully. An angel in a white uniform—the pure, unstained white a balm to his senses—was kneeling at his side. She couldn't have been more than twenty with full, soft lips and tender, and large, melting brown eyes that looked out at him from under eyebrows that described perfect arches.

"*Como estas*?" she said.

He stared, bewitched, first at the dimple in her cheek, then at the tiny mole at the corner of her mouth that moved slightly as she spoke.

She said something more he couldn't understand.

"*Nada español*," he answered helplessly.

"*No hay problema*," she said soothingly, shushing him with a slender finger on his lips. Her touch was as soft as the wing of a butterfly. Quietly, singing a melody Arkady had never heard before, she lifted his head gently to give him some water through a straw. She washed off the dried blood from his face and hands and upper body. Arkady couldn't keep his one eye off of her. His misery evaporated. All alone in this inhospitable hospital, he felt as if he had reached a safe harbor, that all would be well in this lovely girl's soft, merciful hands.

• • •

"You really mustn't get into fights," Miguel admonished him when he picked up Arkady the next day. He had developed a real fondness for his employer.

As he exited the hospital, his head bandaged and leaning on Miguel's arm, Arkady said nothing as he focused on the ground right in front of him. He hadn't seen the adorable face of the nurse again. But she was present in his mind's eye.

Had she been a hallucination? Not impossible, considering the beaten-up condition he had been in, and the amount of alcohol coursing through his veins. But no, it couldn't have been a hallucination. The tune she had sung to him played over and over in his mind. He knew it so well he could have hummed it out loud: That had to be proof that she was real.

Once he got home, Arkady sent Miguel off on a mission. “Find that girl, Miguel! I have to see her again,” he begged after he told him the story of their encounter. And the ever-compliant Miguel obliged.

Miguel returned with a report that very evening. It was encouraging. He found out that the girl, whose name was Yunaisy, was a nursing school student. She was now in Baracoa visiting her parents and would be back in Havana in a week.

“Baracoa? Where’s that?” asked Arkady.

“On the eastern tip of the island. Where Columbus landed on his first voyage.”

Yunaisy. Yunaisy, Arkady repeated to himself, his imagination now absorbed by the poetic syllables of her name. He tried to tell himself that he was being naïve, dreaming about a girl he didn’t know. But he couldn’t get her soft eyes, the cute mole at the side of her mouth that showed up to such advantage her creamy, coffee-colored skin, out of his mind.

Miguel had even better news. He had pulled a favor from a member of the hospital staff and found out the name of the street where Yunaisy’s parents lived. Arkady was delighted. He flung his arms around Miguel, kissed him on both cheeks, and then danced around the room.

“Take me to Baracoa,” he said, flushed with excitement and anticipation.

• • •

Baracoa, the oldest town in Cuba, was surrounded by green mountains and faced a blue bay with yellow beaches. Small and picturesque, its narrow streets were full of rickety houses with red-tile roofs and peeling but colorful walls.

A taxi drove them straight from the airport to the outside of town and, a few minutes later, they were inching down a narrow alley barely wide enough for their car.

As they approached Yunaisy’s parents’ house, Arkady’s heart was pumping overtime, pounding against the walls of his chest. *I’m an idiot*, he told himself. He just couldn’t fully fathom what he was doing.

And then suddenly, standing in the middle of the potholed road ahead of them—there she was. Smaller, in a pale-blue cotton dress with a ruffled hem, and even more delicately built than he remembered from the hospital.

Arkady tore out of the taxi, and stopped short, tongue-tied, before her.

Yunaisy gave him an astonished stare, and with a little cry covered her mouth with her hand. "What are you doing here?" she managed to half whisper in Spanish.

Arkady didn't need any translation to understand the question. He had been preparing for this moment for days. But his ready-made answer eluded him now. She was even lovelier than he remembered. A warm glow of happy certainty washed over him.

His gut feeling had not betrayed him. This girl was a miracle—and he had not been mistaken in seeking her out.

No one in the household knew English beyond a few broken words, and Arkady had never needed Miguel's translation services more than in the following hours. They were all crowded uncomfortably in the sitting room of the family's home: Arkady, Miguel, Yunaisy, her mother, her father, and her two siblings. The room was so tiny—not really bigger than his bathroom back in Moscow—that Arkady had to climb over the back of the single sofa to sit down.

"Your daughter cared for this young man at the hospital in Havana," said Miguel, pointing to Arkady's still-bandaged eye. "He came here to thank her personally," he continued, addressing Yunaisy's father.

It was a very lame excuse, but no one seemed to mind. Slowly, bits of information about the people in the room dribbled back in translation to Arkady. Yunaisy's father was a fisherman. Her mother an elementary school teacher. Yunaisy would be turning twenty in three months. She was a good girl. She did well at school and helped out in the house. Most of all, Arkady learned, she liked to sing. She could have become a professional singer, but the family thought nursing was a safer and more stable career.

Through it all, Yunaisy sat very still, staring down at the floor, her face flushed pink under her olive skin, though she did throw Arkady furtive, darting glances from time to time. Arkady, too, was quiet, trying hard not to keep his eyes glued permanently on the cute little mole at the side of her mouth, or on the dimple that appeared the moment even the most hesitant smile began to break on her face. She looked so young, unspoiled and innocent in her pale-blue dress, the sheen of downy hair on her temples so delicate. And how glossy was her rich, dark chestnut hair, pulled back in a braided pigtail.

A tray with glasses of papaya juice was passed around. It was Arkady's turn to speak through Miguel, who presented Arkady as an ordinary tourist and a university student from Russia.

Later, that evening, Arkady invited Yunaisy and her family to dinner at the seaside. On a wooden deck outside they ate fish fresh from a recent catch. After the meal, they watched the sun set behind the mountains as it painted the sea a soft orange and pink. *What more could one want from life?* Arkady asked himself, breathing in the peaceful air and basking in the warmth of the dying sunrays and the glow of Yunaisy's proximity.

Arkady and Miguel ended up staying the night in Baracoa with a friend of the family. Not that Arkady was going to get much sleep: When he found out that Yunaisy and her father were to go out fishing that night, he immediately decided to join them.

• • •

In the ancient rowboat rocking on the river, Yunaisy, her father, and Arkady were on the lookout for *teti* fish, scanning the dark water. Arkady had no idea what he was looking for. It all felt uncanny: the silence, the moonlight, the soft lapping of the river, the sour smell of salt wafting in from the sea, the impenetrable black patches of jungle-like growth on the riverbanks, the eerie circles of light from the handmade torch that Yunaisy, watching and waiting, kept swinging back and forth over the side of the boat.

She was so close, crouching down right beside him. He could feel himself burning up from the animal warmth of her body. She shifted her weight ever so slightly from one bent leg to another and turned her head shyly in his direction. He needed no words to know what she meant by those almost undetectable movements. The certainty of their mutual attraction was absolute, as if shouted out in all the languages of the world, and it took all of Arkady's willpower to resist pulling her up at that very instant and crushing her body against his.

Her eyes back on the water, Yunaisy suddenly began to sing. Low-pitched at first, then in clear, plaintive tones.

He recognized the lilting melody at once; it was the same one she had hummed to him at the hospital. Incandescent, incomprehensible lyrics echoed through the air and across the river like a siren call. Unlike Ulysses, he made no effort to resist it.

Nor, evidently, did the tiny translucent *teti* fish that appeared out of nowhere in their thousands as if bidden by her singing. They moved along the sides of the boat in long, snaking eddies of shimmering silver, just under the surface of the water. Lit up by the moonlight and their torches, they seemed to mirror the currents that electrified Arkady's heart.

Whatever it was—the mythical dimension of the moment or the place—he fell hopelessly in love with the moon, the girl, and Cuba.

Chatting excitedly, Yunaisy and her father began scooping up the fish by the bucketload. Soon they returned to the sandbank to offload their cargo on the beach. Over two hours, they completed half a dozen short trips. Arkady chipped in, too, working in eager collaboration beside Yunaisy and her father. It was hard work, and the piles of fish in the dirty pails stank, but he felt good in a way he never had before.

• • •

Back in Havana, a few days later, a naked Arkady, with his marble-white skin, and wiry, strong limbs, was all over Yunaisy, his hands following the curves of the soft, yielding plumpness of her belly, breasts, and thighs. The experience was like none other he had had before. With a great shudder, he felt his entire body melting into hers.

They were in the bedroom of his rented house. It was getting dark, and he switched on the light.

"Arkady?" Yunaisy whispered, hesitating with the pronunciation of his name as she stroked his misshapen ear and shaved head.

"*Arkasha*," he corrected her, smiling.

"Ar-ka-sha," she repeated bashfully. The soft enunciation of his nickname called forth the deepest feelings of intimacy and tenderness. When he woke up the following morning, she was still in his arms. He watched her sleep for an entire hour. He was afraid to budge lest he wake her; she looked so peaceful in her sleep. All he wanted, all he would ever want, was to protect her and make her happy: He was in love.

• • •

So many new emotions!

Arkady began to skip meetings with his father's team. After a week, he stopped going to them altogether. What was the point? He didn't give a damn about oil and had no interest in making his father even richer. He had found what he came for.

His undernourished heart brimmed with fulfillment and happiness.

Now that he had time on his hands, he daydreamed about a future that couldn't possibly be brighter, about the possibility of a new and simple way of life that would resolve his inner contradictions.

Could he really live in Cuba? *Why not?* he thought. It's not as if he would miss his family very much. Cuba had not only given him Yunaisy, but Cuba was, as far as he could see, the model of the society that he had been searching for all his life. People here were poor, but children didn't quit school at the age of ten to pick bananas or to work in sweatshops. The twenty-six universities were open to all. And free.

In the short time he had been here, he had already met three poets! And there was equal access to basic—albeit very basic—food, and to healthcare. Equality, justice, and literacy—all of which bestowed dignity on the people.

Watching kids kicking around a football in the street one afternoon, he made a vow to dedicate his life to the place where he could actually make a mark, where he could finally move on from playing revolutionary and nihilist to the real thing and fulfill his yearnings for action against neo-liberalism and globalism.

With his prize money, he and Yunaisy would not only live out the rest of their lives in relative comfort but also have plenty to spare. He would set up an accessible internet café or fund a clinic (which Yunaisy would run). Or help promote what he saw as the viability of the Cuban model to the world outside.

Decidedly, the time had come to claim the $5 million that was his by right. He had won the bet, fair and square: He loved Yunaisy, and she loved him.

He marched into the Hotel Habana Libre downtown and he sent a message to his father on the frustratingly slow computer.

He went to the hotel several times to check for a response, until at last the reply came the next day. But it was from his mother.

Moy daragoy: My dear… In a tone that was distant and almost abstract, she congratulated him and told him she was happy for him that he had found someone to marry. Both she and Papa would love to meet the girl, and she wondered how this could be arranged. Oleg was due to arrive in Havana in a few days, and he would bring the best wishes of the family to Arkady and the bride.

And that was it. Not a word about Arkady winning the bet. Not a word about the money owed to him. He stared at the screen in disgust.

Five million dollars, after all, was no more than what his father was willing to pay for five bottles of vodka.

• • •

Back at the house in Nuevo Vedado, Arkady was nervously pacing the living room in circles. "Sit down, Yunaisy," he told her. "I have something important to tell you." He spoke in a mixture of English and broken Spanish.

She obediently curled up on the sofa, her small body coiled tensely against the pillows, and her brown eyes darting around the room like those of a cornered animal. She sensed that something was wrong—that something momentous was about to happen.

She had never believed her life with Arkady could last. Her father had warned her. Her mother had warned her. Arkady seemed decent and kind, they told her, but his infatuation was doomed to be short-lived, for what possible interest could a poor, simple girl like her hold for a worldly, sophisticated man like him? So, the hour in which he would announce he was leaving her had come at last, she thought, working herself up into a state of utter misery and despair.

Arkady sat down next to her and dried the tear that was rolling down her cheek.

"I haven't told you all about myself, Yunaisy."

She braced herself and threw back at his eyes a look of terrified expectation. *He is married!* she thought wildly. He squeezed her hand.

And he began, haltingly, in broken Spanish, and with a Russian-Spanish dictionary on his lap, to reveal that he was the son of an obscenely wealthy man.

Yunaisy didn't say a word. The content of what he said reinforced her conviction that Arkady was on the point of ditching her.

"Are you listening, Yunaisy? I've kept other things hidden from you as well. I have a violent temper, and I used to binge-drink often. My family is awful. Unlike yours. I've been a student forever. And before Cuba, I never had a job."

It all came out—down to his father's million-dollar vodka and the revulsion he had felt at the Dubai Mall and his simmering bitterness. But as for the story of the wager, on that he remained silent: There was no way in hell he would risk anything that might hurt her.

And then he told her that he loved her. That she had changed him, that Cuba had changed him.

Yunaisy sat very still and with each passing sentence from Arkady's lips began breathing more easily. Her features regained the serenity and sweetness that had enchanted Arkady from the start. She flung her arms around him and covered him with kisses. And she seemed to take the news of his family's riches in her stride. "I love you too, Arkasha. I don't care if you are rich or poor. It makes no difference."

• • •

But somehow there was a difference. In the following days, after Arkady informed Yunaisy of Oleg's impending visit, he noticed that Yunaisy kept glancing at herself in the mirror and flitting about the house like a frightened little bird.

"Is it because of my brother? He won't bite, my love. He's just a businessman. What my family thinks doesn't matter."

But Yunaisy wouldn't calm down. The day Oleg was due to arrive, Yunaisy entered the living room looking lovely in a white dress that Arkady had never seen before.

"It looks new. How on earth did you get it?"

Yunaisy shrugged her shoulders and avoided his eyes. "I borrowed it from a nurse in my ward. I want to look beautiful for your brother. We must be hospitable and invite him for dinner. I bought coffee and sugar and some cakes. And enough for a decent meal."

Arkady took her in his arms and kissed her gently. "You're too good for him. He'll probably be jealous of our happiness," he added with a good-humored twinkle in his eye.

Uncharacteristically, Yunaisy pushed him away.

Sitting down on the sofa of the living room, she suddenly asked him, "What is Moscow like?"

"Big. Cold. No beaches. You wouldn't like it." This was the first time she had ever asked about the world outside.

"I'd love to go one day and see Moscow for myself. And Paris and New York. London, too."

Yunaisy's enunciation of these new aspirations troubled Arkady. He felt as if a tiny cloud had appeared in the spotless blue sky of their paradisiacal existence, an existence that he prayed would last forever.

• • •

Oleg walked up the small garden path to where Arkady was waiting on the covered front porch, eager to share his happiness with the world and brimming with goodwill, a huge smile of welcome beaming on his face.

"I see you've changed your hairstyle, baby brother," were Oleg's first words as he slapped Arkady's shoulder. "Makes you look more manly. Less of a wimp." Getting straight to the point, he asked, "Where is this little treasure of yours?"

"Yunaisy will be out in a moment," said Arkady. "Come on in."

If he was nettled by his brother's swagger, Arkady showed no sign of it. Determined to keep the meeting as pleasant as possible, he inquired politely as they entered the living room, "How was your journey?"

"Fine, fine. I arrived yesterday, actually. Wanted to do a bit of preliminary exploring on my own. Recover from jetlag and all that."

"I see," Arkady replied, surprised.

Just then, Yunaisy made her appearance in her white dress. But with one look at Oleg, she gasped in horror. With a short scream, she scurried back into the other room.

Astounded, not knowing whether to follow her or not, Arkady didn't move. He just stood there in the living room, facing his brother.

"I don't understand," he said slowly. "I don't understand," he repeated. "It wasn't shyness." Not by a long shot. Hadn't he detected a look of terror in Yunaisy's eyes?

"Your future wife is just a frightened little rabbit," Oleg replied coolly.

Ignoring the insult, Arkady asked in a hoarse voice, "Have you two met before?"

"No. No. Of course not. Where? How?"

Something was terribly wrong. When Yunaisy didn't reappear, Arkady's eyes narrowed, and he prodded Oleg in the chest with his finger. He knew in his bones that his brother was lying. "Come out with it. She obviously knows you. How else do you explain her reaction at the very sight of you?"

"You know, baby brother, I'd do anything for your sake—" Oleg began, obfuscating.

"Is that so?" Arkady interrupted him angrily. "Stop fucking around with me!"

He knew Oleg was ruthless, capable of anything.

"Easy, baby brother. Papa was worried you were being taken for a ride by some Cuban gold digger. So, we put a tail on the girl. Followed her every move. I knew where to find her the minute I landed."

"You traitor! How could you?" Arkady spat out in venomous fury. Surveillance state, surveillance family—what was the difference? His family could have easily bought off the entire Cuban police force….

"I only have your best interests at heart—"

"Sure you do. Spoken like a true hypocrite—"

"Shut up, Arkady. That girl is no good," Oleg said, trying to stare him down. "I approached her on that big avenue downtown—the name escapes me now—and offered her ten dollars for the night."

"What?" Arkady roared. "You contemptible, conniving piece of shit!"

"Oh, she's a smart one. Refused me again and again."

"Enough! Of course she did! Yunaisy's an angel! She loves me!"

Oleg seemed to revel in torturing his brother. "Eventually I upped the price to a thousand, and what do you know? She willingly spread her legs and let me fuck her brains out. The bitch doesn't deserve your love, little brother."

In the short silence that followed this revelation, Arkady could hardly breathe. He didn't deserve *her* love! A gold digger? *No*! It was the other way round—it was the accursed family gold corrupting everything it touched. But the scream in this throat couldn't escape: It was as if someone had poured a bag of sawdust into his lungs.

Choking with rage, Arkady lashed out at Oleg, butting him with his head, kicking ferociously, and beating him in the face.

As Arkady landed blow after blow after blow, he was hardly aware of the blur of white cloth that crossed his field of vision for a split second. It was Yunaisy, escaping out the front door and slamming it behind her.

Arkady showed no mercy and swung out at him again, and this time his brother fell, his head crashing into a bronze vase standing on the floor.

Panting heavily, Arkady stared down at him. His brother wasn't moving, his face a mash of distorted red flesh. As the fog of his crazed anger gradually cleared, Arkady gazed down in horror at his brother's blond hair. It was matted with blood.

Arkady shook him, and then shook him again. He searched for a pulse.

There was none.

What have I done? he thought. He crouched down, and wept and wailed, as he cradled, keening, Oleg's head in his arms. It was no use. He could not bring him back. His brother was dead.

• • •

A figure standing in the open doorway cast a shadow that jolted Arkady back into the present. It was Miguel, who had come to join them for dinner. As Miguel quietly closed the door, he stared down silently at Oleg's dead body.

Furiously rubbing the side of his head, Arkady looked up at him, swallowing hard, and ranting, "I never meant to kill him, I swear. I never meant to. It was an accident. I never meant to. I was so angry." And spinning, stretching the truth, he wailed, "He raped Yunaisy."

Miguel nodded. He didn't question Arkady, who had told him many stories about his ruthless family.

"Oh, God, Miguel. What on earth am I to do?" Arkady whimpered.

Miguel didn't reply at first. But after a few moments, he seemed to have decided on a course of action.

"We need to get you out of here right away. If you get caught, they'll lock you up for life, even if you're only charged with manslaughter. But first," he said, looking at the body and the blood-spattered floor, "we have to clean up this mess."

But Arkady could not move at the thought of the monstrous horror he had wrought. *I killed my own brother. I corrupted Yunaisy.*

So it was Miguel who rummaged through Oleg's pockets, retrieving his passport and $33,000 in cash. It was Miguel who dragged the body to the bedroom and shoved it into a closet. "It'll buy us some time," he said, grunting from the effort.

Arkady, still standing petrified, useless, watched with dull, frozen eyes as Miguel proceeded to mop the blood from the floor.

A sudden urgent knocking at the door made them both jump. They frowned at each other in apprehension. Miguel went to open the door.

Two men in striped suits were standing at the threshold. They inquired after Oleg. Miguel assured them Oleg would be out in half an hour, and they left.

"They said they're Oleg's business associates!" whispered Miguel when they had gone.

"They're sure to be back," Arkady whispered, sick with fear.

"It's too risky for the airport. The only way is by sea. I'll find a boat to take you across to Florida."

"But what about Yunaisy? I can't just abandon her!"

"For God's sake, what use will you be to her in prison? Come on," he urged. "Quick. Quick. Forget about Yunaisy. Let's go. Right now."

Forget about Yunaisy? In a daze Arkady followed Miguel outside. As in a nightmare, where the dimensions of space and time are distorted, every motion he made felt unreal. But he did reach the fence somehow. Climbing over it, he emerged into a side street, where Miguel was waiting beside his parked car.

• • •

A few hours later they arrived in a small fishing village on the northern coast of Cuba, not far from Havana. The boat they found was not much more than a beat-up handmade craft. Its owner agreed to take Arkady to Florida for $3,000. Miguel counted out the cash from Oleg's money and handed over the rest to Arkady.

"Is there no other way?" Arkady resisted. "What is Florida to me?" Tears welled up in his eyes.

"There's nothing left for you here in Cuba. Come on. Be reasonable. You still have a future."

It was a moonless night, very dark and very quiet, with a brisk wind blowing. They were standing on the small, half-rotten dock.

"Without Yunaisy, I'm lost," said Arkady.

"There will be other loves."

"No. There won't."

He looked forlornly at the boat, and then at Miguel.

"I have no choice, right?" he said, barely audible.

"You don't. I am sorry," said Miguel.

"Then do me one last favor, my friend. Find Yunaisy. Give her this." He counted out $10,000. "Look after her. Tell her—tell her that I am the one who let her down. That she shouldn't blame herself. And, Miguel…"

"Yes?"

"Tell her to be happy."

• • •

Floridana Beach stretches out for miles and miles in a straight line from north to south, and along a tongue of land separated from the mainland by the Indian River. It is a narrow, sandy beach, not more than twenty yards wide, accessed across low-lying sand dunes. The Atlantic Ocean feels very close, almost intimately close, as its waves crash onto the shore.

And it was along this shore near Palm Bay, five days after Arkady boarded the rickety boat in Havana, that Tyler Wilson could be found, with a gun in his jacket pocket, walking in the dead of a dark, cloudy night.

Wandering along the deserted beach, Tyler stumbled upon an object in his path. In the beam of his flashlight, he could see that it was a soggy leather shoe. Then a few dozen yards away, he stumbled upon another shoe.

Tyler pointed his flashlight northwards along the beach. There was definitely something out there, silhouetted against the darker clumps of seaweed and paler sand.

Tyler quickened his pace.

He passed some broken boards. A torn jacket and a shirt. And then—the remains of a boat, its hull ripped apart, lying on its side.

He had heard of boats and dinghies setting out from Cuba to the Keys shipwrecked and washing up on the west coast of Florida. Rarely so far up north, though. Must have been the hurricane from a couple of days back. Such were his thoughts as he looked around for bodies. Sure enough, after a few more yards, he found a man, lying shoeless and shirtless, face up in the sand.

He prodded the body with his foot and then kneeled down beside it.

The man was missing an ear, his skin blistered by the sun, and his open, lifeless eyes reflected the palest whitish blue in the beam of light from his torch.

Chapter 9

TYLER WILSON

Palm Bay and New York City, USA, July–September 2008

"The central base of world political power is right here in America, and it is our corrupt political establishment that is the greatest power behind the efforts at radical globalization and the disenfranchisement of working people."

—DONALD TRUMP

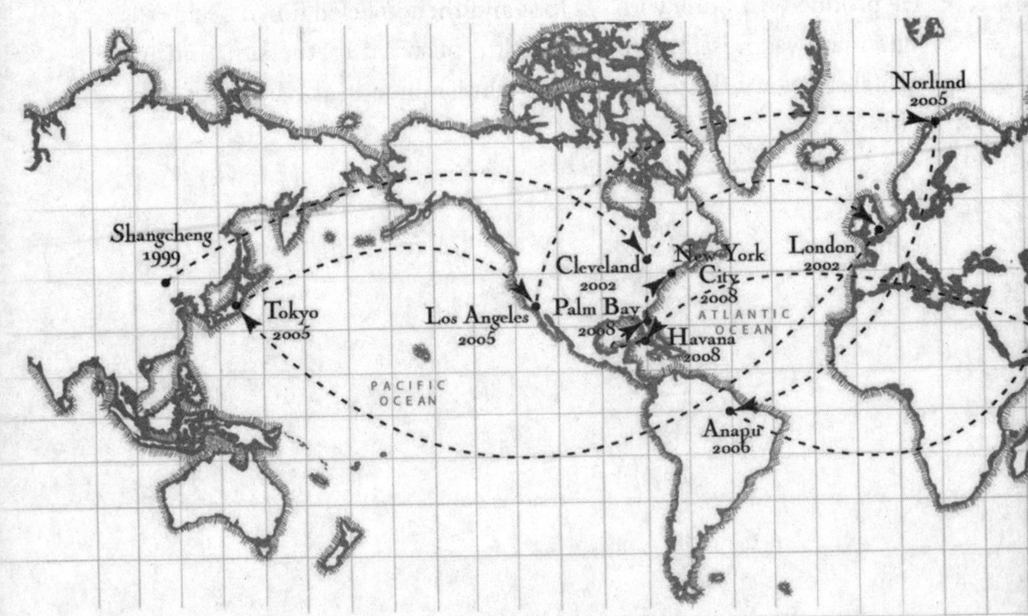

ENGULFED BY THE SOUND OF the crashing surf, Tyler Wilson contemplated the gun weighing heavily in his right hand. He knew it was a sin, but burning in hell could not possibly be worse than what he was feeling right now. He raised the gun to his temple.

Just then the clouds above shifted, and the moon came out of hiding, illuminating with the fullness of its light the dunes and the waves and the surrounding darkness with such a surprising intensity that for a split second, the spectacle of it stayed his hand.

His eyes met the open ones of the dead man he had discovered lying a few feet away that seemed to glint with renewed life from the reflected light of a moonbeam.

Spooked, this graphic reminder of the reality of his future state in the form of that extinguished life gnawed away at his resolve. He lowered his gun. All he could imagine now was the defilement of his own corpse by the prodding shoe and prying hands of whoever would inevitably find him. All he could think of was of the indignity of his own rotting flesh that would result from his pulling the trigger.

Tyler howled at the wild and indifferent ocean, but he just couldn't bring himself to do the deed. Slowly, he put the gun back in the pocket of his windbreaker, sank down on the sand, and crouched next to Arkady's body. He rocked on his heels and covered his face with his hands. He was filled with disgust and shame at his fear of death, at his weakness, at his cowardice. At this, his latest failure.

• • •

What was left to do but call the police? Still kneeling in the sand, he fumbled with his cell phone. No signal. *They've finally cut me off*, he thought, remembering the mountain of unpaid bills. It was useless. He was an impotent man with a useless phone and an unused gun.

He could go to the police in person, but the nearest station was some twenty miles away. In any case, why hurry? The poor fellow was way past help.

Who was he? Tyler flashed his light around the body. He then spotted a rounded object caught in a clump of seaweed. Crawling towards it on his hands and knees, Tyler discovered it was a zippered nylon pouch, half buried in the sand. He picked it up. After struggling with the zipper, gummed up with grains of sand and saltwater, he finally managed to pry it open. Inside was a transparent plastic bag stuffed with a thick wad of hundred-dollar bills, secured with a rubber band.

Tyler looked around him apprehensively. He rose to his feet and swept his flashlight up and down the beach. It was still completely deserted.

He was quite alone with the treasure trove.

His heart pounding, he hurriedly shoved the pouch into his knapsack. And then he ran.

• • •

Tyler ran as fast as his legs could take him across the dune to the parking lot. He got into his car, his hand shaking so hard it took him several tries to insert the key into the ignition. Tires screeching, he sped away, his foot pressed down on the accelerator as far as it would go.

For ten minutes, he drove like a man possessed on the dimly lit A1A. Gradually his breathing and wits returned to normal, but he only slowed down once he was certain no one was following him. Aimlessly, he drove in the general direction of Palm Bay. He was unable to rid his mind of the lifeless eyes staring out past him into the void, of the vivid image of the shaven head and deformed ear and sun-blistered skin.

Then he thought of the money. He turned onto a deserted side road and shut off the motor as the first light was beginning to break. He reached for his knapsack, took out the pouch, and removed the wad of bills from the plastic bag. Carefully, he snapped off the rubber band and began to count.

He whistled in amazement. Sweet Jesus! Twenty thousand dollars! He had never handled so much cash in his life! Why was the man carrying so much? The possibility that this was ill-gotten money eased his qualms about taking it. He, who had never so much as stolen a cookie in his life. But jack squat had that ever done for him.

In any case—*finders keepers.*

He removed a hundred-dollar note, stuck it in his wind jacket's pocket, put the rest of the wad back into the pouch, and leaned back in his seat.

Twenty thousand dollars!

There was a lot he could do with this much money.

But it was too late.

He exhaled in short, shallow gasps as tears began to glisten in his brown eyes and then roll freely down the stubble in his cheeks.

Too late! Too late!

What good would the money do him now?

• • •

At 6:45 a.m. Tyler was driving down Dixie Highway. Feeling a sudden onslaught of hunger, he pulled up in front of Wet Spot, a dive bar that had become a second home for him in the past year.

Even at this early hour, the bar was noisy with regulars, a motley crew of veterans and down-and-outers from the nearby trailer park in baseball caps and sweatshirts, sipping coffee at the wooden counter. The loud voices fell abruptly into respectful silence when Tyler walked in. Most everyone here had been at his son Christopher's funeral the day before.

As Tyler headed over to a table in a far corner of the bar, he could feel the eyes boring into his back.

He slid onto a chair at the table. Out of the corner of his eye he could see Katie coming over with a mug of steaming coffee.

"Hi, Katie," Tyler mumbled.

"Hiya, sweetheart," Katie spoke softly in heartfelt sympathy as she surveyed the desolation on Tyler's drawn face. This good-natured, solid man with the kind brown eyes and full, tender-looking lips didn't deserve the misfortunes that had come battering down upon his head as if on the head of Job.

Katie set down the mug of steaming coffee on the wooden table, the first brew of the day. She knew Tyler liked his coffee strong and black.

"On the house," she said.

"Thanks," Tyler replied with a wan, miserable smile. "And bring me a cheeseburger, will ya? On second thought, make that two."

He was ravenous. And now he had the wherewithal to pay.

But what right did he have to draw breath, let alone eat?

He stared at the empty chair on the other side of the table, his head slumped on his chest.

Back when he could still afford it, he used to take Christopher here every Sunday after church for a cheeseburger and a milkshake. It was a precious father-and-son moment he looked forward to every week.

And now—those moments—never more.

Tyler's wife, Sally, had taken Tyler's pickup to bring Chris to a school event. Her own car wouldn't start. When the pickup skidded at an intersection, the brakes failed, and she and Chris crashed into the back of a bus.

Tyler had known the brakes were worn out, but he kept delaying their replacement. Money was tight. The odd jobs he was doing here and there were barely enough to get them through the month. He thought he was only putting himself at risk and never imagined Sally might take his pickup.

It was as if he had killed Chris with his own hands. He should have scraped up the money for the repair somehow. Borrowed. Stole.

Standing at the edge of the grave, he'd been deaf, dumb, blind, incapable of making a sound, not even to cry as his son, as his Christopher, was lowered into the ground in a small box.

He missed him so much—his sweet, tow-headed boy. The searing pain was unbearable, and Tyler felt as if he was drowning in it.

He was only eight years old.

Tyler clenched his fists to keep himself from sobbing out loud.

Tyler had no need for the money he had found now: It was not going to bring Christopher back.

His son, whom he had cherished above all others, was gone forever.

• • •

A burly, thickset man in a scuffed leather biker jacket, his black hair receding, approached the table and sat down. He was carrying two beer bottles, and he handed one to Tyler.

"How are you coping?" he asked him.

Tyler looked down glumly at his uneaten cheeseburgers.

"I know you blame yourself, but it's not your fault," Ray said.

"You didn't do anything wrong. You worked hard. Paid your taxes. Took care of your family. You never hurt anyone."

Tyler sat very still, stone-faced. He took a long swig of beer and wiped his lips with the back of his hand.

"Your attitude's all wrong, man," Ray pushed on. "They got you thinking it's your fault. They *want* you to think it's your fault. Because this way they can keep on doing to you what they've been doing all along."

Tyler's eyes remained fixed on the beer bottle.

"The New World Order is to blame. Not you."

Slowly, Tyler shifted his eyes. They were vacant, like empty rooms with the lights switched off.

"What?" he said in far-off voice. *My sweet tow-headed boy.*

"You know, it's the global power elites I've been telling you about, the ones who control the banks, the corporations, the media. The ones who are trying to take over the entire country. They're trying to take away everything we have so when they are ready to seize power, we'll have nothing left to fight them with. Didn't you read the books I gave you? They explain everything."

Tyler shook his head. He wasn't much of a reader. When it came to the affairs of the world, he was content to leave them to people smarter than himself. He tried to muster the last quantum of energy he had left.

"Please, Ray...lay off it. I can't. Not now."

"Hush, hush. I know, buddy." Ray placed a tentative, beefy hand on Tyler's shoulder in an awkward attempt to comfort him. "I'm just trying to help you see the light. Ease the burden. Because there are people to blame, you know. There are people out there who should pay the price."

Tyler's face remained locked in pain.

"They shipped our jobs to Mexico and then to China. *Free trade*, they call it! But no new jobs ever come to replace them. Then they created the housing bubble. They got everybody to buy a house so that when the bubble burst they could take away all our savings. We are left with no jobs, no house, no savings. You think all this is just a coincidence? These people are responsible for your losing your job and your house. They're the ones who killed Chris."

"Ray, this is not a good time. Please," Tyler pleaded.

"Of course. I'm sorry. I'm an insensitive bastard, I know," said Ray, getting up. "But when you feel better, think over what I said."

• • •

Tyler knew Ray meant well, but in truth, he didn't feel like a victim. Blaming others was not in his nature. He was the one responsible for his family. It was his cross, and his alone, to bear. But there was no denying that the thirteen years he had given to Sea Star had made no difference when the crunch came, even with him having been made foreman and all. Job's going to China, they said.

Thirteen years, and he was laid off without so much as the slightest warning, with a measly six-month severance pay.

Nobody had put a gun to his head when he bought their house just before he lost his job, but everyone had assured him that the value of real estate could only go up. That it was a no-brainer investment. They were all wrong. After interest rates went up and the housing market crashed, the bank repossessed their house. His family was evicted, and they lost all their savings.

Sally had always told him that he was too trusting. Too naïve. Sally was always right.

It was time to go home, if only to have a word with Sally.

They had not spoken since he picked her up at the hospital. Tyler would never forget the drive home. It was as though the entire universe had lost its structure. Even the tires of the car felt as though they couldn't move forward, spinning uselessly in the tar of melting asphalt.

Tyler remembered glancing into the rearview mirror to check on Sally. He wanted to comfort her, to say they would overcome as they always did—as a team. But she had retreated into a world of her own. She sat so still that she scarcely seemed to breathe. Tyler had never seen his high school sweetheart like this before. Scared, he didn't dare break the silence.

But now there was a glimmer of hope. He patted the comforting wad of money, securely ensconced in the inner pocket of his windbreaker.

• • •

When Tyler entered the trailer, Sally was busy packing a suitcase and didn't look up to greet him. Tyler followed her every movement, his eyes darting after her nervously.

"What are you doing?" he finally sputtered.

"What does it look like, Tyler? I'm leaving," she said in a deadpan voice.

Tyler tried to take her into his arms, but she wriggled out of his embrace.

"Honey. Listen to me. You're in shock. We're both in shock. But hey, I've found some money. We can fix things. Start over."

"Start over? How dare you," she exploded, choking over the words. But it was the alien expression in her grey-blue eyes that really got to him. He was looking into a stranger's eyes. There was so much loathing in them that Tyler took a step back. He felt suffocated, as if the very surfaces of the trailer were closing in on him and the air was slowly being sucked out.

"My god. You're serious. You can't just get up and leave!"

"I am. I can."

The sound of jangling car keys filled the space between them.

"I don't understand."

"Nothing to understand. It's over between us."

If only she would scream or yell or hit him.

"All you do is bow your head to fate. The world stomps all over us and you do nothing. Nothing. I can never forgive you. Not now that Chris is gone. Not ever."

Tyler stood helpless as the door of the trailer slammed shut. He was completely alone. Bereft of everything.

• • •

The following morning, Ray climbed into the trailer carrying three pizzas and three coffees.

"How you guys doing? Thought you might be hungry," he said in his grainy, baritone voice. "How's Sally?"

"Sally?" Tyler repeated dumbly. And with an almost imperceptible movement of his head, and a wave of his hand he added, "She's gone. She's gone and left me."

"What? When?"

"Yesterday."

"But why?"

Tyler sighed. It was much more than a sigh: it sounded more like the plaintive moan of a wind blowing on a bleak, treeless hill.

"She despises me," he uttered at last, in a whisper that cracked through his shame. "She said she'll never forgive me."

"Oh, man. That really sucks. You gotta do something, for Chrissakes. Gotta get her back.

"How?"

"I'll tell you how. You gotta show her that you won't allow this to stand, that you will hold to account all those who are responsible for Chris's death. You've gotta to show her that Chris didn't die in vain."

Tyler stared despondently at the floor.

"You've got to make those bastards pay." Ray egged him on. And raising his voice, he continued, "We're all victims here. Turn your sorrow and grief into anger. Anger is better. Anger is useful."

"I don't know..."

But Ray was unstoppable.

"Can't you see that there is a terrible conspiracy against us out there? The New World Order is trying to bankrupt this country, to make way for a world controlled by the United Nations, the billionaires, and the globalists. A new world currency will replace the dollar. We'll lose our sovereignty, our independence, our heritage. Very soon, we won't just be working for the big corporations anymore. We'll be their slaves."

Tyler had known Ray for a few years now. They had both worked at Sea Star, a local shipyard. But they were not close. Ray was a loudmouth with a reputation of being something of a troublemaker. Besides, they led different kinds of lives. Ray was divorced and didn't have a family to tie him down.

But after the two of them were laid off and became neighbors in the trailer park, their common misery drove them to seek each other's company. Tyler discovered that Ray was smart. He had stuck out a couple of years at college and read many books. But when he found out that Ray was an Iraq War veteran, Tyler's respect for him grew. His own father had fought in Vietnam. Besides, Tyler enjoyed listening to him, even though he didn't always quite understand what Ray was talking about.

"That's crazy talk, Ray," Tyler said, finally forced to defend himself against Ray's barrage of words.

"The economy is going down the toilet, man. The dollar is crashing. Inflation will run wild," Ray went on ominously, his dark eyes smoldering. "Alex Jones is warning on Infowars that the Supreme Court will soon ban gun ownership. Immediately after that, they'll impose martial law and suspend the Constitution! It's coming, I tell you. Mark my words, Tyler. It's coming."

There was a heavy silence. Eventually, Tyler replied, sighing, "We're just two powerless, unemployed jerks from Palm Bay."

"Stop underestimating yourself," Ray chided him. He then threw a quick glance through the window of the caravan to make sure they could not be overheard outside and went on in a low, hushed voice.

"Look. I have a plan, see. And let me tell you, it's a damned good plan, and I've been figuring it out for a long time. It's good to go. I'm just waiting for a little money to get the ball rolling."

Tyler's ears perked up. Maybe he could do some good with the money, after all.

"Remember how a few years ago Mayor John Mazziotti made that call to ban Chinese imports?"

Out of the fog of his misery, Tyler nodded. "Uh-huh."

"Well, Tyler, I think a ban is exactly what the country needs. We gotta get his message out to the rest of the country. To do that, we need to go up to New York, where all the rich and powerful live."

"New York?"

Tyler sounded completely bewildered.

"Yeah, ya know, home to Wall Street and the UN and all that."

"I've got some money," Tyler said in a voice so low that Ray wasn't sure he'd heard him correctly.

"You do?" he asked in disbelief. "How much?"

"Twenty grand."

Ray's voice dropped a register. He was practically drooling. "That much? Cool. Did you rob a bank or something?"

"No. Of course not. It's a long story."

"Never mind, now that we have the funds."

In his misery Tyler never noticed Ray's wily insertion of the plural *we*.

"Come on, buddy, are we in this together or not? For Chris's sake? To make Sally proud? Regain her respect?"

Tyler was beginning to wonder if Ray didn't have a point. Maybe the New World Order really was responsible for what happened to him and his family. Maybe the money he found was some kind of sign from God for him to take matters into his own hands. Anyway, what did he have to lose?

Wasn't it high time to *do* something, as Ray said, stand up for his family?

"For Chris and Sally," Tyler repeated. *For Chris and Sally,* he repeated over and over to himself, surrendering to Ray's enthusiasm.

• • •

Ray, for his part, could not believe his luck and had no intention whatsoever of giving Tyler a chance to change his mind.

He decided to put his plan in motion at once.

The following morning, he announced to Tyler that an incredible opportunity had just presented itself.

"In two weeks, the leaders of the New World Order will be gathering at a conference in a hotel in New York City. We have to move fast."

If Tyler was having second thoughts, he said nothing. He had given Ray his word. He didn't want to let him down, the only person in the world who had not given up on him.

To make sure Tyler had no time to think, Ray kept him busy.

He put him in charge of organizing transportation and supplies. He sent him to Tampa to buy an unregistered car and to Jacksonville to pick up a stolen plate. And then he sent him to Miami to buy suits, shirts, ties, socks, shoes.

"Spare no expense for the new threads. If we are going to penetrate the inner sanctum of the rich and the powerful, we have to look the part. I'll take care of the guns."

"Guns?" Tyler asked in a tremulous voice.

"Don't worry. If everything goes according to plan we won't have to use them."

Tyler was mollified by Ray's assurance. Ray had it all figured out. Ray was his lifeline and his leader now. His crutch. Ray's enthusiasm was infectious. For the first time in his life, Tyler felt he was doing something important. He brushed away any thought about consequences.

• • •

"Slow down, will you."

They were traveling on the I-95 in the white Ford Mustang Tyler had bought. The speedometer was touching 100 mph, and Tyler was feeling sick. They had just passed Atlanta, still had sixteen more hours to go, and Ray hadn't shut his mouth for the past two.

"Stop the car! Stop the car!"

Ray swerved onto the shoulder of the road. Tyler heaved and heaved.

"Are you sure we should go through with this?" asked Tyler, still trembling from the nausea when he climbed back into the car. His nerves had been getting the better of him since they left Palm Bay, with the reality of their mission finally dawning on him. This was no movie.

"Never been more sure about anything in my life," Ray breathed. "It's going to be great. So many people have responded to my call to arms. Dozens will come, I tell you. Maybe even more. Ordinary citizens just like us, from all over the country."

Like-minded activists Ray had met on the internet would be joining them in New York City. "They're all patriots, and they're champing at the bit. And," he added, "some of my old buddies from Iraq are coming, too.

"They are boiling mad that four thousand of our boys died in Iraq—for nothing. There were no weapons of mass destruction. It was all lies. The lies of our overlords, the elites.

"So, find your balls. We're going to make history. I've drafted a declaration. The entire country will hear it. We'll be broadcast on prime-time TV, on the radio. We're going to be a force to be reckoned with.

"You'll see," Ray went on. "We're going to surprise these rats in their stronghold. We're going to hold them accountable for what they're doing to the country. They won't know what'll hit them until it's too late."

• • •

At 3:00 p.m. on September 14, 2008, two men in dark navy-blue suits with tennis bags slung over their shoulders approached the Waldorf Astoria, a Park Avenue hotel in Manhattan, where the leaders of the New World Order were gathering to plot their takeover of the world.

At the fore, Ray marched through the revolving doors, up the stairs, and into the lobby with all the assurance of a regular guest.

Tyler, assailed by trepidation, was barely keeping up. As soon as he had stepped into the entrance with its gilded ceiling and mosaic floor, Tyler knew he was in way over his head. This was not a place for people like him. This place where presidents stayed. In a place like this, they would see right through him in an instant. Who was he going to fool in his suit?

The tie around his neck was suffocating him and he could feel a panic attack coming on.

But the thought of Chris and Sally steadied his nerves. *Get a handle on yourself.* Ray promised they'd be in and out in a matter of a few hours.

When he saw Ray gesturing for him to hurry, he quickened his step.

Let's get this over with.

Ray stopped near the tall, landmark clock in the middle of the lobby, the agreed-on meeting place. Tyler glanced at his watch. Three twenty-five, it said. They were five minutes early.

The five minutes ticked by quickly. The lobby was full of people, but no one came up to the clock as Tyler paced impatiently to the left and to the right, unable to stand still.

"Are you sure they'll come? Are you sure they'll recognize us?"

"Stop worrying. It's the tennis bags, remember? We all agreed to carry them. That's our signal."

They waited. It was 3:45. "Let's give it a bit more time," said Ray, scratching the bald patch at the back of his head. "Most are coming from out of town. Maybe they're stuck in traffic or something." But he was beginning to look seriously worried.

And still nobody showed. Ray and Tyler strained their eyes, combing through the crowds of hotel guests and convention attendees. Not a single tennis bag was to be seen.

"You're not mistaken, are you? About the meeting time, I mean?" asked Tyler.

Ray shot him a dirty look. "Have a little faith, goddamnit!" Tyler shut up.

The clock above them chimed. It was already 4:00 p.m. Ray's face, glistening with sweat, reddened, and he loosened the tie around his neck. "*Fuck. Fuck. Fuck,*" he swore under his breath. "Where in the hell is everybody?"

"Let's get outta here," Tyler rejoined, his eyes growing fearful.

Ray dug in. "Not on your life. There's still the two of us, right? We'll just take our chances and try to get into the convention hall."

"But the entire place is full of security," Tyler protested. Sure enough, there were uniformed guards everywhere, stationed around the staircases and positioned outside all the elevators.

"Yeah. The rich and powerful sure don't spare no expense for their own protection even though they want to take our guns away," Ray snorted angrily.

"Never mind that, Ray!" Tyler cried out, seriously beginning to doubt his friend. Maybe Ray didn't have it all figured out after all.

A security guard was making his way in their direction. Abruptly Ray turned around and, without warning, broke into a run.

"Hey! Stop!" the security guard called out. Tyler dashed down the stairs at the side of the elevators after Ray. Sprinting down two steps at a time, they reached the lower level.

The security guard, now joined by a couple of others, was closing in.

"Quick, quick! In here!" Ray yelled as he headed around the corner that led to yet another short stairwell down to the Bull and Bear Prime Steakhouse. Suddenly, he pulled out a handgun from the back of the waistband of his pants and fired toward the top of the stairs.

"What the hell?" Tyler cried out, startled by the gunshot. But Ray pushed him forward through the open double doors, bolting them behind them.

Then Ray aimed at the security guards behind the glass panes of the doors. "If you try to get in, I'll shoot whoever's in here!" he hollered.

The security guards backed off.

"OK, we're safe for now."

"Was that necessary?" Tyler spat out furiously.

"Calm down. No one got hurt, did they? Put on your mask and unpack your rifle. Right now!" Ray ordered as he quickly surveyed the burgundy-carpeted expanse of the restaurant opening up before them. "Come on, crybaby," he said. "We're on to plan B."

It was only 4:45 p.m. and the place was still empty but for a small clutch of people standing and sitting around an oversized mahogany bar with a bronze sculpture of a bull and bear at its center.

The sound of the shot and the sight of two masked men brandishing weapons storming into the bar sent the small crowd into a frenzy. Ray ran towards the bar, rapidly shouting out orders. "All staff, out! Through the street door. Now! The rest of you—down, down, where I can see you!"

Amid a storm of overturning barstools and breaking crockery, everyone in the restaurant dropped on the carpet.

Everyone, that is, except for a tall, broad-shouldered man in an expensive-looking suit standing at the far side of the bar. Holding out his wallet for all to see, he advanced carefully a few steps toward Tyler.

"Hi, I'm Charlie, Charlie Creek," he said smoothly. "What do you say you guys leave quietly, before you get into real trouble, eh? Take all I've got on me. That's five hundred bucks, and I'll throw in my Rolex watch. It's the real McCoy."

"On your knees, you dumb fuck!" Ray exploded. "We don't give a rat's ass for your fancy watch!" he roared, waving his Colt in Charlie's face frozen by the sudden assault. "The nerve! Your kind always thinks you can buy off anybody. Well, not this time, buddy! Not this time! We ain't interested in your money."

Ain't interested in your money! Good Lord, if it wasn't money they were after, then it must be—it could only be—a terror attack! Under Ray's wild-eyed stare, Charlie's ruddy face turned pale and his thin lips trembled, his belief in the power of Rolexes shattered. He promptly folded his large, muscular body onto the floor, trying to make himself as small as possible.

Noticing the quivering of Charlie's lips that moved as if in silent prayer, Tyler felt an unfamiliar, and thrilling, sense of power.

"Listen up, folks," he said, almost apologetically. "Just cooperate and we'll go easy on everyone."

"That's right," said Ray. "Just clam up and switch off your phones and you'll be all right."

A ginger-headed man in jeans and a navy polo shirt, crouching next to Charlie, was speaking quietly into his cell in a distinct British accent.

"Sell a thousand October S&P contracts for me at market. Have to hop now."

"You heard him, didn't you? Switch off your phone," Tyler exclaimed nervously.

Simon lifted up his hands. "It's off. All done," he said with more brightness than he felt. The trader's instinct had gotten the better of his fear. The already wobbly stock market was sure to take a dive once the news of a terrorist attack inside the prestigious Waldorf Astoria Hotel got out. Simon, running his own hedge fund now, just couldn't let this sure win pass.

"No more phone calls!" Ray glared at Tyler and grabbed the phone from Simon.

Just then, a dark-haired waiter in a white shirt and black vest sauntered out of the men's room.

Immediately he froze in his tracks and flung up his arms. He sank to his knees.

"Hey, you! Get up! Get up! What's your name?" Ray shouted.

"Er-Ernesto," stammered the young man, rising uncertainly to his feet.

"OK, *chico*. Grab everybody's cellphones and dump them over there," said Ray, gesturing to an empty table.

Ernesto shuffled reluctantly through the small group. Suddenly, he stopped and peered down at a small Asian woman in a red dress.

Ray pushed Ernesto roughly. "Hurry up. I don't have all day." Then he turned his attention to the Asian woman.

"And who are you?" Ray asked.

"Tomoko Watanabe," the woman answered, in a hard, high-pitched voice.

"Chinese, ain't you?"

Tomoko shook her head. "No. Japanese."

"Japs. Chinks. What's the fucking difference?"

"Leave her alone," protested a blonde woman beside Tomoko.

"Shut up!" snarled Ray.

Tyler ground his teeth. What had gotten into Ray? There was no reason for him to talk like a gangster.

"Don't think for a moment we've forgotten Pearl Harbor. Uh-uh. We won't forget, ever," Ray went on, unstoppable.

Tomoko sat very still, her small, plump body folded into a defiant ball. *Don't you dare lay a finger on me, you chikushou.* Tomoko had done well with her investments, having cashed out of her carry trades just in time before they crashed in 2007. She had even written a bestseller on investing. She was in New York to promote its US publication.

The blonde whispered something into Tomoko's ear.

"Didn't I tell you before to shut the fuck up?" Ray snapped. His eyes fell on the conference nametag around her neck: "Bridget Johannessen, on your feet."

Birgit got up.

"Who else is here for the Global Economic Forum conference? Come on—show yourselves!"

Two men cautiously stood up as well.

"My, my," said Ray. "Look what we have here!" he called out mockingly. "The fish we've been angling for. We wanted a full net, but three will do nicely.

"So, Bridget, what are you doing at the conference?"

"It's Birgit," she corrected him calmly. "I'm here to speak about deforestation in the Amazon and its impact on global warming. If you don't let go of us soon, I'll miss my session."

"Global warming, huh? You're one of those eco-freaks telling us we'll fry if we don't do as you say, huh? We know what you're up to. Creating panic about environmental disaster to distract us from the real problems in the world."

"Global warming is a fact, so you can put your conspiracy theory to rest," she countered, looking Ray fearlessly in the eye. If there was one lesson that Birgit had learned from the past two years fighting for the rainforest in Brazil, it was the imperative to stand up to thugs.

"Why should I trust your facts? Global warming is a sham trumped up by the New World Order to make people believe that only an authoritarian world government can prevent the end of the world. We know your tricks."

He then scowled at a lean, handsome, middle-aged man right behind Birgit, looking at his nametag.

"Listen up, everybody. This is Ryan. Ryan Forrester. What sins does he have to fess up to, I wonder?"

Ryan kept his cool.

"Take it easy, man, will you? Why don't you stop venting and cut to the chase? Just tell us what it is you want. Maybe there's something we can do to help," he said, enunciating every word at an even clip, as he pulled out a pack of cigarettes and a lighter from his trouser pocket.

"Are you kidding me?" Tyler suddenly interjected. "You can't smoke in here!"

"Really?" Ryan retorted. "When do you care about breaking the law?"

Tyler, who had always played by the book, looked away shamefacedly, his face flushed.

Ray, on the other hand, didn't let up: "So what are you here for?"

"I'm one of the keynote speakers."

"Speaking about what?"

"Global competitiveness and the benefit of offshoring."

"Oh, ho! Look who we've got here!" Ray glanced back at Tyler. "Thank him for bringing down the price of your flat-screen TV."

Misinterpreting Ray's reaction, Ryan breathed easy for a moment. At last, maybe these crazies would knock it off for a while. But he then made a mistake.

"Yeah. I actually help American companies stay competitive by outsourcing to China," he added with evident pride.

"Very nice. Very nice," said Ray with a forced smile before abruptly screaming in Ryan's face.

"Christ! You haven't thought it through, now, have you, you dumbass? That by moving all the jobs to China all we ever do is watch fucking flat-screen TV!" Ray hopped from foot to foot, the volume of his voice turned up to full-blown screech. Then he hunched his shoulders and shoved the muzzle of his rifle into Ryan's cheek, forcing his head sideways.

"Traitor! *Scum*!"

"Stop it. Stop right now," Tyler cried out, rushing to Ray's side. *Jesus.* Ray was losing it!

"Cut it out. If not, I'll walk away right this second," he whispered breathlessly in Ray's ear. "Calm down, will ya? No one gets hurt. You promised."

Ray lowered his weapon.

"Who's your friend here?" said Ray smoothly as if nothing untoward had happened, and he turned his attention to an Asian man in his early sixties standing next to Ryan.

"My Chinese business partner," Ryan exhaled in a shaky voice.

"Great. Another fish in our net! What's your name, Chinaman?"

The man looked steadfastly ahead, signaling his condescension by remaining silent. He had the air of someone used to issuing orders rather than obeying them.

Ray squinted at his nametag.

"Lang Chang. Chang Lang. Can't make it out. Hey, Chink, I'm talking to you," Ray taunted him.

Tyler wet his lips nervously. What Ray was doing wasn't right, regardless of what these people might have done.

Without flinching, the man finally broke his silence. "Listen to me, you good-for-nothing turtle egg. If you don't release us immediately, I, Liang Dacheng, will personally make sure you will live to regret it," he snarled.

All heads turned to get a look at the man who dared defy someone with a gun in his hand. "And who do you think you are to threaten me?" Ray exploded, jerking up his weapon. "You ain't in China now, in case you didn't notice. I bet you've made millions stealing our jobs. And now you come here and act like you own the place. You're the one who'll be sorry, believe you me."

Liang said nothing. After pulling off the sale of the factory in Shangcheng, he had gone on to become a successful dealmaker. He was now a powerful tycoon with controlling interests in manufacturing, real estate, and mining spanning the globe, and he commanded respect wherever he went. Even prime ministers and presidents spoke to him with deference.

A faraway wail of police sirens penetrated from the street outside.

"The police are arriving," said Liang. "You're running out of time. You'll never get out of here." The authoritative tenor of his voice seemed to lift up the captives' spirits.

"If we thought we were gonna get out of here, we'd never have come in the first place," replied Ray.

Tyler was hit by the ominous implication of Ray's words. What a fool he was to have believed Ray, that this was going to be an in-and-out job. They would be lucky to get out in one piece.

Just then, the cordless phone on the bar counter rang.

Ray picked up the phone.

"Hello?"

A few seconds passed. Ray stuck out a raised thumb in triumph, signaling excitedly to Tyler.

"It's for us," he said in an awed voice. But Tyler wasn't paying attention, sunk in his own anxious thoughts. What had he gotten himself into? Sally. *She* would know what to do. Oh, how he missed her.

Back on the line, Ray said, very loudly, "Yes. Yes. I'm the one in charge. My name? It's Ray Cox. We have eleven, no, twelve hostages. What do we want? Very simple. We want the secretary of commerce to ban all imported goods from China.... No, I ain't joking. We ain't going nowhere until our conditions are met." And he slammed down the receiver.

Tyler couldn't believe that Ray had revealed his real name. That wasn't part of the plan. For sure there was no getting out of here now.

The hush in the room was intense.

"Are you out of your fucking mind?" It was Ryan, finally losing his cool. "Do you even understand what you're demanding? You're asking our president to declare a trade war on China!"

"Hell, yes!" Ray countered. "If this is what it takes to make stuff in this country again. We used to manufacture a lot of stuff. The best in the world. No reason we can't do it again."

Ray was right, Tyler thought sadly. He'd give anything to get his old job back at Sea Star, building and repairing beautiful yachts and sailboats.

"You make it sound so simple," said Ryan. "Do you think the Chinese will take it in their stride? They will retaliate. They'll boycott *our* goods."

"And we'll dump US government bonds and the dollar, too," added Liang Dacheng. "You won't be able to pay your bills without our money. You'll go bankrupt."

Ray charged up to Liang.

"Shut your mouth, Lang Dang," he fulminated with spittle-flecked lips. "Who asked for your opinion? Boycott all you want. You export a lot more to us than we export to you. You have so much more to lose than us. You take our jobs and steal our technologies and we've done nothing about it. Believe me, that's about to change. We won't make nice anymore."

"Even in the very unlikely event the secretary were to respond to your demand, you do realize, don't you, that a trade war between the US and China would trigger a collapse of the world economy?" Simon interjected, trying to strike a more conciliatory note. "No one would be spared!"

But Ray spun around like a top. "So what? *Spared?* All it will do is hurt rich people like you. Little people like us are hurting already. We ain't got nothing to lose."

Damn right, said Tyler quietly to himself. *They take and take and take until you don't have a darn thing left in the world. And once you have nothing to lose, the tables turn.*

"The secretary will never agree to your demands," said Ryan.

"In that case, I'd start preparing for the long haul, if I were you," Ray replied.

This had the effect of shutting everyone up.

• • •

Nobody spoke again while they waited for the secretary's response. Time passed with nail-biting slowness. After an hour, a strident ringing cut through the oppressive atmosphere of the restaurant. Ray jumped on the phone.

He clearly didn't like what he was hearing—

"What do you mean 'the commerce secretary won't accept our terms'? How do we even know you're telling the truth? How do we even know somebody actually spoke to him? I need proof, man. Why should I even trust you?"

Ray stopped talking and hung up. But the negotiator at the other end of the line wasn't giving up. The phone immediately rang again.

"Yeah, yeah," Ray barked into the receiver. "And in the meantime, buddy, we have a new condition. Yeah. An interview on CNN. We want to make our case to the public. Let the public decide…"

The negotiator made no promises.

There was nothing for Ray and Tyler to do but wait for him to call back. Ten minutes passed, twenty minutes passed, an hour passed.

Finally, the phone rang.

"Is this CNN? Oh, it's you! What do you mean CNN won't cover the story? That's impossible!" Ray sputtered. "You think I was born yesterday? Let me tell you, if we don't get what we're asking for in one hour, something really bad is going to happen."

What did Ray mean by that? Tyler wondered in dread. The whole situation was already much worse than he had imagined it would be. He couldn't take much more of this.

Ray swayed from side to side, his free hand gripping his forehead, looking like a trapped animal.

"Folks, the media and the government are trying to cover up our story," he announced. "Typical. They don't want people to know about us, because they know the public is on our side. See? That's the America we live in.

"But," he said, turning to Tyler, "we refuse to be silenced."

Tyler took Ray aside and grabbed him by the collar. "What in the hell did you mean by 'something really bad is going to happen'?" Tyler asked.

"No options left, pal. We gotta show them we mean business," Ray muttered, looking sideways to avoid Tyler's gaze.

"What is that bad thing?" Tyler insisted.

"Sorry, Tyler. We're in a bind. We can't allow the bastards to ignore us. We gotta carry out our threat."

"Stop fucking with me! What threat?"

"Taking out the hostages."

• • •

Tyler opened his eyes wide in horror and disbelief. Since when had this been part of the plan? Ray was off the rails!

"No. Oh, no, Ray." Tyler panted heavily, retreating. "Oh, no. No way in hell I agree to this." He hadn't come here to get blood on his hands!

"Don't you see?" Ray pleaded. "We *must* get in the news. We must. Otherwise, the other side wins."

Ray was on the phone again.

"We're running out of patience," he roared. "I don't care a fuck what your excuses are. We're gonna start shooting one hostage every hour until you give us what we want. You can tell the commerce secretary it'll be on his conscience."

Not a single sound could be heard in the restaurant as the hostages, terrified, drew closer to each other and cowered as one body.

Tyler paced around the bar counter, circumnavigating, again and again, the heavy, bronze statue of the bull and bear in the center of the bar.

Then Tyler looked up at the TV tuned to CNN: no breaking news flash, no headline banner, no nothing. The anchors smiled and frowned and babbled as usual. *Fuck.* Ray was right about one thing at least; they were being ignored. A hostage situation was unfolding in New York City, and the news of it was being suppressed. No one, *no one*, seemed to know or give a shit.

He shook his fist at the indifferent box and the indifferent world it contained, barely able to control the urge to take his gun and open fire at the set.

It was now 11:00 p.m. They'd been in the bar for six hours.

"They don't believe we're capable of doing it, buddy," Ray mumbled into Tyler's ear. And then he called out loudly, "Listen up, everyone. They're forcing our hand. Who wants to be first to die?"

The raw brutality of the question sliced through each and every hostage like a cleaver.

All the blood drained from Tyler's face.

"No!" he screamed. "No one dies! No one gets hurt!" He jumped right in front of Ray, waving his arms and hopping up and down, as if this would stop him.

But Ray was past any reason. Pushing past Tyler, he abruptly yanked Tomoko from the group of sitting hostages.

"No, no. Not her!" cried Tyler, pulling back the hapless Tomoko.

"OK, smarty pants. Who, then? Take your pick. Who won't be missed? Who can the world not shed a tear for? You have some great candidates here."

Tyler didn't answer. He couldn't believe—didn't want to believe—that Ray actually intended to carry out his threat.

"Take me. Shoot *me*," he answered quietly.

A gasp arose from every throat as Tyler stood defiantly between Ray and the hostages huddled together on the floor.

Then he turned to them, desperate.

"Who here has some connection with a media outfit? Any media outfit? We must get our message out!"

No one answered.

"We just want to be heard! Is it so much to ask?" Tyler went on in a trembling voice.

"We don't mean no harm, folks We ain't thugs. We're decent people like you. We work hard. But we've been abandoned. We're like the Israelites wandering in the desert. Our jobs are gone, and we can't take care of our families. We're not asking for your charity. We just want our old jobs, and our lives, back."

An uncomfortable hush followed. Ernesto, squatting under the overhang of the bar counter, couldn't help but identify with this skinny guy who seemed too small for his suit. Ever since leaving California, Ernesto had been wandering in a desert of his own. Traveling from town to town, America had let him down, his dreams crushed.

"Time's up, people!" Ray yelled as he gestured with his rifle to Charlie.

"Why me?" Charlie yelped. Great globs of perspiration appeared on his face and dark stains spread under his armpits.

"Never liked you," Ray jeered. "You and your gold Rolex."

"I don't deserve this!" Charlie cried. "Somebody help me!" he implored the entire company. But everyone looked away. In his terror he appealed to Birgit: "Birgit, please help me. I beg you, please help me. It's not my fault that the mortgage bonds defaulted. I intended to warn you, Birgit, I swear."

Birgit, who had recognized Charlie the moment she entered the bar, averted her face. Charlie indeed had not warned Gunnar and the town back in Norway about the collapse of mortgage bonds as US house prices fell. He had broken his promise.

"Get out here in front of me," Ray barked.

"Have pity," Charlie squealed, as he desperately tried to crawl away and hide behind a toppled barstool. Charlie was big, but Ray quickly overpowered him and dragged him, kicking and punching blindly into the air, out into the middle of the floor.

"Kneel. Hands behind your neck!"

Ray raised his rifle and pointed it straight at Charlie's bowed head.

The inner voice Tyler had been hearing the whole afternoon welled up as loud as the thunder of God in his head.

He lunged for Ray's rifle.

But Tyler was no match for the heavyset Ray.

Soon Ray had him pinned to the floor.

The hostages looked on, aghast.

But nobody budged. Simon, a hero of the markets, had no taste for physical risk. Tomoko had no heavy studded handbag with which to repeat her whack-the-bad-guy-over-the-head stunt. Ryan's days of playing superman were over. Charlie was a blubbering mess. As for Liang Dacheng, his courage didn't quite measure up to his previous bravado.

It was down to one man's pluck. To everyone's surprise, Ernesto suddenly sprang into the fray, furiously trying to pull Ray away from Tyler. The hostages cheered when Ernesto succeeded in wrestling Ray's rifle from his grip.

But it wasn't over.

A shot went off.

Somehow, Tyler had managed to grab Ray's handgun from his belt.

And there was Ray, languishing in a pool of blood.

In a daze, Tyler slowly got back his feet. He looked down at the immobile body sprawled on the floor with horror and incomprehension. What had he done?

At precisely that moment, FBI agents and police officers, in black helmets and protective gear, stormed into the bar amidst the sound of shattering glass. Through the big double doors from inside the hotel, from the street entrance, from the windows, they came pouring in in an unstoppable wave.

The game was up. Tyler dropped his weapon to the floor and raised his arms. Ernesto did likewise. But it was too late. Their gestures of surrender failed to make an impression on the agents, who had instructions to fire at will.

Multiple shots rang out.

Slowly Tyler and Ernesto crumpled onto the burgundy carpet.

Birgit rushed to Ernesto's side. He was dead.

But Tyler was not.

Blood dribbled out of his nose and ears and mouth and trickled down his chest, staining his collar and the front of his shirt and tie. His eyes fluttered open. Grunting with pain, he edged his neck around to the side to see Birgit, kneeling beside him, her fingers on his pulse.

"He needs help!" Birgit cried out, tearing up Tyler's shirt and trying to apply pressure to the wound in his chest. "I can't stop the bleeding!"

But she couldn't get anyone's attention.

Sometimes seeming coincidences are not coincidental.

All the hostages' eyes were riveted on the TV screen. It was past midnight, and the banners and anchor screamed: Lehmann Brothers Filed for Bankruptcy! There would be no government bail-out. This was more than just a major Wall Street bank going under. The glue holding up the global machine was becoming unstuck. Wall Street would never be the same again. The whole damn world would never be the same again!

Surely this was the beginning of the end. Surely a market crash was coming. Mouths agape, nobody gave a penny's-worth thought to poor Tyler.

And when the police instructed the hostages to clear the bar, they fled as fast as they could. Back towards their own affairs, back to a future which in the space of a newsflash had become as uncertain and murky as it had been certain and triumphant before.

Birgit was left on her own.

"Shame on you! Shame! He saved us! They both saved us!" she screamed after the departing figures, beside herself with fury.

"Hold on there," she told Tyler, squeezing his hand. "Help will soon come."

Tyler squeezed it back weakly, and as he tried to say something, she put her ear to his moving lips.

His eyes were open, and he could see that she had tears in hers.

With a sigh as slight as the rustle of a bird's wings, the image of Chris, his tow-haired little boy, flickered behind his eyelids. Then, with one last effort, he managed to whisper "thank you" before his head rolled limply to the other side and he finally shut his eyes.

ACKNOWLEDGMENTS

WE ARE DEEPLY GRATEFUL TO our agent, Felicia Eth, for believing in this book and never giving up on it. Our thanks also go to Patricia Mulcahy and Karl French for their invaluable editing work, and to Jesse Coleman, Benny Ziffer, Howard Marks, Jagdish Bhagwati, and Katie Hope for their encouragement. A special thanks to Kedem Shinar who designed the maps and to Adi Shinar who contributed the brilliant title for the book and many helpful suggestions.